MARKETING

FOR

BUSINESS

GROWTH

MARKETING
FOR
BUSINESS
GROWTH

First edition published in 1969 under the title "The Marketing Mode"

THEODORE LEVITT

Graduate School of Business Administration
Harvard University

McGRAW-HILL BOOK COMPANY

New York   St. Louis   San Francisco   Düsseldorf   Johannesburg
Kuala Lumpur   London   Mexico   Montreal   New Delhi
Panama   Paris   São Paulo   Singapore
Sydney   Toronto   Tokyo

Library of Congress Cataloging in Publication Data

Levitt, Theodore, 1925–
   Marketing for business growth.

   First ed. published in 1969 under title: The
marketing mode.
   1. Marketing. I. Title.
HF5415.L483   1974   658.8   74-8413
ISBN 0-07-037415-5

   890 BPBP 832

The editors for this book were W. Hodson Mogan and Patricia A. Allen,
the designer was Naomi Auerbach, and the production was supervised
by Teresa F. Leaden. It was set in Times Roman by Monotype Composition Co

It was printed and bound by The Book Press

When people don't want to come, nothing in the world will stop them.   SOL HUROK

CONTENTS

Preface

A PRODUCT is something people buy. If they don't buy it, it's not a product (or a service). It's a museum piece. A business is not a business if it can't stay in business. It can't stay in business if it doesn't attract and hold enough solvent customers—no matter how efficiently it operates.

Marketing is about getting and keeping customers, all the big exhilarating things and the even more abundant little agonizing things that help make people finally want to do business with you.

The primary purpose of this book is to talk with the chief executive (whether of a company or a corporate division) about what he ought to know about marketing, how to manage his marketing chief, and how to balance the opportunities and threats of his *external environment* (the world external to his firm) with the resources and aims of his *internal environment* (the "world" of his firm—its plants, balance sheet, people, products, customer goodwill, and so forth).

The chief executive must know something about marketing, though not really very much. But what he must know is enormously important. This book confines itself largely to these important matters.

Simultaneously, the book talks to marketing chiefs and other high-level marketing executives—on three general topics, which I think will also interest the chief executive: (1) how to think about and get more from the products, people, and the resources you have; (2) how to think sensibly about and get innovation and imitation in marketing; and (3) how to think about marketing's claim on company resources relative to other considerations which must go into charting the purposes and managing the various functions of the whole organization.

Actually, this book is a revised, cut-down, and augmented version of *The Marketing Mode,* published in 1969. It isn't that things have changed all that much since then, except that I thought the book needed to sharpen its managerial focus—to get to the point faster, make a point more emphatically, target the audience more clearly and write to management's special needs and problems with less circumspection. Compare only the two titles. *The Marketing Mode,* though in my product-oriented bias pleased me enormously as a title, has a tone of detachment and abstraction. The tone actually belied the book's practical substance. By contrast, *Marketing for Business Growth* sounds more like it is there where the action is. Moreover, this new book has been rearranged, thinned out and new material added to make the action more palpable and the reading more quickly rewarding.

That gets us to a problem. I don't know that men who manage read prefaces of books. They are more likely to dive right in. If you haven't already, watch out for Chapter 1. It's awfully long, and may seem not at all to get quickly to the point. I'm sorry, but please hang in there with me to its termination. The moment of a baby's birth and first traumatic breath is its most critical and agonized instant. Things get lots easier after that, and in the case of this book, will seem more directly utilitarian for the reader. I urge you to get born with me by going through Chapter 1 first rather than trying for instant adulthood via some more titillating later chapter.

There is, finally, the last section of the book, which is a bit different. One chapter deals with the future, in which all of us are destined to spend the rest of our lives, and the other with the question of the morality of the commercial lives we lead. My hope is that these chapters that wind down the book will wind up its readers in a special way—their insights, their actions, and their spirit.

Theodore Levitt

SECTION ONE

The View from the Top

Chapter One

The Marketing Chief and the Chief Executive

MARKETING IS NOT the devious art of separating the unwary consumer from his loose change. While it encompasses many commercial arts—selling, pricing, product policy, merchandising, promotion, advertising—marketing is these things and lots more.

Marketing is concerned with all the exhilarating big things and all the troublesome little things that must be done in every nook and cranny of the entire organization in order to achieve the corporate purpose of attracting and holding customers. This means that marketing is not just a business function. It is a consolidating view of the entire business process.

Obviously, then, marketing is not just for marketing specialists. Marketing is also for presidents—which is what all other corporate departments also say so urgently about themselves. The lieutenants of each department constantly tell the president that his direct personal support is immediately needed lest the enterprise suffer irreparable harm. Every department calls for the chief's undeviating and sympathetic attention—production, finance, personnel, community relations, labor relations, R & D. If the poor man responded fully to everybody, he would scarcely have time to be president.

Though marketing is for the president, few things in marketing actually need his attention. Those which do can have a powerful impact on the life and earnings of his company. Unless the chief executive is thoroughly experienced in the subject, the things in marketing that require his direct attention can pose treacherous problems. Because marketing deals so inescapably with intangibles and with data that are simultaneously incomplete, unreliable, and not usually very relevant, marketing is not an art easily mastered in mid-life, like finance.

One thing that distinguishes marketing from other corporate functions is its unique operating environment. Instead of performing mainly against standards—as, for example, manufacturing does—it performs mainly against competitors. Manufacturing has cost and operating standards. It has a lot of control over its environment—production processes, machines, and employees. These are organized and manipulated under one corporate roof to produce maximum efficiencies. In contrast, marketing is all over the map: it has very little comparable control over its environment.

Both manufacturing and marketing must roll with the punches, except that marketing gets punched more often and more unexpectedly. It is in more continuous and direct contact with the enemy. Outside conditions constantly impose new and unexpected demands. Because of that, marketing's main thrust is less with efficiency than with magnitude. It is less immediately interested in how well (to continue the metaphor) it conserves its fighting strength than in how often or by what margin it wins the fight, no matter with what absence of style or grace. The expansion of sales is generally viewed as more immediately relevant than the reduction of costs. Volume understandably becomes the name of the game—magnitude, not efficiency.

Of course marketing is interested in efficiency. But the most palpable fact of its existence is that it cannot easily control the events or conditions that produce efficiency. The major events or conditions of its operations are the actions of its competitors and the behavior of its customers. More than any other corporate functions, marketing constantly faces energetic adversaries against which it must struggle for success. Success is defined as consumer patronage. What makes success especially hard to attain is the fact that the consumer seems constantly to change the conditions under which he will deal with one rather than another supplier.

Marketing may not be harder than manufacturing, but it is enormously different. One of the most exasperating ways in which it is different is the difficulty of knowing whether marketing is doing a good job. Even more difficult is determining which of several candidates will make a better marketing vice-president. Marketing is filled with uncontrolled, uncontrollable, unstandardizable, and unpredictable hazards. Like politics and sex, marketing is a squishy subject.

It is precisely because of that that the boss can be so easily and disastrously misled—whether the boss is a president directing and evaluating the marketing vice-president or whether he is a marketing vice-president directing or evaluating a sales manager, a product planner, an advertising director, or a market researcher. No wonder the chief executive whose background lies outside marketing would rather deal with almost any other subject, like manufacturing and finance. Their seemingly solid and tangible manageability provide a reassuring comfort.

Because marketing deals with the sources of revenue, it can make a strong case for the chief's one-sided support—support he generally feels compelled to give because he has come to appreciate marketing's importance. For those in marketing, this is highly felicitous. Unfortunately, it may not be for the company. What's good for a segment of a company may not be good for the whole company. Marketing decisions, because they deal with squishy matters, often require a good deal more wisdom, judgment, and prophetic insight than careful deductive reasoning. Without the experience that helps provide these abilities, the danger is that the chief boss either will reject, for lack of proper documentation, what his marketing lieutenants urge, or will support too strongly what he should not support, or make wrong decisions on things he hardly understands and about which he won't admit his ignorance and discomfort. Terrible mistakes have been the unhappy yield of precipitous and wrongheaded presidential rejections of marketing viewpoints and, on the other hand, of a lopsided and euphoric presidential love of marketing's lyrical promises.

Of course, the chief executive is not alone. He has staff, line lieutenants, and others to help him with decisions. He can insist, if proper documentation is not possible, certainly on proper reasoning from his marketing aides. Yet anybody who has diligently worked his way up to the upper echelons of an organization knows how easily the bodies can get buried, how easily bosses can be misinformed and even deceived by well-meaning subordinates taking fragile little liberties with the facts.

One major purpose of this book is to help two categories of corporate bosses—the chief corporate executive and the chief marketing executive— to get better control over the marketing job, to make better choices regarding what to look at in marketing, and to make better decisions on what they end up looking at. Another major purpose is to help both presidents and marketing executives understand, in a more practical and balanced fashion than has recently been the case, the pervasive yet limited role of marketing in achieving the corporate purpose.

The marketing department can do only part of the corporate job. To attract customers takes more than having the right price and the right pitch. It also takes having the right product. But marketing does not run the engineering department or the R & D department, which is generally where the products come from. Nor should it. Neither does it run finance, which has a lot to say about budgets. Nor should marketing run the plant, where product costs are generated and where customer shipments come from. And marketing certainly does not make mergers down on Wall Street, where a certain kind of action is. Yet marketing makes the sales, where the revenue is.

This is a book for marketers that is designed also for presidents—to give the chiefs of marketing new insights regarding the character and responsibilities of their jobs and to give the chief executives a modestly improved basis for thinking about their role in marketing. It is designed to help the marketing man do a better job in these troubled and changing times and to help presidents understand more clearly their own responsibilities in the context of the corporation's marketing function.

It is not a textbook. It is certainly not a dandy "how-to" book. Nor is it a book which, like a detective novel, proceeds with mathematical precision from some obvious beginning, step by step to a clear resolution in the end. Only in fairy tales and pulp romances are things smoothly resolved in such a way that everybody "lived happily ever after," except of course the evil villains, who get their just desserts. Real life is, as the real story goes, "one damned thing after the other." Hence, this book makes no lyrical promises of liberating solutions. Nor does it present marketing in a highly structured order, as if to suggest that if we knew enough, we'd see both sense and order in the world with which we deal. Each day our scientists see how uncompromisingly non-Euclidian our world is. This explains why physicists working furthest out on the frontier of knowledge so often become philosophers. Science is too limiting—only speculation fulfills curiosity.

Our job in business is not to discover sense and order. It is to achieve other and more urgent ends. There is no presumption that sense and order are the roads to attaining these ends.

This is a book with a point of view. It is designed to help men of high and awesome responsibility to think through the major problems of their corporate affairs in terms that have not always been accorded the privileged place of such exalted activities as finance. Finance deals with the ultimate reconciling end—the famous "bottom of the line." Marketing deals with the means—the generation of the customers whose patronage produces the revenues that go into the bottom of the line.

Every organization needs a purpose, some notion of why it exists and what it wants to accomplish—its goals, its objectives, and the kind of environment it wants to create for the people on whom it depends to achieve its purpose. Without some notion of purpose and direction, of knowing where it wants to go and why, it will drift in the competitive wind like a fallen leaf on an autumn day. It will do at any particular time whatever the transient pressures of the moment compel. Its life and posture will be determined not by what it has decided for *itself* but by what others have decided for *themselves*.

We are all fated to live in environments and under conditions not of our own making. For that reason we are all fated to lives of accommodation and compromise. But if we develop for ourselves a reasonably clear notion of specific purpose and direction, we can, given effort and resolution, achieve considerable control over our destinies. We need not invoke the doctrine of free will to declare that we can be active agents of our environment.

The purpose of this book is to talk about marketing and the corporate purpose in operable terms—terms that are both relevant to the day-to-day activities of the men who work in marketing and crucial to the men who run the companies that must so inescapably perform a marketing function. Consider the following:

In the year 1900 the American Wind Engine and Pump Company was a magnificently thriving enterprise. Its majestic windmills stood like powerful giants astride the farms of America's vast prairies. The workmanship was superb. Fittings were honed in solid brass by craftsmen of unimpeachable dedication. Prairie farms dependently got their drinking water, their machine energy, indeed their lifeblood from the output of this uncommonly profitable company. When finally new forms of energy crept over the horizon, its owners said with the same uncompromising pride that produced such superior fittings that "God put the wind on the prairies so that man might use it, and God will not take it away unless he wants man himself to perish." Today the company exists under a different name and with a vastly different balance sheet. It makes gooesneck table lamps, and in microscopic quantities.

Who was responsible for this company's awful fate? In the end, it is the chief executive who must be blamed, but if the company had been organized like today's large corporation, the original blame would have to rest with the marketing vice-president. His department is the company's eyes and ears to the world, the only world to which the company addresses all its efforts. His department is responsible for selling what the company makes. But it must also take important responsibility for deciding what it should make. His department is responsible for being in touch with the constantly evolving reality of the customer's world—what the customer needs, how he behaves, what he values, how he makes purchasing decisions, and the competitive options that are constantly becoming available to him.

The corporation's president, together with his inner cabinet, has many tasks and many demands on his time and attention. He depends on his lieutenants to get today's ongoing jobs done, but he also depends on their advice to decide what should be done tomorrow. The lieutenant in charge of marketing, because of his department's intimacy with the market, should have the major originating responsibility for advising what should be produced for sale, at least in the relatively short run. The execution of this responsibility is best handled in the larger corporation by establishing a formal product-line planning activity in the company. Product line planning belongs in the marketing department.

Product-line Planning and Corporate Strategies

According to Prof. E. Raymond Corey, one of the pioneer authors on the subject, "Product planning may be defined as the determination of the company's basic objectives, of what products it will make and sell, and of what the specification of these products will be."[1]

What a product's specifications shall be requires, first, understanding that a product or service is not what most people think.

If we define a product in its simplest commercial terms it is this: A product is something people buy—that is, in some magnitude that makes it profitable. If people don't buy it, it's not a product. The key is, "Do they buy it?"

Why do people buy products? Leo McGivena once said, "Last year one million quarter-inch drill bits were sold—not because people wanted quarter-inch drill bits but because they wanted quarter-inch holes."

People don't buy products, they buy the expectation of benefits.

People spend their money not for goods and services, but to get the value satisfactions they believe are bestowed by what they are buying. They buy quarter-inch holes, not quarter-inch drills. That is the marketing view of the business process.

But it goes even further. The marketing view also demands the active recognition of a new kind of competition that is in galloping ascendance in the world today. This is the competition of product augmentation: not competition between what companies produce in their factories, but be-

---

[1] E. Raymond Corey, "The Rise of Marketing in Product Planning," *Business Horizons,* February, 1961, special supplement from the *First International Seminar on Marketing Management.*

tween what they add to their factory output in the form of packaging, services, advertising, customer advice, financing, delivery arrangements, warehousing, and other things that people value.

WHAT IS A PRODUCT?

When the outputs of competing factories are essentially identical and their prices the same, the conversion of an indifferent prospect into a solid customer requires a special effort. Whether the product is cold-rolled steel or hot cross buns, whether accountancy or delicacies, competitive effectiveness increasingly demands that the successful seller offer his prospect and his customer more than the generic product itself. He must surround his generic product with a cluster of value satisfactions that differentiates his total offering from his competitors'. He must provide a total proposition, the content of which exceeds what comes out at the end of the assembly line.

Take cosmetics. The industry has factory sales of over $3 billion. Yet not a single American woman buys a single penny's worth of cosmetics. Charles Revson, the entrepreneurial genius who built Revlon into the thriving enterprise it is today, has said, "In the factory we make cosmetics. In the store we sell hope." Women use cosmetics, but they don't buy them; they buy hope. Mr. Revson has built his magnificent edifice on the correct understanding of human drives. He knows that chastity is the rarest of all sexual aberrations.

"Hope" is the extra plus—the special promise of customer-satisfying benefits—that gives cosmetics their special appeal. It is not with the generic product that Revlon addresses itself to the consumer, but with the special promise of differentiating glamour, personal fulfillment, and sex appeal. What is important is not so much what Revlon puts inside the compact as the ideas put inside the customer's head by luxurious packaging and imaginative advertising.

Pressure valves, polypropylene, and screw machines cannot be similarly glamorized, nor does glamour itself attract any solvent customers for screw machines. But hope does—the buyer's hope that in choosing your company's screw machines, he has made a safer and better choice. Of course, the customer expects quality equipment and competitive prices. He expects on-time delivery. But successful companies increasingly find it pays to give the customer more—to supply him with extras he was not himself aware he wanted. Having been offered these extras, the customer finds them beneficial and therefore prefers doing business with the company that supplies them. By augmenting his generic product with unsolicited extras that produce extra customer benefits, the seller produces for himself extra customers.

In recent years computer manufacturers have been especially active in augmenting their products with application aids, programming services, information-systems advice, and training programs for their customers. These services are so important for sales success that it has become perfectly clear that the computer manufacturer with the biggest share of the market is not necessarily the one whose computers are always the best or the cheapest. Indeed, subpoenaed documents in the IBM-Telex litigations disclose IBM judging any number of its competitors' computer products better than its own. Success and leadership have gone to IBM largely because of its better total package of customer-satisfying and therefore customer-getting values. The most important part of this package turns out to be something quite profoundly different from the computer hardware itself. It is the so-called "peripheral" services and aids with which the generic product is so effectively surrounded.

Fertilizer, Sex, and Cigarettes

Computers are not distinctive in their capacity to lend themselves to this kind of service augmentation. It works with perhaps even greater force for the most mundane commodities. Take fertilizer. The International Minerals and Chemical Corporation sells a prosaic mix of fertilizer ingredients—phosphate, super-phosphate, and potash—very much more successfully than its competitors. It does well not because its prices are lower, its delivery more reliable, or its salesmen quicker at grabbing the luncheon check. It succeeds so well because it has carefully analyzed the overall business problems of its prospects and then has done something imaginative about its findings. It provides its customers with free business consultancy services as part of its total product package. As the result, it has given its prospects a special set of reasons for preferring to do business with IMC rather than with its competitors. IMC does not offer a better product, but it offers a *different* product—a product with new and superior benefits for its users.

For years, almost instinctively, consumer goods manufacturers have recognized that the generic product is perhaps the least important part of the product itself. In clothing, it is not dresses one sells, but fashion. In retailing—the retail store—it is often atmosphere, selection, speed of service, or delivery that matters as much as the quality of the products themselves. In cigarettes, the point reaches its most extraordinary extreme. Only a particularly prudish observer can fail to come to any conclusion other than that American cigarette companies literally sell only one product —sex. Even the "low-tar-and-nicotine" brands embellish their many ads with suggestive scenes of sexual prowess and allurement. The most successful of all American cigarette campaigns in over thirty years is pure sex—the Marlboro Country ads. The rugged outdoor simplicity of the American frontiersman appeals to the male animal for what it implies about his virility. It suggests a powerful masculinity undiluted by contaminating urban softness. And it appeals to the female just as effectively by implying that a woman who smokes Marlboros is an uninhibited primitive of irresistible attraction.

It is not too wild to suggest that the large retail department store should view itself as being in show business. The customer goes there as much to be titillated and entertained as to buy what is displayed. She goes to have her senses heightened and her spirits elevated. Indeed, unless her senses are properly titillated and her spirits lifted, she probably will not buy, or buy in the desired quantity. It is relevant that Abe Feder, responsible for the magnificent lighting effects in the original Broadway production of *My Fair Lady,* received so many offers from large retailers that he established a successful lighting consulting firm.

The necessity of creating the proper buying atmosphere, of producing properly promising packaging, and of offering sufficiently appropriate customer services is so obvious to today's businessman that he is largely unaware that he is responding to that necessity. Yet to do these things well, he must be aware of the fact that he is doing them at all. Any number of companies, upon being told of International Minerals and Chemical's customer consulting services, will respond with impressive examples of how they have done the same sorts of things for various customers. They may indeed have done the same sorts of things, but they have not done the same thing. They have helped customers on an ad hoc basis when a particular salesman has taken the initiative, when a particular prospect actually requested the help, or when a particular customer was in visible trouble. That is all very well. The point is that IMC does it on an organized, fully budgeted, continuously programmed basis. It has men with the full-time responsibility of analyzing its prospects' and customers' problems for the purpose of constantly producing product augmentations designed to help with these problems and hence help give customers special reasons for dealing with IMC. As a consequence, IMC has created within its vast organization a powerfully prevailing culture in which the customer is viewed not as the object of a military encounter—to be targeted, banged away at, gotten the big guns out for—but as an entity with problems that he is trying to solve, problems in whose solution IMC should participate.

The Problem of Defining
the Problem

The marketing concept views the customer's purchasing activities as being problem-solving activities. This view of what the consumer does can have a profound effect on how the supplier or seller conducts his affairs. It affects more than how he does business and how much business he does. It affects what business he tries to do and what his product line should be. By looking at what the customer is actually trying to do, the seller will see that his problem as a seller is quite different from what it is usually assumed to be. Only after he defines his problem properly can the seller decide what is proper for him to do. Never is this necessity more urgent than when competition is most severe. The most severe kind of competition is warfare. It is not surprising, therefore, that war strategy has so often focused so carefully on a prior definition of the specific problem at hand. Since one gets few second chances, it is essential that the first try succeed.

During the early days of World War II, the United States suffered heavy shipping losses to German submarines on the North Atlantic supply runs. Detailed study showed that losses were inversely related to convoy size and that the ratio of required escorting military vessels was inverse to the size of the convoy. A rash and dangerous conclusion would have been to greatly expand convoy sizes. This would have reduced losses while felicitously economizing on the use of escorts. That would have been a sound solution only if the problem had been to reduce shipping losses. But that was not the problem. The problem was to win the war. Significantly larger convoys would have produced great logistical tie-ups at embarkation and debarkation, thus greatly aggravating security problems and greatly increasing Allied vulnerability to enemy attack at these points. Moreover, if the strategy began to work on the high seas, German submarines would have been diverted to fight in other critical combat areas, where the results might have been even more devastating.

Incorrect definition of the problem—or incorrect statements of the objective—can produce similarly incorrect conclusions about the appropriateness of a given strategy in business. A current example is the burgeoning demand for aid to the aged that has been generated by life-sustaining drugs and Medicare. The ratio of elderly people in hospitals is rising. At the same time the demand for nursing homes is booming, in part because of drugs and Medicare, and in part because of the great availability of retirement pensions and the rising independence of adult children who don't want ailing parents to live with them. A superficial look suggests great commercial opportunities in hospitals and nursing homes. Such opportunities do indeed exist, but they are exaggerated. A more analytical look shows that many hospital beds are occupied by postoperative patients who are too well to require hospital care and too well to require nursing-home confinement. What they require is convalescent care—a transition facility between in-patient surgery at hospitals and ultimate nursing-home confinement. The availability of such transitionary convalescent centers would greatly relieve pressures on hospitals and greatly enhance the dignity of patients who are too well for terminal nursing-home residence. Recognition of precisely this problem has created companies like Extendicare, Inc., and American Medicorp, Inc., which provide convalescent-home services while many others are still busily building terminal nursing homes.

This is a case of companies whose careful examination of the full range of conditions to which they addressed themselves resulted in a product-line activity that, in effect, altered the business into which they might otherwise have gone. Servicing hospitals or running terminal nursing homes is completely different from running convalescent centers.

Ergo, Air Cargo

Similarly, supplementing a factory-produced product with services is completely different from running a factory, and it is different from the usual way of selling the product. A classic example is the work of American Airlines during its early efforts at promoting air freight. The motivation was obvious. Airplanes carried people all day long and halfway through the night. But from midnight until dawn these costly but highly mobile fixed assets remained idle. Searching for new uses, American sought out the Distributor Products Division of the Raytheon Corporation as a possible air-cargo customer. The DP Division supplied transistors and vacuum tubes to distributors who resold largely to small radio and television repair shops throughout the nation. It had five warehouses supplied from a single factory warehouse near Boston.

American studied Raytheon's distribution operations in infinite detail. The result was a proposal to eliminate all five field warehouses and supply distributors directly by overnight air cargo. American proposed that all daily orders be assembled at the factory each night, picked up by American at the plant, and transported by air cargo overnight to fourteen break-bulk locations throughout the nation. From there common carrier truckers would deliver the orders immediately to distributors.

But American did not stop there, leaving it to Raytheon to work out the details. American enlisted the help of the Friden Company and Western

Union. Together the three companies designed an elaborate automatic data-transmissions system with feeder terminals in the field and print-out readers at the plant. Electronically transmitted orders were received by a computer at the plant and automatically converted into shipping invoices, slotted into shipping schedules, and fed into inventory control and production schedules. The net result was that Raytheon received a systems proposal that was so complete and persuasive in every detail that it became easy for Raytheon to make a decision in favor of air cargo.

What was American Airlines' product? To say that it was air cargo is to miss the point. It was the provision of that fashionable commodity, a system. Air freight alone was a minor, and by itself insufficient, element of the system. American surrounded this particular element, the generic product, with a cluster of augmenting benefits that became the deciding variables in the transaction. The product was not air cargo; it was a fully integrated, automated, and complete communications-distribution system.

American might have stopped with the mere proposal to substitute air cargo for the warehouses. It might have said simply that communications and teleprinters and computers and trucking were not its business and that it knew nothing about such things. But it systematically and conscientiously did more. It arranged to do the whole task that was needed to solve Raytheon's problem. As a consequence, it created a customer where none existed—where the customer was not even aware that he was a prospect.

This is today's hidden competition, the nongeneric component of the product, the clear fact that, for its buyer and for its consumer, a product is more than what is made in the factory. And this "moreness" is not just "packaging"—the cosmetics of its container or design. A product is everything with which it is surrounded and elaborated and reinforced that has the power to affect consumer choice—that contains, in effect, the power to influence choice in its favor. In the case of industrial goods and services, the nongeneric character of products is particularly prevalent in the relations among large companies whose customers are relatively small and fragmented, or whose competences are limited—institutions where suppliers can bring to customers help and support that they cannot easily provide for themselves. This is not the visible competition among televised toothpastes or the headline-getting competition among giant suppliers of aerospace systems to NASA. It is the new competition of product augmentation.

We shall look closer at this idea—an idea which we shall call the "augmented product concept"—in the next chapter. Let's look now in detail how the things we've been talking about get us back to Professor Corey's prescriptions about product-line planning and its central role in helping define and achieve the company's objectives.

Professor Corey cites as a model the operating responsibilities of the product-line planning function in one large multiproduct, industrial-products corporation:

(1) Appraise products and product trends in relation to competing products as viewed by customer; (2) analyze customer needs and habits and evaluate with respect to existing and contemplated markets; (3) prepare product specifications of performance, physical characteristics, quality level, dependability, serviceability, safety design features, product identification, packaging and appearance; (4) determine product timing and establish master product calendar; (5) formulate prices at which products should be sold to achieve the volume position and profit objectives of the business; (6) control product lines by development and administration of policies, programs, and plans to accomplish the marketing objectives of the business; (7) process product ideas as a means of formulating plans and programs for innovations; (8) provide product information for building advertising and sales promotion and for manuals, catalogues and price books; (9) recommend appearance design and contract for appearance design models of new products; and (10) coordinate planning of product programs of Sales, Engineering, Manufacturing and Finance Departments.[2]

Obviously, product-line planning is based on a thorough understanding of the consumer, the market, and all the forces that impinge on them. Hence, ". . . the very nature of the product policy problem makes it an area of vital interest to top management. . . . [Because the] kind of products that a company includes in its product line determines whom it can serve and with whom it must compete . . . this factor goes far toward determining the nature of the firm's business."[3]

The Role of Marketing

Since product-line planning bears so visibly on the company's future posture, the chief executive has a particular responsibility to expect that the marketing department will supply him with the data and the advice necessary for informed decisions as to what is to be produced, now and in the future.

---

[2] Hadley Company, International Case Clearing House, 2M31, copyright 1957 by the President and Fellows of Harvard College, pp. 14–15.

[3] Edgar A. Pessemier, *New-product Decisions: An Analytical Approach,* McGraw-Hill Book Company, New York, 1966, p. 7.

Data Are Not Information

The enormous prodigality of the computer has so accelerated the process of data accumulation that we often actually know less than we did before. Great masses of data are disgorged in impressively magnificent print-outs. Yet they seldom improve our grasp of the elaborately quantified situations that are depicted.

Data are not information. Information is not meaning. Just as data require processing to become informational, so information requires processing to become meaningful.

Yet the more abundant the information, the less meaning it will yield. We know that the surest way to destroy a man's capacity for discrimination is to overwhelm his senses with the relevant stimuli. The greater the variety of food consumed at a meal, the less you appreciate each dish. The louder the noise, the less impressive the message.

When we call for more information to guide product policy, this must mean a call for more meaning. What is needed is discrimination in the use of data, not its sheer abundance. Abundance is not a liberator. It is a suffocator.

Discrimination cannot be exercised in a vacuum. It has to be relevant to the purpose for which it is exercised. This means that the effective use of information requires a clear understanding of the exact purpose of its use: What is the question it is designed to answer, what is the problem it is designed to illuminate, and what is the issue it is designed to focus?

Take the case of the Irish Tourist Board. For years it was enormously successful in building tourist business, congratulating itself for having constantly overfulfilled its objective of generating overseas trade revenue. But the true facts were quite the reverse. The Board had targeted high-income, high-spending tourists. When they got to Ireland they stayed in luxurious foreign-owned urban hotels, drank imported Scotch whiskey, ate imported beefsteak, and rented imported motor cars. Had the target been lower-income tourists satisfied with staying in less luxurious domestically owned hotels, eating in native restaurants, taking trains and buses, and saving by buying picnic lunches of locally grown foods at locally owned stores, less might have been spent by each tourist but Ireland would have earned more.

Before data can be effectively processed, before information can be effectively arranged and converted to meaning, considerable thought must first be given to their specific uses and purposes. Otherwise, the recipient will be deafened by an orgiastic outpouring of noise, or deceived by data that lack the needed information.

Thinking: The New Necessity

The irony is clear: The more data we get, the less time is available for their effective use. Hence the more effective we get at providing data, the greater the requirement that we spend more preparatory time deciding specifically what we want them for—what are the relevant issues and questions? The necessity of thinking is intensified, not obviated, by the prodigality of data and information.

The feedback consequences of this are also clear. The computer must be harnessed to give the executive more time to think so that he can effectively use the computer. If the computer fails to do that, it will consume itself. It will be like a giant weed whose ungovernable growth creates a self-destructive imbalance in its metabolism.

In the new world of abundant data, especially data masquerading as information, now less than ever can an executive be effective without first thinking carefully about what the relevant questions really are. Otherwise, he'll be swamped.

Thinking: By the Boss or by His Staff?

Yet high-echelon executive decision making in the large corporation seldom exhibits evidence of very much careful thinking. The decision-making process is generally assumed to involve a heavy input of judgment. The implication is that thinking is what guides judgment. Yet when we look at the criteria by which men are chosen for top positions, no one will deny that it is successful *experience* that predominates, not evidence of competent thinking. Men are systematically rotated into various assignments in order that they may get a "breadth of experience in all our operations" before being elevated finally to the upper ranks.

This premium on experience is powerfully attested to by the authority accorded to men who in meetings "talk from experience" and by the devastating approbrium implied by the observation, "That may be all right in theory, but. . . ." "Theory," which is the Siamese twin of "thought," is held in low esteem. To think your way through to a solution is to imply a failure of the only legitimate way to get it, by experience and brute energy.

Where careful thought *is* acknowledged as a prerequisite for effective executive action, this capability is so widely presumed to be inappropriate for the line executive that a separate organizational entity has been created in order that thinking may have a legitimate corporate residence. This entity is called the "staff." And of course staff work is viewed as inferior. It is done by people who think, not act; people so thoroughly lacking in authentic business competence that they are structurally excluded from any line authority, where they might do some terrible harm. Contrary to what one might expect in these increasingly more complex days, an increasingly distinct separation is actually being made between line and staff. In most corporations where the staff is expanding, so is its structural isolation from decision-making authority.

Yet this isolation is only a presumption. In operating fact, the more difficult and the bigger the decision, the greater the likelihood that the staff, or an outside group of consultants or financial advisers, will make that decision.

Decision or Choice?

Managers are increasingly withholding complex decisions until "all the facts are in" and the situation has been "thoroughly studied." Judgment is suspended until the staff has reported. But finally, when the decision is made at the corporate top, it is neither a decision nor a judgment. It is a choice—and generally not even a choice between alternatives; rather, the choice is between accepting or rejecting the staff's elaborately documented and heavily supported proposal. It is, moreover, a choice in which the line executive does not so much make a judgment based on his own independent thought as it is his going through a process by which he gives or withholds his blessing of the staff's recommendation. In more advanced or sophisticated, but rare, situations, he is given a set of alternatives from which to choose. He must make a choice or judgment as to which to use, but it is always expected in such cases that the staff will indicate its own preference.

Whatever serious thought goes into the decision-making process will have been done by the staff. Things will be carefully laid out to the busy line executive with elaborate simplicity. His job is to approve, or at best to choose. What thinking is involved is operationally equivalent to deciding at which restaurant to have lunch, or whether to have lunch at all.

In the large organization this process is a daily occurrence, far different from the situation in the old days, when seat-of-the-pants decisions put a heavy burden on the executive to synthesize for himself the meager facts available to him. The result today is the extreme danger of high-level executives developing a trained incapacity for independent thought and analysis and, as a consequence, a trained capacity to make only routine bureaucratic choices. What passes for thinking is generally little more than rambling committee discussions of the ins and outs of issues carefully predigested, documented, resolved, and set forth by the staff. There is seldom a quiet moment of independent contemplation, rarely a staff document that is thoroughly studied and weighed by its recipient, rarely a decision of any consequence made on the basis of deductive reasoning at the upper level.

This severe indictment is not made lightly or without acknowledging many laudable exceptions to the dismal picture. To the extent that it is the general picture, this is not to suggest that staff work is undesirable or that seat-of-the-pants decision making is to be preferred. Far from it. What is suggested is the necessity for top management to recognize exactly what is happening and to appreciate its awful implications. As men rise higher in the managerial hierarchy, they get more staff to do their thinking for them. As in any skill or art, disuse produces disability. Hence men who increasingly rely on their staffs to do their thinking for them are increasingly incapacitated to do precisely what is so vital at the higher level—to think about the corporate purpose and about strategy, tactics, and entrepreneurial opportunities.

Few men of rank and achievement will agree with this unflattering assertion. Self-respect and the plaudits of friends, subordinates, family, and stockholders require a more prepossessing self-image. Yet one may ask the high executive to sit down quietly and make a careful list of situations in the last month in which he has made decisions—and then ask which of these have been choices and which decisions, which based on staff or subordinate recommendations and which decided from scratch. How often in the last year has he sat back and, with anything resembling a systematic evaluation of the state of his corporate affairs, consciously and alone pondered how to handle them? A fair response to these questions cannot be flattering. And yet there is always an "and yet." It is that the failure lies not in the respondent to the question, but heavily in the nature of the system. He needs the staff and the subordinates to do so much of his work, but then almost automatically he lets slip into their hands work that should be preserved for him alone. This is the easy but treacherous posture into which it is essential that he not slip. His biggest job becomes, almost, to hold on to what his job really is.

The Task at the Top

Let us once again look at the special role of the chief executive and see how it imposes on him the special necessity for independent strategic thinking.

The central task of a business is to create and keep a customer. The chief function of the business's chief executive is to see that the business will constantly succeed in that endeavor. A great many chief executives confine their efforts in this regard to assuring that appropriate financial and management resources will be available. Some have answered very elaborately the question of "available for what?" They know where they plan their companies to be. Others know it by instinct. Many know only that they want to "keep going."

The larger the organization, the greater the lag between a decision at its apex and an action at its appendages. This fact alone is enough to tell us that the chief executive's primary concern about the company's customer-getting task can apply only to the future, not to the present. He is too far removed from the scene of routine operations to have any appreciable day-to-day effect on them. More than anyone else in the enterprise, his decisions are characterized by the most profound fact of all decisions, namely, that decisions have futurity. They affect what *will* happen, not what *is* happening. What is happening has already happened. It cannot be changed. Only the future is changeable. And for the chief executive, only the relatively distant future is changeable—not tomorrow or next month.

If the job of management is to organize, coordinate, command, and control, it must first know where it wants these efforts to take the company. Then it needs a strategy for getting there. It must have a plan and it must have a strategy, no matter how crude, amorphous, inarticulate, or subconscious. Otherwise, there is drift, taking the company where the competitive forces created by others send it, not where management wants it to go.

In a large organization the chief executive's subconscious plan is not good enough. The plan must be known and clear to his lieutenants. Otherwise they may take actions which, perhaps unintentionally, subvert the plan. Each action is like that of a bricklayer carefully putting down a brick. The accumulation of bricks produces a result that is in some way confining. He may end up with a cathedral or a delicatessen, or merely a tantalizing Rube Goldberg concoction, none of which conform to what the silent architect at the top had in mind. While each brick (or policy or strategem or tactic) may have aggressively dealt with an existing situation, the danger is clear that it may be incapable of dealing with future situations.

What's at Stake

More is at stake than the life of the business. Also at stake is the kind of life the business will lead and the kind of people available to run the business. The manager of the R & D department may return from the campuses with magnificently promising "A" students who will produce products that the silent architect does not want. He wants only low-cost imitations of other companies' proved products. The R & D head could have saved himself lots of headaches and the company lots of money by going after solid "C" students. The marketing head in the meanwhile would have gone after the campus's fast-moving promoters rather than careful product planners. The solitary silence of the architect at the top will have produced frustration, resignations, and really none of the objectives he so jealously kept to himself.

His staff and his consultants can provide the president and his close lieutenants with information helpful in deciding what the company's future posture and strategies should be. But it is precisely because the final decisions have so much futurity, precisely because their consequences will be felt so far out into the uncertain future, that the available facts are considerably less relevant to such decisions than to, say, operating decisions. The "facts" available for decisions about things only vaguely perceived are different from facts about things that are solidly contemporary. It follows that the decision-making process at the top must also be different in important respects from that at lower levels.

Look for a moment at the tremendously successful Xerox 914 copier. The nation's three most prestigious consulting firms recommended against it during the planning stage, and so did the corporate staff with considerable vehemence. The example is instructive, and the more so because it is not uncommon. The 914 is a high-velocity, multicopy reproducing machine with the speed of a printing press but none of its costly and time-consuming setup requirements. The consultants very sensibly concluded that only companies with large and far-flung staffs were reasonable prospects, plus selected smaller ones with special paperwork needs. Interviews and analyses of such companies' paperwork activities finally produced potential market-size estimates of relatively microscopic dimensions.

Xerox's decision to proceed with the 914 was based on inputs the consultants had not effectively considered: that there was an accelerating increase of staff activity in all organizations and that its output was paper work; that increasing organizational decentralization was producing an accelerating expansion of organizational entities and increasingly larger superorganizations; that there was an expanding trend toward written rather than oral communications within a business; that increasingly business decisions would be group decisions and that these would be preceded by written reports and heavy documentation; that the resulting proliferation of bureaucracy would raise the tendency to associate effort with the output of reports, memorandums, and correspondence, all of which would become widely distributed in order to broaden the appearance of activity; and that once this practice was set into motion by one person, it would proliferate competitively to others within the organization. Not only would the resulting flow of paper work grow exponentially, but most significantly for Xerox, this growth would be heavily in the form of identical documents circulating among many different people.

Limits of Scientific Management

What distinguishes this analysis from the more common type of forecasting and staff reporting is that it is qualitative and projective rather than quantitative and extrapolatory. It requires creative and cerebral inputs rather than quantitative and arithmetical ones. The available "facts" with which Xerox's top management dealt were entirely different from those used by the consultants and the staff. Not that the consultants and the staff were incapable of such inputs; rather, their reason for existence was precisely to avoid such inputs. Consultants and staff exist in order that decisions will be based on "solid facts," not on the old seat-of-the-pants intuition or "feel for the market." They exist specifically to replace what is viewed as the risky method of the past—the intuitive guesswork of self-willed entrepreneurs. Because that is the reason consultants exist, it is hardly legitimate for them to repeat, even in elaborately rationalized form, what they have been hired to replace.

It is not hard to see the ironic trap we are building for ourselves. Escape from uncertainty induces the creation of staff and the development of "scientific" management. These create a management style that emphasizes rigorous quantification of alternatives and directions. But the more distant the impact of choice, or the greater the departure of a proposal from experienced ways of doing things, the less quantifiable it is. Hence the less likely that the choice or the proposal will meet the "scientific" tests of the new managerial style. As the result, the company will increasingly reduce itself to the effective management of the here and now rather than the creation of the uncommonly new. As suggested in a remarkably perceptive book by Donald A. Schon, "In this environment the corporation minimizes innovation. The strategies it has developed to control uncertainty increase the probability of failures."[4] The danger is that the entire long-range decision-making process will become shrouded in a pervasively restrictive illusion—namely, that at last things are being done in a scientifically pure and therefore superior fashion. This presumption becomes the final guarantee against the legitimacy of inspirational thinking, against what, indeed, is thinking itself. All that remains is choice. Judgment becomes a dull exercise in ancestral piety, invoking at best only the limited particularism of past experience.

[4] Donald A. Schon, *Technology and Change: The New Heraclitus,* Delacorte Press, Dell Publishing Co., Inc., New York, 1967.

Unhappily, the structure of the modern, large organization systematically militates against the exercise of thoughtful entrepreneurship at the upper levels. The staff is presumed and expected to provide all the inputs necessary for making difficult decisions. If its work is thorough, its recommendation must therefore be incontrovertible. The president or executive committee or board of directors that objects more than occasionally to the recommendations of its staff will be committing an act of profound insubordination. It will be reverting to an older style of management whose replacement the creation of the staff symbolizes. The only way for the chief executive to legitimately reject the staff's work is for him to commit the redundancy of getting a sycophantic second staff of his very own.

This is, in fact, not uncommon. It takes two highly ceremonial and legitimizing forms. One form is the outside consulting agency. The second is the establishment of the "office of the president." President Nixon has been a particularly avid user of the latter, especially in foreign affairs. The elaborate staff of the State Department has been systematically neutralized by his own personal White House staff of foreign-affairs experts. Nor did things change when Mr. Kissinger took over at State. His real office remained in the White House.

But a measure of how powerfully entrenched the new requirement of quantification for high-level decision making has become in modern, large-scale organizations is that even these second staffs are compelled to adhere to the organization's rigid method lest the decision maker disqualify himself for modern leadership. He cannot afford to seem to be a Henry Ford. He must be an Alfred P. Sloan, ragardless of whether that style is always appropriate.

The Power of Management Styles

The rigid requirements of management style are not without their helpful purposes, however. Therein lies the awful dilemma of modern leadership. The chief executive helps set the management style. If he does not for his own decisions insist on the requirement of completed staff work, neither will his subordinates. The result would certainly be catastrophic. The large, complex organization cannot effectively execute its day-to-day tasks without constant, careful study of its operations, without carefully systematic and documented inputs to its operating decisions. The Henry Ford fashion of hunch, inspiration, energy, and unrelenting personal pressure to reduce costs is not enough.

Yet at the apex of the organization the central decisions about the future cannot be effectively facilitated with the kinds of materials that the method of "completed staff work" provides. Top decisions of certain limited kinds, of course, can be facilitated by this kind of staff work—decisions regarding legitimate extrapolations about the required size of future plan facilities, location of certain distribution points, international markets to enter with existing products, and the capital requirements for such ventures.

But the more difficult decisions about entirely new product categories to enter, new businesses to develop, elaborate new ways to distribute products, new and untried services to offer, new ways to control and manage the business, new ways to develop young managers—none of these decisions are easily facilitated by the conventional methods of completed staff work. Yet these are preeminently presidential decisions, decisions which in this world of rapid and disabling newness are imposed upon the president with unabating frequency.

How can the necessity of his making important decisions in the more old-fashioned manner be reconciled with the necessity of his insisting on the new-fashioned manner for his subordinates? More important, how can the man trained and accustomed to the new-fashioned manner learn, and reconcile, and accustom himself to the old manner when his elevation to the top is based on his effective mastery of the new manner?

Old and New Management Styles

Just as there is no single emancipating way to get new products, no elegantly single best way to organize a company, or no inspirationally best style for leadership, so there is no best single way to deal with this unique dilemma. All that is obviously clear is that the dilemma will not get attention if its existence is not clearly recognized.

Some things follow from that recognition:

1. The chief executive must project two entirely different, but not opposite, management styles.

2. He must legitimize both styles.

3. He must see that the organization understands the reasons for, and the specific appropriateness of each style.

4. He must encourage the capacity of younger and more recently trained executives to think more carefully about the purposes for which the new expansion of data is to be employed.

5. He must establish via his own example the legitimacy of projective thinking—of data that are inductive and intuitive, rather than simply quantitative and deductive.

6. He must communicate the nonquantitative rationale for intuitive decisions, not only to avoid the unintentional legitimization of seemingly capricious decisions, but also to encourage within his organization the habit

of thinking out solutions and programs, rather than merely deriving them from others.

7. He must abandon the heavy customary reliance on formal internal communications; these thoroughly screen out the nuances of argument and alternative, in which so often reside some of the most provocative and promising ideas.

The common tendency today to depend so heavily on formal, written communications rather than on informal, face-to-face contact has several causes and consequences. These are worth a brief examination. One reason for their heavy use is that formal, written reports and memorandums are in some ways clearly superior to face-to-face communication. They impose on those who write them a discipline not otherwise required. A second reason is that they simply save time. Third, they produce a record for subsequent consultation.

All these are good reasons. It is this very fact that produces their abuse. A good thing is not improved by its multiplication. Every effort has a price. The usual practice has become not only to have formal, written reports, one of whose presumed purposes is to eliminate some of the wastes and slippages of face-to-face communication, but to also augment these with formal meetings to discuss the reports. In other cases the cause and effort work in reverse; a meeting is required, for the record, to be augmented with a formal report to be distributed at the meeting.

The entire process involves elaborately costly preparation. There are extensive drafts and redrafts of the presentation that is planned for the meeting. Several dry runs precede the final presentation itself, complete with several monitoring people called in for their reactions and advice. Numerous subsidiary meetings precede the ultimate big meeting, which becomes bigger in its perceived importance to the "presenters" as the preparation proceeds. But often the executive who suggested the meeting in the first place will have had only the most casual motive—to keep himself modestly informed of a department's or a project's progress. Yet in a culture where "completed staff work" and "scientific management" have been elevated to the proportions of a medieval faith, this single limited purpose of keeping informed will, at the lower levels, be elaborated into preparatory proportions of elaborate dimensions. Everything stops to prepare for the "big" meeting.

A similarly wasteful process is set into frantic motion when a high-level boss telephones a subordinate (or, more likely, writes a letter) for a memo or a note on a particular situation. Several days' work of several men is the predictable overreacting result.

It would make a great deal more sense for the inquiring executive to have lunch with his subordinate or to call him to his office on short notice for a brief chat. In a great many cases that is all that is needed or intended, and yet infinitely more generally happens. The result is that staffs are generally about twice as large as they need to be.

Where the Action Is

There is no question that a large, complex organization needs formal procedures and standards. But it is precisely because it needs them that it needs to guard against their unrestrained proliferation. Even more, it needs to guard against their becoming a crutch of management and a substitute for the executive getting his hands dirty.

For example, there is a tendency in many large organizations to operate almost exclusively through written reports and to make judgments almost exclusively on the basis of variances between budgets and actuals, on the basis of the difference between formal standards and hoped-for estimates. As a result, often not enough attention is paid to the character, the methods, and the spirit of the men whose performance and promise are being evaluated in the process. There is, in short, not enough of a premium put on direct face-to-face evaluation of, and "feel for," the man.

Any executive can measure the extent of his delinquency on this matter merely by remembering how often he has "spotted" a promising man in the organization virtually by accident—by having inadvertently met him during a field visit, having heard him speak at a meeting that he might easily have missed had some urgent, last-minute event necessitated his absence, and so forth. In other words, higher executives may be too much insulated from their subordinates, and particularly from the field.

When the top man does go into the field, too often he gets a synthetic, red-carpet treatment. His reception and tour have been planned like a military operation. All effort is diligently devoted to his getting nothing but the most rosy and attractive picture of life in the lower-echelon hinterlands. He gets a badly distorted view of reality.

The solution is to have more field visits, more informal drop-ins in subordinates' offices, more unannounced "circulation" by the boss.

This kind of circulation makes possible as few other actions can the achievement of some of the special things suggested for the chief executive in this chapter. Nobody in any organization is as visible as its chief, even when he remains anonymously closeted behind protective secretaries, busy assistants, and heavy oak doors in a luxuriously carpeted distant corner of the upper floor. Visibility is a function of rank, not nearness or accessibility. No eyes are more sharply trained or ears more carefully tuned than those of subordinates looking upward. The boss's every utterance and every action—even his inactions—and the particular gait of his walk to the elevator each morning are measured, interpreted, and talked about. There is an eager audience for the observations of people who happened to be on the elevator that morning with some high-level boss—that he looked worried, or wise, or impatient, or heavier, or that his "Good morning" sounded genuine or abstracted or bored or hurried.

Unintentional Communication

The higher the person's rank, the more fully his unintentional communications will be seen and the more elaborately they will be interpreted. The higher his rank, the greater the significance that will be attached to his unintended rather than his intended communications. Everybody knows that the rules are less important than the ropes. The rules are that the intended communications be very carefully structured. The president's speeches are prepared with the penultimate care given to state documents. The object is to sound a ceremonial note of purpose, dedication, and progress without at the same time saying anything either too specific or too insufficiently promising. His letter in the annual report is so antiseptically conventional that, except for a few numbers, it would be perfectly suitable for the reports of a dozen other companies drawn out of a hat. Those are the rules. Anybody who knows the ropes knows that the trick is to hear what the boss is *not* saying. That requires careful attention, and it is to what he is not saying that everybody listens so carefully.

That is why so much elaborately involuted and expensive corporate activity is so often generated by the boss's most casual comments. His little questions at little meetings, often intended only as ritual offerings to the necessity that he say *something,* set off vast activity below. In one large corporation a sudden coughing spell by a group vice-president at the moment when a proposed project's budget was preliminarily presented to the executive committee was seriously interpreted by the subordinates as meaning that he viewed it as excessive. During the entire meeting none of the executive committee's members ever mentioned costs, though there was considerable discussion about details that affected costs. The project team concluded that the committee's concern with the details was an attempt to find ways to reduce excessive costs. As a consequence the team greatly modified the program. The costs were equivalently reduced. It was precisely these modifications which subsequently caused the project, at enormous cost, to fail.

In another situation, an executive committee member innocently wondered whether the specially constructed building for an entirely new kind of service business should perhaps be planned for an alternative use in case the proposed test failed. The building was originally to be located in a declining section of the test city in which real estate values were depressed but which would not affect its volume of business. The result was a compromised, redesigned structure in a costly, high-traffic location. The new multipurpose building was so inadequately suited to its primary purpose and the new high-cost location so steeply raised the break-even point that the test failed.

Obviously, in both these cases it could be asked whether the men who presented the original plans did not cause these failures by their own sheepish behavior. Had they been forthright and, in the second case, explained the risky and high-cost consequences of a different building in a different location, the deciding executives would certainly have responded favorably. It is a reasonable question, but also the wrong one. The right question concerns why mature and trusted men behaved so sheepishly to begin with. The answer is that the organization taught them to know the ropes, to learn to become trusted by responding to the casual and often unintended signals of their superiors. A man is considered trustworthy and responsible when he is effectively responsive, without requiring a lot of details to be spelled out to him.

This is all very well, even desirable perhaps, on routine operating matters. Bosses rightly expect things to happen in response to casual comments that have an easy, suggestive tone rather than an abrasively authoritarian ring. The options that are in any case available to the subordinate are highly limited. The result is actions not likely to depart measurably from the boss's suggestive intentions. But this style is not appropriate when the options are many and varied and the consequences of departure from the intended idea can be devastating.

The power of unintended communications expands as the communicator's rank increases. This means that top management must be constantly aware of what their most casual words and deeds convey to others. They can be thoughtlessly employed to stifle, misdirect, misinform, and even destroy. Or they can be thoughtfully employed to achieve within the organization adherence to a desired norm of completed staff work as well as to stimulate imaginative entrepreneurial audacity. In the end, the things that rule the process are the signals perceived by others, not the rules written by organizational engineers.

What the Chief Must Do

Information, discipline, planning, structure, and order—these are inescapable organizational requisites. The larger the organization, the more they are required. But the more they are required, the more their re-strictive consequences must be offset by more emancipating styles at the apex.

Marketing is the one corporate function that is least effectively governed in a traditionally orderly manner. Unfortunately, it is the implicit recognition of this fact which so often causes marketing to be governed so sloppily. A great deal more order, system, planning, control, and even rigidity can be injected into most marketing organizations without injury to their success. The typical plea is that marketing deals with too màny intangibles to be effectively governed in the conventional manner. In many cases this plea merely masks a congenial preference for a free-floating, undisciplined shop. Often it represents an unwillingness to face the demanding require-ments of professional and responsible behavior. The chief executive can and should expect more from his marketing department than persuasively plausible arguments that "marketing is different."

On the other hand, the chief executive must recognize that not all his dissatisfactions with his marketing operations are all that justified. Market-ing is a uniquely vulnerable activity. It suffers from having an almost in-finite potential for improved performance: prices could always be higher, and sales always better. The production department operates in a happy contrast. Costs have a solidly limited capacity for reduction. Wage rates, material costs, plant overhead, fringe benefits—all these are fairly fixed and irreducible. Productivity is measurably improvable only with the help of big, new capital expenditures or if the sales department can deliver bigger orders for standardized products. With these limitations, it is on marketing that the quest for profit expansion finally focuses. Marketing can produce more because production cannot cut more. Marketing is uniquely concerned with upward potentials, and as the astronomers tell us, up is infinite. Hence, marketing is constantly on the griddle.

"The chief executive cannot claim credit for marketing success," Clarence E. Eldridge once wisely said, adding, however, that neither can he avoid being blamed for marketing failure. Marketing operates decisively and inescapably in two quite different worlds—on the one hand, in the world of today's products and today's competitive environment, and on the other, in the uncertain world of tomorrow. It is in a powerful position to recommend and influence the company's products and operating posture for tomorrow because a properly run marketing organization will look ahead with more perceptive detail and concreteness than other operating departments. Looking ahead is one of the primary functions of product planning, and it is the president's duty to see that his marketing department executes this function effectively and with imagination.

Organized Entrepreneurship

The president, whose ultimate job is to secure the organization's future, cannot escape the fact that its successful future requires the creation of customers. This means that marketing's talent of studying the consumer must be developed and enlisted, while the entrepreneurial audacity to capitalize on its findings must be cultivated and employed, especially at the upper levels.

Unfortunately, it is difficult for persons with little or no intimate exposure to the entrepreneurial process to know what it really is. Few men who, by common consent, are viewed as having achieved great deeds of entrepreneurship would agree that this term describes any of the things that large organizations call by that name. In the large organization the process of creating new things is distinguished by the risk-reducing efforts that surround it. Large organizations do not have the gambling instinct. Innovation, like other functions of the firm, is viewed as an orderly process in which uncertainties are sedulously avoided unless they can be converted into manageable risks. Indeed, as Schon shows, the whole process of innovation in the large organization may be described as that of converting uncertainty into risk—that is, of describing probable outcomes in budgetary terms. Where this is not possible, nothing is ventured. The large organization cannot operate in uncertainty, but is well equipped to handle risk. Risk lends itself to quantitative expression. Its probabilities can be calculated. It can be controlled by the formal mechanisms of justification and review.

Uncertainty is different. It requires action but resists quantitative analysis. One can act, but cannot estimate the risks or rewards of his action. The large organization, whose size and structure exist largely to manage a complex but proved process, is typified by its insistence on the quantification of risk (whether via sophisticated probabilistic devices or by the more common budgetary tools) and by the mechanisms of justification and review. Dramatically new ventures that do not easily fit these procedures simply do not get support.

This goes a long way toward explaining why the great new innovations of the post-World War II era so uniformly originated either in small, new companies that were not dominated by this culture of scientism in management or in large companies dominated by men who, because of historic tenure or family power, were not constrained by normal procedures. The list is instructive: Polaroid, Xerox, Holiday Inns, McDonald's, IBM, Korvette, Leasco, Digital Equipment Corp., Texas Instruments, Reston, Northwest Industries, Diners' Club, Walt Disney Productions, McLean Industries, Beeline Fashions, Sara Lee, the Shaheen enterprises. Each of these companies was, in effect, a one-man show, tightly run by single men or a family.

Deeds of genuine entrepreneurship are by definition assaults on uncertainty. If they succeed they are heroic deeds. If they fail few people hear about them, and few lessons are derived for us to read about. Attempts in large organizations to achieve this kind of entrepreneurship have generally failed because of the insistence upon measured quantification that reduces risk to the corporation's normal proportions. These proportions are generally stated in terms of minimum expected sales or return on assets employed. The small, new entrepreneur, either unaccustomed to this discipline or impatient with it, plows ahead into the darkness with nothing to sustain him but his vision, his energy, and often his blindness to the pitfalls. It is a style the large, bureaucratic, team-operated organization cannot tolerate. That is why the successful entrepreneur does not recognize as entrepreneurship what the large corporation calls by that name, and can seldom live with the large corporation after he cashes in his chips by getting acquired by it.

Yet because of its enormous resources and staying power the large corporation can actually risk the uncertainties of genuine enterpreneurship even better than the impecunious upstart. This disjunction between what it does and what it can do reflects a disparity between its fiscal resources and its management style. It is a style designed largely to manage the here and now, at best to take measurable risks but not to plunge headlong into uncertainty.

Various companies have tried various devices to achieve the entrepreneurial equivalence of smallness. They have tried task forces, new-venture teams, joint ventures, and other types of entrepreneurial enclaves. These attempted institutionalizations of entrepreneurship have invariably run into disabling troubles, as we shall see in Section II of this book. The dominant culture of scientific management and review in which they operate tends to impose restrictive standards and procedures. The men who must ultimately approve their budgets cannot easily alter their accustomed habits. Moreover, this kind of institutionalization requires an enormous tolerance for repeated failure, unfulfilled promises, erratic and emotional people, constant delays, and the simultaneous presence of all these in a variety of continuing projects. Failure of management to approve the continuation of any one project before it is decisively beaten in the laboratory or in the marketplace becomes interpreted by all the others as a wanton breach of promise, a denial in deed of what is so resolutely affirmed in word. Demoralization and resignations are the predictable outcomes.

Unfortunately there is no easy solution—if, indeed, there is any solution at all. The idea of institutionalizing entrepreneurship is probably inherently self-contradictory. The fostering of what, for it, passes as the entrepreneurial spirit in the large corporation is, on the other hand, probably an essential condition of survival. And only the chief executive of a corporation or a large, autonomous operating division is in an effective position to try to foster it. Everybody else is too rigidly and quite necessarily obliged to conform to the budgets, reviews, and controls without which the ongoing corporate job cannot get done. Perhaps the best that can be hoped for in the large organization is an occasional massive entrepreneurial thrust whose origin is serendipitous rather than specifically ordered or planned. Indeed, the entire history of entrepreneurship is a history of capitalizing on unexpected and unanticipated opportunity—often nothing more than the suddenly inspired creation of opportunity, where none seemed to exist, by a single uncommon man. If uncommon things are to be done, they will require methods that are uncommon to the corporation and styles that are uncommon to the manager whose accession to the top rank generally represents his mastery of what the corporation commonly does and in an acceptable or common way.

Managers of large organizations and gigantic processes are constantly faced with Whitehead's seminal reminder that change and adaptation are the central requisites of survival. Anybody who aspires to more than simple survival, who, in short, wants to survive gallantly, not just vegetatively, must do more than simply adapt to change. He must make change, and not just elegant little changes at the margin. How the large organization can effectively do more than that is the great unanswered, perhaps unanswerable, question. It may be that we are limited to doing little more than making our best efforts, to simply trying to foster the unexpected and attempting an occasional massive burst of inspired heroism.

Unfortunately, none of the elegant new tools of modern scientific management and evaluation will help. Almost certainly they will hinder the processes. Ambiguity and disorder are the ruling requisites. Analogies abound. Speaking of a government's management of foreign affairs, Thomas C. Schelling has written that it

> . . . is a complicated and disorderly business, full of surprises, demanding hard choices that must often be based on judgment rather than analysis, involving relations with more than a hundred countries diverse in their traditions and political institutions—all taking place in a world that changes so rapidly that memory and experience are quickly out of date. Coordination, integration, and rational management are surely desirable; but whether it is humanly possible to meet anything more than the barest

minimum standards is a question to which an optimistic answer can be based only on faith. . . . The best—the very best—performance that is humanly possible is likely to look pretty unsatisfactory to the Congress, to Washington correspondents, to the electorate, even to the President who presides over the arrangement.[5]

In the case of entrepreneurship in the large business organization, if we substitute in the above quotation "board of directors" for "Congress," "business school professors" for "Washington correspondents," and "stock-holders" for "electorate," the point is much the same. The possibility of doing things satisfactorily, or right, or in an orderly manner is a chimera. The corporate president fortunately is well paid to make the best of this unhappy reality.

All this is intimately connected with marketing, for it is there that ambiguity is most rampant. It is the company president's special burden to insist that he get from the marketing department the inputs and the inspiration necessary to deal with the ambiguities of the marketplace that in the end determine the corporate future.

[5] Thomas C. Schelling, "PPBS and Foreign Affairs," *The Public Interest,* Spring, 1968, pp. 26–36.

Chapter Two

What's Your Product and What's Your Business?

WE HAVE REFERRED to the "augmented product concept"—the idea that a product is more than the generic thing produced in the factory. We have referred to cosmetics as hopes, quarter-inch drill bits as quarter-inch holes. People buy the expectation of benefits, not the generic products themselves. This distinction has enormous significance for how to view your business.

Take the construction industry. Life used to be enormously uncomplicated for its manufacturers. They simply supplied boards or beams or tiles and let somebody else worry about assembling them. But as new materials and new products generated new competition, one manufacturer after another has been forced into strange and complex new businesses— not only to protect traditional markets but also to help produce new ones.

Aluminum Company of America not only makes construction extrusions, but finances the skyscrapers that use them; Armstrong Cork manufactures not only ceiling tiles, but also integrated lighting systems; and Weyerhaeuser Company, the nation's largest lumber producer, has developed perhaps one of the most elaborate and fully encompassing "products" with which to compete in the residential housing field—the Registered Home Program. This program attempts to shore up the position of its dealers against the inroads of big-tract home builders and housing component makers, who often bypass dealers and buy lumber directly from competing manufacturers. Weyerhaeuser correctly believes that there is a continuing and sizable market for the output of the small builder, but that he needs help of a kind he is often incapable of providing himself. As a consequence, Weyerhaeuser has gotten deeply involved not only in selling the lumber but also in pushing sales of the houses themselves and everything that goes with them: architects' plans, financing, sales training, merchandising aids, and color-coordinated interiors.

What Weyerhaeuser is trying to do is put its dealers into home construction, or at least into producing and supplying prefabricated components for custom home building. Working through local mortgage houses, Weyerhaeuser offers to make funds available to dealers and mortgage companies from national sources. Weyerhaeuser guarantees the top 15 percent of the mortgage and gives a twenty-year written warranty to the home buyer on all lumber it supplies to a new house. This is considered a potent argument to a generation accustomed to warping doors and sticking windows. In return, the dealer commits to buy all lumber for Registered Homes from Weyerhaeuser.

While this is an example of an extremely complex form of product augmentation, some are much simpler and more venerable. The Campbell Soup Company has for years offered management-training programs for retail food-store owners and management-level employees. The Pillsbury Company offers its Creative Marketing Service International to small retailers. Under this program, retailers pay for otherwise costly merchandising services from Pillsbury, but it costs no money. They pay with points earned from the purchase of Pillsbury products. W. R. Grace & Co. offers a complete package of ten key services to the customers of its various plastics. Butler Buildings pays half the cost of consulting studies designed to make dealer operations more effective. General Electric has created a considerable incentive for multibrand dealers to push GE major appliances with its Major Appliance Marketing Program. The dealer carries only floor samples and does nothing more than complete the selling transaction. Then GE takes over, drawing the appliance out of its own warehouse, delivering it to the buyer, installing and demonstrating it, and, where needed, servicing it. United Van Lines, the moving and storage company, offers a free, detailed community information service for its prospective movers.

The new competition is costly but inescapable. In a world of highly undifferentiated generic products, there is an inevitable shift to new forms of competition. This shift clearly requires an analysis of customer and consumer needs that extends beyond the generic product itself. And since it is not really the generic product that people buy, but the benefits it bestows, to think of the "product" in terms more encompassing than in the past is not only competitively wise but also ontologically sound. It is the benefits that *are* the product.

Survival for the Small Company

Because this new competition is costly, it creates survival problems for the small members of industries dominated by large firms. It is to be expected, therefore, that survival for the small firm will increasingly take the form of carving out highly specialized niches in markets that the large, think-big firms have not yet organized themselves to reach, or indeed cannot reach.

In the major-appliance field Gibson and Speed Queen have done exactly that. Faced with the thriving aggressiveness of mass-merchandising stores that sell well-known major appliances at relatively rock-bottom prices, major department stores have difficulty impressing on the community that they are low-priced sellers. Their cost structures generally prevent them from selling these highly advertised commodities at competitively low prices. Speed Queen and Gibson have helped them to make a competitive, low-price impression. They have chosen not to compete with the major producers in terms of either advertising volume or in the same distribution outlets; they offer their appliances almost exclusively to large metropolitan department stores at highly attractive prices. These stores use their own reputations and local advertising power to promote these brands, thus enabling themselves to make an impact as low-price sellers of major appliances while giving otherwise obscure brands the benefit of their reputations.

While large companies can do more for their distributors and dealers and thereby outsell their small competitors, the small recipients of these services from large suppliers become more competitive because of these services. Thus, Du Pont systematically makes cost analysts available to fabricators of its plastics. Large fabricators have their own analysts and don't need Du Pont. The small ones do, and get the benefit of the nation's largest plastic producer. But Du Pont's customer-service activities extend far beyond this. They include making available to its customers, at out-of-pocket costs, its own internally developed training programs, including even training of lathe operators.

The F. W. Means Co., the Chicago-based linen supply firm, has a free interior decorating service for the restaurants that use its linens and uniforms. But not all ancillary supplier services come for free. Distillers Corporation—Seagrams, Ltd., offers to its 450 independent wholesalers the services of its Distributor Consulting Service at a standard fee—$60 a day per consultant. The rate is less than half the fee of outside consulting firms, but the service is felt to be equal in quality. The consultants are given full independence. Typical jobs run to $10,000, but have been as high as $15,000. The service takes on almost any job: warehousing, computer installation, truck routing, administrative procedures, market studies, compensation.

CREATING ACTIONABLE
PRODUCT DEFINITIONS

Only philosophers can afford to define products in ontological terms, and that is only because for them it makes no operational difference what the definition is. For anybody to whom it makes a difference, the definition must have actionable content. It must suggest a concrete course of action.

The examples of the augmented products cited above have in common a single attribute: they contain features that produce results—a competitive plus. These key features, the features that distinguish these products from those of competitors, are invariably external to the generic products in the old-fashioned terms in which we are in the habit of defining industries.

In some cases the things with which a product is surrounded are so visibly important to its success that we thoughtlessly take their importance for granted. Their significance is totally overlooked. Quick examples are clothing (it is style and color that are bought, not shelter or coverage), cosmetics (images and packaging, not chemicals), and even cars (styling, size, comfort, operating expense, and accessories, not transportation).

With some "products" the surrounding attributes have a virtual absolute life-or-death power over the success of the product, and yet we are seldom aware of it. For example, one survey suggests that people think of airlines as selling seats on planes going from point X to point Y. The product is viewed as sit-down rapid transit between airports. Yet if the airlines viewed that as their product, they would die. Their product has a powerful and deciding hidden attribute—the supporting software reservation services. Without it, the product would be entirely different, such as Eastern's famed no-reservation shuttle service. The no-reservation service is economically possible only on exceptionally high-traffic routes for people who travel largely on a routine basis rather than on special occasions. It would not work today, for example, between New York and Miami, even if the traffic equaled the New York–Washington volume. The reason is that the purposes of the two traffics are different. New York–Washington traffic consists of highly repetitive flying by single businessmen constantly on the move. New York–Miami traffic consists of vacationers, generally traveling in twos and only once a year. They require a scheduled, planned, well-ordered certainty about their travels because their travels are special, once-a-year occasions flanked at origin and destination with highly elaborate preparations for departure and arrival.

The consequences of a breakdown in an airline's reservations system would be as revenue-destructive as the breakdown of the airplanes themselves. A product is something that is capable of producing revenue. When an airline seat cannot produce revenue because the computerized reservations system has broken down, it becomes painfully clear that the reservations system is a central part of the airline's product.

A product therefore consists of all its attributes that produce solvent customers. By this standard, it can be said without excessive stretching that the Edsel automobile was not a product. It did not produce enough customers. But the Edsel's magnificent failure demonstrates the importance of yet another vital nongeneric aspect of product attributes. This is the element of excitement.

Payoff from Excitement

Excitement is a fragile and abstract commodity not likely to attract the serious attention of solid executives schooled in the arcane arts of finance, law, and manufacturing. Yet it is as crucial for new-product success in cars, computers, and cutting tools as in cosmetics. That is why the annual machine-tool trade show in Chicago increasingly has the extravagant appearance of Pucci's Paris showings. Elderly, gray-haired presidents of stolid Milwaukee machine-tool companies, austerely encased in tightly buttoned herringbone vests, appear pridefully beside their huge machines in McCormick Place amid a flashing circus of crepe-paper banners, rotating psychedelic lights, and alluringly underdressed young ladies hired to produce fetching come-hither looks that draw like magnets other equally austere men into the fiscal vicinity of $100,000 milling machines designed to cut massive hunks of steel into smaller sculptured pieces. These stone-faced presidents, who watch so carefully over each fleeting penny in their manufacturing operations, are converted into big-spending good-time Charlies in Chicago, where hospitality suites are a twenty-four-hour staple, and where there is an obvious presumption that ballyhoo, babes, and booze not only will attract the transient attention of well-educated engineers armed with pocket slide rules, but will actually help convert them into serious prospects who might then and there possibly place an order.

The machine-tool manufacturer who enters this annual extravaganza with nothing more than his new equipment sitting on a bare floor against a bare wall, with a trusty old pipe-smoking machine designer handing out specification sheets, is headed for failure. The "product" does not sell itself.

It needs to be ballyhooed and adumbrated. It needs to be surrounded by an excitement no less palpable than Pucci's.

Edsel's fatal failure was in major part a failure to sustain the excitement that extensive preintroduction promotion had produced. William H. Reynolds, who was at Ford during the great debacle, suggests in a highly informative and perceptive retrospective look that "it is possible that the advertising caused the public to expect too much. . . ." Ford's promotions created enormous excitement and expectations. These were quickly shattered, Mr. Reynolds suggests persuasively, by

> . . . a decision to try to get as many Edsels as possible on the road immediately after introduction. Ford wanted people to see the car, and to look upon it quickly as an established mode. A resulting failure to adhere to quality standards resulted. Many cars that should not have been released from assembly lines without extensive rework were sent to dealers. The Edsel acquired very early the reputation of a poorly constructed car. Most of the "bugs" . . . were ironed out fairly quickly, but not until after the damage had been done.[1]

Reynolds argues that Edsel's famous horse-collar styling blooper was not nearly as decisively destructive as the fluently uninformed popular critics so confidently contend—that indeed the vertical grille had fine classical antecedents in the La Salle and Pierce Arrow, and was comparable in appearance to those of then-popular European sports cars such as the Alfa-Romeo and the Bugatti.

Nothing sells itself, not even the most venerable and tantalizing of all commodities—sex. It has to be embellished, elaborated, amplified, enriched, perfumed, styled, corseted, colored, and cosmeticized. If even sex needs that kind of doctoring, no experienced male can conceivably argue that other things don't. No purchasing decision for any product, no matter how sophisticated its engineering or critically crucial its economics, is ever made exclusively by the strict determinism of the slide rule.

The Slide Rule versus the Human Rule

The issue is a simple one: What is the relative importance of the slide rule versus the human rule? The "human rule" is more important, even in selling slide rules, than is generally conceded, more important than sellers are generally aware. The ingredient of excitement and other embellish-

---

[1] William H. Reynolds, "The Edsel Ten Years Later," *Business Horizons,* Fall, 1967, p. 42. See also John Brooks, *The Fate of the Edsel and Other Business Adventures,* Harper & Row, Publishers, Incorporated, New York, 1963.

ments are central characteristics of the products themselves. They must be viewed as part of the essential characteristics built into the product from the beginning.

The importance of this is further and perhaps best illustrated to the executive who frequently flies via commercial airlines. Consider the setting. Here is a man of solid perspicacity and great responsibility about to enter a massive tube of aluminum, plastics, glass, textiles, and copper wire. The tube will take him at incredible speed six miles up into the heavens, where the arctic winds can freeze him into an instant icicle and the air pressure can crush him like a champagne glass. A faulty part in the engine, a minor defect in the pressurizing equipment, a suddenly berserk pilot, and the executive's life is extinguished. And how does our paragon of the managerial arts decide between TWA, American, or United for the 8 A.M. trip from New York's La Guardia Airport to Chicago's O'Hare? Ask the man from Mars, and he will not hesitate a moment to tell you that when his life is at stake, man will be rational and decide on the basis of slide-rule calculations regarding the safest airline to take. He will want at least to consult CAB records for the airline with the best record. All else is applesauce. Yet it is for the applesauce that our sensible executive with three minor dependents and a nervous wife finally lays out his company's money—for the airline that has the most interesting breakfast menu, sterling (not plastic) tableware, the most attractive and cheerful stewardesses, the most pleasing decor, the fastest baggage-handling system, the most reliable schedules, and in-flight stereo music.

Even the most prosaic products with no relation to life or death require the sustaining ingredient of excitement. That is one reason why there is such a booming demand for the services of companies who stage elaborate "show-biz" sales meetings and business conventions. One of the most successful practitioners of this approach is Anthony E. Cascino of International Minerals and Chemical. Says he, "It is not just that a sales meeting imparts information; it must also provide inspiration and enthusiasm. Even the most revolutionary marketing approach will suffer if it lacks emotion and empathy. Salesmen need excitement and stimulation, and a sales meeting should provide the atmosphere through which these characteristics can be generated."[2]

The way a generic product is engineered and positioned affects the ultimate consumer. But it can also be used to engage the enthusiasm and energy of the middlemen who handle it through the distribution chain.

[2] Anthony E. Cascino, "Organizational Implications of the Marketing Concept," in William Lazer and Eugene J. Kelley (eds.), *Managerial Marketing*, rev. ed., Richard D. Irwin, Inc., Homewood, Ill., 1962, p. 373.

Melville shoes has successfully gone from giving its various items not just identifying numbers, but also excitement-generating names such as Twisters, Possums, Teardrops, Voodoos (for boys) and Voodoo Dolls (for girls). There was even a GTO shoe, "with bucket-seat heel pad, accelerator heel, seat-belt buckle, and four-on-the-floor." Francis C. Rooney, Melville's effervescent and solidly businesslike president, says flatly, "People no longer buy shoes to keep their feet warm and dry. They buy them because of the way the shoes make them feel—masculine, feminine, rugged, different, sophisticated, young, glamorous, 'in.' Buying shoes has become an emotional experience. Our business now is selling excitement rather than shoes."

As a consequence of this view of his product, Rooney, who declares himself a "lousy shoe salesman," more than any other man in the $6-billion shoe industry has fomented the revolution that has changed the business from one in which price was the dominant factor to one concerned with "what people want and how to get them to buy it." In the process Melville stimulated not only sales but a revived enthusiasm and commercial spirit among sleepy store managers and salesmen. The net result has been both excitement in the store and the conversion of Melville into an exciting stock on Wall Street.

The Sensate Society

Three factors combine to emphasize the accelerating necessity to build excitement into the very core of business activity. One is that we live in a society in which so many people have so many more things and so much more money than they need to sustain life at some reasonable level of amenities. Second is that there is so little to set one generic product off from another. And third is the inevitable routinization of man's daily task, whether in business, at home, or at play.

Routine is a consequence of mechanization. Premechanized society routinized life according to the cyclical regularity of natural phenomena: the daily rising and setting of the sun, the periodic cycle of the seasons. Machines, however, have produced many more routines, and these in important respects deprive man of his freedom. The preindustrial farmer, even though the sun predictably roused him to the fields, had enormous freedom regarding how he could spend his time until sunset. On balmy summer days he could without a second thought take a siesta under an apple tree. In the fall he might hunt, and in the winter sleep. Industrial man does not use the sun as his alarm clock. He gets to work not at about eight o'clock, but at 8 A.M. sharp. That is when the assembly line is turned on and the office begins to hum. The siesta, no matter how tempting, is obsolete, as the rising industrialization is making clear in Latin countries. The machine cannot economically be turned off for the civilized midday privileges of preindustrial life. Not even so profoundly important a national ritual as baseball's World Series commands enough authority to slow the machine. Where the machine itself does not directly pace industrial life, such as in the office, the World Series gets attention only via the subterfuge of the transistor radio hidden in the desk drawer.

This fact tells us as well as anything how powerful are the routinizing and regimenting consequences of the underlying technology. The simple twelve-hour rhythm of the preindustrial day is converted to the complex and demanding clockwork of the present. The industrial day is a series of highly involuted and programmed cycles, from the harsh ring of the morning alarm clock to the scheduled rush to work; from the periodic rest and coffee breaks to the standardized dinner hour at home; and finally to the closing weather report on late-night television. The necessity of such routinization is so profound that we understandably begin acculturating the smallest child. Demand feeding of infants gives way to scheduled feeding. By the time the child is old enough to go to school, he doesn't view getting there on time as anything but routine. Even the acceptance of the necessity of organized routine is routine.

"Tripping Out" and the Adult Dilemma

In such a world, combined with generic-product standardization and far-above-subsistence living, it is not surprising that man responds eagerly to the fascinating shock of the unexpected. The enormous attractions of marijuana, contact sports, television violence, and literary "sex and sadism" are understandable. They provide man with escape—not escape from reality but escape back to reality. He wants to escape from the artificiality that the machine has imposed on his life and return to a more primitive involvement of his senses with nature in the raw. The only reason teenagers and college students are greater consumers of marijuana than adults is simply that adults have greater obligations to the machine. They cannot "drop out" because they are too deeply in. They are prisoners of the world they made.

This accounts for the intensity of the adult furor over the seemingly aberrant life styles of their children. It represents less adults' concern about the health and happiness of their children than the fact that they are envious of their children's freedom. The young people who take trips and smoke pot need it least because they are already so much less thoroughly bound to society's rigid routines. The people who need most to escape, who are most firmly imprisoned by the world from which the trip is an escape and who have the greatest need to drop out, are the adults. They are understandably unhappy about the liberated behavior of their children.

The adult's reward for a life of hard work and scheduled dedication to his job is the anomalous necessity to work even harder and with more dedication. The juvenile beneficiaries of his inescapable attachment to the machine are most intent on escaping the machine. No wonder the adult world is so outspoken about the younger generation. It shows no gratitude for parental sacrifices—indeed it pooh-poohs them and seeks artificial escapes from what is already a condition of great relative freedom. The invocation of moral platitudes and self-righteous calls for order and discipline have been the predictable outpourings of envious adults and social arbiters ever since Isaiah.

The adult too searches for and needs excitement—the felicitous injection into his life of benignly unexpected events. That is why excitement will increasingly, in spite and perhaps because of computers and management science, become a powerful ingredient in business success. The man, the company, the product that denies this most in practice will suffer most in the market.

SYSTEMS SELLING

It is fashionable to talk about systems selling. It is not so clear what it means and where it applies. The term originated, in fact, not with the seller but with the buyer. The federal military establishment developed the practice of buying major weapons and communications packages through a single prime contractor. Instead of buying individual items for a battleship, such as the ship's shell, the artillery, the electronic submarine-sighting equipment, and the telecommunications devices, it bought them as a single package from a single company, even though no single company produced all the components. Package contracts were awarded to companies with the capability to design, engineer, build, assemble, and service the complete package. The package was the system, and prime contractors were compelled to bid on the system as a whole, getting in turn their own subsystem or component bids from item suppliers. That is the origin of the systems phrase, although in practice it was antedated by general contractors in a vast variety of fields from building dams to constructing oil refineries.

The growing complexity of products that have elaborate interindustry characteristics has made systems buying an increasing necessity. Computers must be tied into communications networks, and warehouses tied into computers and transportation networks. The combination of competences, resources, and equipment needed to make a single piece of industrial equipment or to organize a totally efficient activity requires the elaborate coordination of a constantly expanding network of varied competences and resources. This has consequences that go far beyond marketing itself, but marketing plays a central role.

Conglomerates and Marketing

One of the best examples is Litton Industries. The company is known as a conglomerate, and yet many of Litton's acquisitions were a process of creating under a single roof the competence to provide customers with an integrated mix of benefits they might otherwise have to buy separately on the open market. Thus, some years ago, Litton acquired and combined the Monroe Calculating Machine Company and the Swedish cash register company, Sweda. Subsequently it acquired Kimball, the company that manufactures the unit-control punched tickets used by soft-goods retailers for monitoring product movement and inventories. Then later Litton acquired Streeter, a manufacturer of retail display cases.

The pattern was obvious. Litton was developing a vertically integrated competence to supply packaged systems to retailers—systems that handle all the materials, information flow, and record keeping from warehouse to display counter to cash register to computerized inventory, purchasing, and financial centers. Litton was creating a new "product," a retail processing system. It hoped to alter the way large retailers planned and bought the equipment that was involved—buying not the individual components from separate suppliers, but a whole system from a single supplier.

To call this effort a conglomerate is to mistake the apparent structure for the operating substance. Looked at in terms of how retailers traditionally operate, Litton expanded itself in order to provide its customers with a single, integrated product system. But looked at in terms of what this did to Litton (at least one segment of the company) the result was anything but conglomerate. We would not say that Ford Motor Company's acquisition years ago of its own steel mill and tire factory got it started as a conglomerate. We would call that "vertical integration." What Litton did in the retailing field is also vertical integration. The difference is that whereas Ford created or bought a series of suppliers for which it became the single customer, Litton put together a series of suppliers such that their customers might have a single source. Thus instead of Litton in this case being engaged in some sort of fiscal razzle-dazzle, it was performing the perfectly respectable function of trying to better serve a new kind of customer buying need.

Three Kinds of Systems Selling

In doing this, Litton demonstrated that there are, using the conventional terminology, three different kinds of systems selling—three different kinds of augmented products: the product system, the contracting system, and the service system.

A conventionally defined product system consists of products combined through engineering and design into an operating unit to perform a specific function. The example of the battleship fills that bill admirably, as does Litton's integrated mix of retailer equipment.

Systems contracting does not sell systems, but uses systems to sell. Thus, while our earlier example showed American Airlines creating a product system, the result for Raytheon was its offering to its distributors a Friden–Western Union communications device that would better enable them to buy Raytheon products. Similarly Beals, McCarthy & Rogers, Inc., an industrial distributor in Buffalo, New York, is a good example of providing a contracting system. It manufactures nothing, but offers customers the use of its computer and data-transmission system to facilitate ordering, faster distribution, less paper work, and reduced acquisition costs. Litton's retailer system has the eventual potential of providing similar benefits by linking the Kimball control information directly from the selling floor to suppliers.

The service system achieves the ultimate of total integration. It sells a system, while the system sells both itself and a service. It is essentially an information-processing and pseudo-decision-making mechanism to help customers manage their affairs better and in the process deal more constantly with their originating vendor.

The Carborundum Company also pioneered an interesting system. Instead of merely selling bonded abrasives in the usual fashion, it decided on the necessity of developing a completely integrated capability in steel conditioning. This resulted, as a first step, in its acquisition of the Tysamun Machine Company. At enormous cost over several years, Carborundum developed a method of machine chipping to augment the grinding process, such that the user in one continuous activity could remove scale and surface defects from a cylinder of steel in one hour and fifteen minutes rather than in the eight hours required by former methods.

What characterized Carborundum's effort was not merely the development of a better method, but the discovery of the necessity for it. Instead of looking only at what its potential customers were doing, it looked more comprehensively at what they would have to be doing in the future. Carborundum concluded that the steel industry would have to convert to continuous casting, which would require hot cutoff and hot grinding, instead of the old methods of doing these jobs after the products cooled.

By making an arborless grinding wheel, with a series of small holes instead of a large center opening, the wheel's running speed was increased by 25 percent. Then Carborundum's Bonded Abrasives Research Center devised a machine to grind hot steel at 1800°F, so that cooling, moving, grinding, and reheating could be eliminated. Combining this machine with the arborless grinding wheel, it became possible to more than double the amount of steel that could be removed in an hour.

As Carborundum knew all along, the resulting technological breakthrough, with all its visible virtues, would not sell itself. That would be an even more difficult and costly task. One hundred and fifty steel industry representatives were flown to the research center in Niagara Falls for a detailed demonstration, then to the Pittsburgh Hilton for a two-day applications seminar. This was followed by a second conference later and numerous private sessions with the engineers and machine men in the various prospects' plants. Carborundum also made on-the-spot studies of prospects' production and changeover problems and analyzed their workmen's capabilities. After eight months it was possible to produce detailed proposals for custom-made Tysamun machines, adoption units, and workmen education programs. The final price tag for the package to the customer ranged around $500,000.

Carborundum not only created a new product—an elaborate cluster of value satisfactions—but in the process performed the preeminent task of the business function: it created a customer.

Not all systems are that elaborate, but all have elaborate elements. The Metalcraft Corporation of Chicago in its factories produces low-priced picture frames sold largely through variety chains and mass merchandisers. Instead of merely selling these, Metalcraft devised a series of display, layout, and inventory packages much along the lines of what has been done so well for years by Hallmark in the greeting card field. By expanding its field sales organization to include detail men who set up and constantly arrange store displays, counsel salesclerks, and maintain inventories, both Metalcraft's volume and its share of market quickly expanded. New customers were rapidly added as stores perceived the virtue of these services. Additional fallout benefits to Metalcraft were a more predictable flow of orders, which helped in turn to reduce manufacturing costs and finished-goods inventories.

To Augment or Not to Augment?

Systems selling is the name for an activity that is more aptly described in terms of the benefits produced for the customer than in terms of what the seller does. It involves the creation of an augmented product that enables the customer to do business with the supplier more easily. For the supplier it can be a costly and risky process—as it is for the patient men who go through the pitfalls and agonies of producing the augmented product. But these agonies do not alter the prevailing necessities.

To compete in this world, it is not enough to have a big and efficient plant, lots of working capital, armies of enthusiastic salesmen, and steady nerves. As machines get more complex, as equipment and business processes get more interdependent, and as competition for the customer's favor gets more intense, the seller cannot depend simply on good engineering, aggressive selling, and low prices for his due. He must find new ways to serve those he seeks to convert to his custom. This means a shift of orientation from the problems of pure production to the problems of marketing—to the creation of an augmented product whose parameters are determined more by the buyer than by the seller. To be sure, the seller has a choice. He can choose to limit his product and his efforts, but increasingly he must make an informed choice rather than simply assume that his obligations are automatically exhausted by the production of the simple pieces of product that have traditionally come out of the plant.

We live in an age in which our thinking about what a product or a service is must be quite different from what it ever was before. It is not so much the basic, generic, central thing we are selling that counts, but the whole cluster of value satisfactions with which we surround it. It does little or no good to make a better mousetrap when "betterness" now has a new, more subtle meaning; and that is where modern marketing comes in. Modern marketing consists of orienting a company toward trying to find out what at any given time the customer will define betterness to mean. This requires the entire company to be more effectively organized and oriented toward fulfilling the customer-getting requirements implied by that definition.

It is through the vigorous and enthusiastic fulfillment of these requirements that competitive strength is achieved. And we must emphasize the notion of enthusiastic fulfillment. Grudging fulfillment almost certainly leads to underfulfillment, which even more certainly leads to failure and disillusionment. But enthusiasm—enthusiasm that says, in effect, that the service benefits with which I surround and augment my generic product are really my competitive edge—produces in a company the continued vigil whose purpose is to understand and serve the customer. This orientation in turn endows its possessor with the greatest of all commercial power —the power to supply the customer with what he wants in an atmosphere of competitive superiority. This spells for such a company leadership, vigorous growth, and enduring profits.

THE ORGANIZATIONAL SIGNIFICANCE OF PRODUCT AUGMENTATION

If the product is something more than its generic content, then obviously its design is something more than should be left to the engineers. If Mr. Revson's factory-made cosmetics have a customer-satisfying intention that extends beyond what his chemists put into the package, then other elements of the product such as its packaging, its advertising, its pricing, and its channels of distribution must at the outset be designed in a manner consistent with the satisfactions that the entire mix is designed to deliver. A $9.95 facial cream does not belong and will not sell in a dime store. A $6.95 lipstick will not sell in a simple brass container.

Things are no less different in the case of a $100,000 numerically controlled milling machine or a standard grade of polyester fiber. Polyester fiber sold by a manufacturer's representative whose entire previous experience and reputation has been in selling rerun or scrap plastics on a strictly price basis is not, in the eyes of the prospect, the same product as when it is offered by the experienced and helpful applications engineers of Celanese. The numerically controlled milling machine with a carefully designed IBM look is not, in the prospect's eyes, the same as the same machine with a Spartan look of engineering practicality.

A product is not just what the engineers say, but also what is implied by its design, its packaging, its channels of distribution, its price, and the quality and activities of its salesmen. A product is therefore a transaction between the seller and the buyer—a synthesis of what the seller intends and the buyer perceives.

What the buyer perceives can in part be controlled by what the seller puts into the product—by how he packages it, how he prices it, and how he promotes and sells it. And how he does these should be a function of his intentions vis-à-vis the customer, not just vis-à-vis the generic product. The seller must ask himself not just what the milling machine is intended to do with a piece of steel—the speed and accuracy of its operation and the ease of setup time, for example—but also what the total mix of things with which it is surrounded is intended to communicate to the prospect.

When we view the product as something far more than its generic content, we are immediately faced with the necessity of a new way to plan for its creation and a new way to manage the process by which we attract and hold customers. It means that products must be planned, not just designed. It means that the people charged with selling the product must participate in its creation at the outset, not just after they get it from the manufacturing department.

This has profound implications regarding how a company is managed because it spells the end to what is in many firms a rigid separation between R & D and marketing, between engineering and marketing, and even between advertising and sales promotion. If the product consists of everything these functions do in respect to the generic commodity, then none of these functions can be permitted to operate independently from each other. What advertising tells us we must say about the commodity must help condition what the engineers put into it; what field selling says are the appropriate channels of distribution must condition both the packaging and the sales promotion.

Consumer packaged-goods industries—particularly those with a high advertising-to-sales ratio—generally organize themselves to achieve the product results I have suggested are necessary to make the product succeed. The usual method is to have product managers and new-product development managers who establish the criteria, set the standards, and assure the performance that will make the entire product mix a consistent and effective whole. In these companies, gone are the bad old days when the chemists turned out a new cake mix for which an isolated artist designed what he felt was a suitable package, and then turned it over to somebody else to price, to still another party to advertise, and finally to the sales organization to get rid of. Indeed, even in less sophisticated companies such crude procedures are rare today. There is generally some semblance of coordination and advance consciousness of what the total combined mix is to be.

But a problem does remain—and that is that the coordination which occurs is only that, coordination. It is rare that except for setting general pricing parameters the total mix is as thoroughly prethought and preplanned as our definition of the product would require. If the product is far more than its generic core, and if on a generic basis there is increasingly less to distinguish one company's product from another's, then competitive effectiveness increasingly requires that the whole augmented product be as carefully preplanned in all its variety as its generic content is preplanned by the engineers.

Without this kind of conscious preplanning, the coordination that occurs later tends to become a process of accommodation rather than of creation. Since there was insufficient preplanning and an inadequate total definition of the product, the various marketing specialists from different sectors of the company will each tend to advocate "solutions" or approaches that derive more strongly from the logic of their respective specialties than from the competitive purpose that was vaguely in mind when the product was initiated. Coordination therefore becomes accommodation, with the probable result that the product which emerges has considerably less competitive power than it should.

The same thing applies not only to old products that are being revised or renewed, but also to the annual plans for existing products. There must be at the outset a clear statement about what satisfaction the product is presumed to deliver to its prospects and about how the product is intended to be perceived and bought by those prospects. This done, all the things with which the generic product will then be surrounded can be consciously planned to achieve the desired effect.

Acceptance of this process has enormous organizational consequences. It means that there must be very detailed product and market planning. It also means that people in charge of these processes—whether for particular products or for product lines—must be invested with responsibilities and powers that sometimes cross over more traditional lines of authority.

We know from companies that have newly adopted the product-management or the market-manager system that managerial activities which cut across traditional functional responsibility can produce enormous organizational strains and people problems. We also know that product management works best in companies with a long history of its use. This means that because the management of the augmented-product process tends to violate the traditional rule according to which people must be given authority equal to their responsibility, the system will work well only after the organization has had enough experience to learn how to make it work. The modern organization that accepts the necessity of the augmented-product concept will find itself encountering strains and problems much like the organizations that accepted and switched to product and market-management marketing systems. To succeed they will face a new necessity—to do what is right rather than merely what is customary or comfortable.

Chapter Three

Your Factories in the Field: Customer Service and Service Industries

THE SERVICE SECTOR of the economy is growing in size but shrinking in quality. So say a lot of people. Purveyors of service, for their part, think that they and their problems are fundamentally different from other businesses and their problems. They feel that service is people-intensive, while the rest of the economy is capital-intensive. But these distinctions are largely spurious. There are not such things as service industries. There are only industries whose service components are greater or less than those of other industries. Everybody is in service.

Often the less there seems the more there is. The more technologically sophisticated the generic product (e.g., cars and computers), the more dependent are its sales on the quality and availability of its accompanying customer services (e.g., display rooms, delivery, repairs and maintenance, application aids, operator training, installation advice, warranty fulfillment). In this sense, General Motors is probably more service-intensive than manufacturing-intensive. Without its services its sales would shrivel.

Thus the service sector of the economy is not merely comprised of the so-called service industries, such as banking, airlines, and maintenance. It includes the entire abundance of product-related services supplied by manufacturers and the sales-related services supplied by retailers. Yet we confuse things to our detriment by an outdated taxonomy. For example:

■ The First National City Bank (Citibank) is one of the biggest world-wide banks. It has nearly 40,000 employees, over half of whom deal directly with the public, either selling them things (mostly money and deposit services) or helping them with things they have already bought (cashing checks, taking additional deposits, writing letters of credit, opening lock-boxes, managing corporate cash). Most of the other employees work back in what is called "the factory"—a massive congeries of people, paper, and computers that processes, records, validates, and scrutinizes everything the first group has done. All the corporate taxonomists, including the U.S. Department of the Census, classify Citibank as a service company.

■ IBM is the biggest worldwide manufacturer of computers. It has nearly 300,000 employees, over half of whom deal directly with the public, either selling them things (mostly machines) or helping them with the things they have already bought (installing and repairing machines, writing computer programs, training customers). Most of the other employees work back in the factory—a massive congeries of wires, microminiature electronic components, engineers, and assemblers. All the corporate tax-onomists, including the U.S. Department of the Census, classify IBM as a manufacturing company.

Something is wrong, and not just in the Bureau of the Census. The industrial world has changed more rapidly than our taxonomies. If only taxonomy were involved, the consequences of our contradictory classifications would be trivial. After all, man lives perfectly well with his contradictions: his simultaneous faith, for instance, in both God and science; his attachment to facts and logic when making important business decisions, but reliance on feelings and emotion when making far more important life decisions, like marriage.

Our contradictory notions about service may have malignant consequences. Not until we clarify the contradictions will companies begin to solve problems that now seem so intractable. In order to do so, they must think of themselves as performing manufacturing functions when it comes to their so-called "service" activities. Only then will they begin to make some significant progress in improving the quality and efficiency of service in the modern economy.

Field versus Factory

People think of service as quite different from manufacturing. Service is presumed to be performed by individuals for other individuals, generally on a one-to-one basis. Manufacturing is presumed to be performed by machines, generally tended by large clusters of individuals whose sizes and configurations are themselves dictated by the machines' requirements. Service (whether customer service or the services of service industries) is performed "out there in the field" by distant and loosely supervised people working under highly variable, and often volatile, conditions. Manufacturing occurs "here in the factory" under highly centralized, carefully organized, tightly controlled, and elaborately engineered conditions.

People assume, and rightly so, that these differences largely explain why products produced in the factory are generally more uniform in features and quality than the services produced (e.g., life insurance policies, machine repairs) or delivered (e.g., spare parts, milk) in the field. One cannot as easily control one's agents or their performance out there in the field. Besides, different customers want different things. The result is that service and service industries, in comparison with manufacturing industries, are widely and correctly viewed as being primitive, sluggish, and inefficient.

Yet it is doubtful that things need be all that bad. Once conditions in the field get the same kind of attention that conditions inside the factory generally get, a lot of new opportunities become possible. But first management will have to revise its thinking about what service is and what it implies.

Limits of Servitude

The trouble with thinking of oneself as providing services—either in the service industries or in the customer-service sectors of manufacturing and retailing companies—is that one almost inescapably embraces ancient, pre-industrial modes of thinking. Worse still, one gets caught up in rigid attitudes that can have a profoundly paralyzing effect on even the most resolute of rationalists.

The concept of "service" evokes, from the opaque recesses of the mind, time-worn images of personal ministration and attendance. It refers generally to deeds one individual performs personally for another. It carries historical connotations of charity, gallantry, and selflessness, or of obedience, subordination, and subjugation. In these contexts, people serve because they want to (as in the priestly and political professions) or they serve because they are compelled to (as in slavery and such occupations of attendance as waiter, maid, bellboy, cleaning lady).

In the higher-status service occupations, such as in the church and the army, one customarily behaves ritualistically, not rationally. In the lower-status service occupations, one simply obeys. In neither is independent thinking presumed to be a requisite of holding a job. The most that can therefore be expected from service improvements is that, like Avis, a person will try harder. He will just exert more animal effort to do better what he is already doing.

So it was in ancient times, and so it is today. The only difference is that where ancient masters invoked the will of God or the whip of the foreman to spur performance, modern industry uses training programs and motivation sessions. We have not in all these years come very far in either our methods or our results.

Promise of Manufacturing

Now consider manufacturing. Here the orientation is toward the efficient production of results, not toward attendance on others. Relationships are strictly businesslike, devoid of invidious connotations of rank or self.

When we think about how to improve manufacturing, we seldom focus on ways to improve our personal performance or present tasks; rather, it is axiomatic that we try to find entirely new ways of performing present tasks and, better yet, of actually changing the tasks themselves. We do not think of greater exertion of our animal energies (working physically harder, as the slave), of greater expansion of our commitment (being more devout or loyal, as the priest), or of greater assertion of our dependence (being more obsequious, as the butler). Instead, we apply the greater exertion of our minds to learn how to look at a problem differently. More particularly, we ask what kinds of tools, old or new, and what kinds of skills, processes, organizational rearrangements, incentives, controls, and audits might be enlisted to greatly improve the intended outcomes. In short, manufacturing thinks technocratically, and that explains its successes. Service thinks humanistically, and that explains its failure.

Manufacturing looks for solutions inside the very tasks to be done. The solution to building a low-priced automobile, for example, derives largely from the nature and composition of the automobile itself. (If the automobile were not an assembly of parts, it could not be manufactured on an assembly line.) By contrast, service looks for solutions in the *performer* of the task. This is the paralyzing legacy of our inherited attitudes: The solution to improved service is viewed as being dependent on improvements in the skills and attitudes of the performers of that service.

While it may pain and offend us to say so, thinking in humanistic rather than technocratic terms ensures that the service sector of the modern economy will be forever inefficient and that our satisfactions will be forever inefficient and that our satisfactions will be forever marginal. We see service as invariably and undeviatingly personal, as something performed by individuals directly for other individuals.

This humanistic conception of service diverts us from seeking alternatives to the use of people, especially to large, organized groups of people. It does not allow us to reach out for new solutions and new definitions. It obstructs us from redesigning the tasks themselves; from creating new tools, processes, and organizations; and perhaps, even from eliminating the conditions that created the problems.

In sum, to improve the quality and efficiency of service, companies must apply the kind of technocratic thinking which in other fields has replaced the high-cost and erratic elegance of the artisan with the low-cost, predictable munificence of the manufacturer.

The Technocratic Hamburger

Nowhere in the entire service sector are the possibilities of the manufacturing mode of thinking better illustrated than in fast-food franchising. Nowhere have manufacturing methods been employed more effectively to control the operation of distant and independent agents. Nowhere is "service" better.

Few of today's successful new commercial ventures have antecedents that are more humble and less glamorous than the hamburger. Yet the thriving nationwide chain of hamburger stands called "McDonald's" is a supreme example of the application of manufacturing and technological brilliance to problems that must ultimately be viewed as marketing problems. From 1961 to 1972, McDonald's sales rose from approximately $54 million to over $1 billion. During this remarkable ascent the White Tower chain, whose name had theretofore been practically synonymous throughout the land with low-priced, quick-service hamburgers, practically vanished.

The explanation of McDonald's thundering success is not a purely fiscal one—i.e., the argument that it is financed by independent local entrepreneurs who bring to their operations a quality of commitment and energy not commonly found among hired workers. Nor is it a purely geographical one—i.e., the argument that each outlet draws its patronage from a relatively small geographic ring of customers, thus enabling the number of outlets easily and quickly to multiply. The relevant explanation must deal with the central question of why each separate McDonald's outlet is so predictably successful, why each is so certain to attract many repeat customers.

Entrepreneurial financing and careful site selection do help. But most important is the carefully controlled execution of each outlet's central function—the rapid delivery of a uniform, high-quality mix of prepared foods in an environment of obvious cleanliness, order, and cheerful courtesy. The systematic substitution of equipment for people, combined with the carefully planned use and positioning of technology, enables McDonald's to attract and hold patronage in proportions no predecessor or imitator has managed to duplicate. Consider the remarkable ingenuity of the system, which is worth examining in some detail:

To start with the obvious, raw hamburger patties are carefully prepacked and premeasured, which leaves neither the franchisee nor his employees any discretion as to size, quality, or raw-material consistency. This kind of attention is given to all McDonald's products. Storage and preparation space and related facilities are expressly designed for, and limited to, the predetermined mix of products. There is no space for any foods, beverages, or services that were not designed into the system at the outset. There is not even a sandwich knife or, in fact, a decent place to keep one. Thus the owner has no discretion regarding what he can sell —not because of any contractual limitations, but because of facilities limitations. And the employees have virtually no discretion regarding how to prepare and serve things.

Discretion is the enemy of order, standardization, and quality. On an automobile assembly line, for example, a worker who has discretion and latitude might possibly produce a more personalized car, but one that is highly unpredictable. The elaborate care with which an automobile is designed and an assembly line is structured and controlled is what produces quality cars at low prices, and with surprising reliability considering the sheer volume of the output. The same is true at McDonald's, which produces food under highly automated and controlled conditions.

French-fried Automation

While in Detroit the significance of the technological process lies in production, at McDonald's it lies in marketing. A carefully planned design is built into the elaborate technology of the food-service system in such a fashion as to make it a significant marketing device. This fact is impressively illustrated by McDonald's handling of that uniquely plebian American delicacy, french-fried potatoes.

French fries become quickly soggy and unappetizing; to be good, they must be freshly made just before serving. Like other fast-food establishments, McDonald's provides its outlets with precut, partially cooked frozen potatoes that can be quickly finished in an on-premises, deep-fry facility. The McDonald's fryer is neither so large that it produces too many french fries at one time (thus allowing them to become soggy) nor so small that it requires frequent and costly frying.

The fryer is emptied onto a wide, flat tray adjacent to the service counter. This location is crucial. Since the McDonald practice is to create an impression of abundance and generosity by slightly overfilling each bag of french fries, the tray's location next to the service counter prevents the spillage from an overfilled bag from reaching the floor. Spillage creates not only danger underfoot but also an unattractive appearance that causes the employees to become accustomed to an unclean environment. Once a store is unclean in one particular, standards fall very rapidly and the store becomes unclean and the food unappetizing in general.

While McDonald's aims for an impression of abundance, excessive overfilling can be very costly for a company that annually buys potatoes almost by the trainload. A systematic bias that puts into each bag of french fries a half ounce more than is intended can have visible effects on the company's annual earnings. Further, excessive time spent at the tray by each employee can create a cumulative service bottleneck at the counter.

McDonald's has therefore developed a special wide-mouthed scoop with a narrow funnel in its handle. The counter employee picks up the scoop and inserts the handle end into a wall clip containing the bags. One bag adheres to the handle. In a continuous movement the scoop descends into the potatoes, fills the bag to the exact proportions its designers intended, and is lifted, scoop facing the ceiling, so that the potatoes funnel through the handle into the attached bag, which is automatically disengaged from the handle by the weight of the contents. The bag comes to a steady, nonwobbling rest on its flat bottom.

Nothing can go wrong—the employee never soils his hands, the floor remains clean, dry, and safe, and the quantity is controlled. Best of all, the customer gets a visibly generous portion with great speed, the employee remains efficient and cheerful, and the general impression is one of extravagantly good service.

Mechanized Marketing

Consider the other aspects of McDonald's technological approach to marketing. The tissue paper used to wrap each hamburger is color-coded to denote the mix of condiments. Heated reservoirs hold pre-prepared hamburgers for rush demand. Frying surfaces have spatter guards to prevent soiling of the cooks' uniforms. Nothing is left to chance or the employees' discretion.

The entire system is engineered and executed according to a tight technological discipline that ensures fast, clean, reliable service in an atmosphere that gives the modestly paid employees a sense of pride and dignity. In spite of the crunch of eager customers, no employee looks or acts harassed, and therefore no harassment is communicated to the customers.

But McDonald's goes even further. Customers may be discouraged from entering if the building looks unappealing from the outside; hence considerable care goes into the design and appearance of the structure itself.

Some things, however, the architect cannot control, especially at an establishment where people generally eat in their parked cars and are likely to drop hamburger wrappings and empty beverage cartons on the ground. McDonald's has anticipated the requirement: its blacktop parking facilities are dotted like a checkerboard with numerous large, highly visible trash cans. It is impossible to ignore their purpose. Even the most indifferent customer would be struck with guilt if he simply dropped his refuse on the ground. But, just in case he drops it anyway, the larger McDonald's outlets have motorized sweepers for quick and easy cleanup.

What is important to understand about this remarkably successful organization is not only that it has created a highly sophisticated piece of technology, but also that it has done this by applying a manufacturing style of thinking to a people-intensive service situation. If machinery is to be viewed as a piece of equipment with the capability of producing a predictably standardized, customer-satisfying output while minimizing the operating discretion of its attendant, that is what a McDonald's retail outlet is. It is a machine that produces, with the help of totally unskilled machine tenders, a highly polished product. Through painstaking attention to total design and facilities planning, everything is built integrally into the machine itself, into the technology of the system. The only choice available to the attendant is to operate it exactly as the designers intended.

Tooling Up for Service

Although most people are not aware of it, there are many illustrations of manufacturing solutions to people-intensive service problems. For example:

■ Mutual funds substitute one sales call for many; one consultation for dozens; one piece of paper for thousands; and one reasonably informed customer choice for numerous, confused, and often poor choices.

■ Credit cards that are used for making bank loans substitute a single credit decision (issuing the card in the first place) for the many elaborate, costly, people-intensive activities and decisions that bank borrowing generally entails.

■ Supermarkets substitute fast and efficient self-service for the slow, inefficient, and often erratic clerks of the traditional service store.

In each of these examples a technological device or a manufacturing type of process has replaced what had been resolutely thought of as an irrevocably people-requiring service. Similar devices or processes can be used to modify and alleviate the customer-repelling abrasions of other people-intensive service conditions.

Consider the airlines. This industry is highly unusual. It is exceedingly capital-intensive in the creation of the facilitating product (the airplane), but it is extremely people-intensive in the delivery of the product (travel arrangements and the customer's flight experience). The possibilities for revenue production that a $20-million airplane represents are quickly vitiated by a surly or uncooperative reservations clerk. The potentials of repeat business that the chef so carefully builds into his meals can be destroyed by a dour or sloppy stewardess.

In fact, stewardesses have a particularly difficult job. A hundred passengers, having paid for reasonable service, understandably expect to be treated with some care. While three young ladies are there to serve them, a number of these passengers must inevitably get their drinks and meals later than others. Most experienced travelers are understanding and tolerant of the rushed stewardesses' problems, but a few usually harass them. The pressure and abuse can easily show in the stewardesses' personal appearance and behavior and are likely to result in nearly all passengers being reciprocally mistreated. This is human. Besides, the ladies may have been on their feet all day, or may have slept only a few hours the night before.

"More and better training" is not likely to help things very much. When the pressure is on, service deteriorates. And so does a stewardess's cheerful manner and appearance, no matter how well schooled she is in personal care and keeping her cool or how attractively her clothes are designed.

But it might help to put mirrors in the airplane gallery, so that each time a stewardess goes in she sees herself. There is some reason to expect that she'll look into the mirror each time she passes it, and that she'll straighten her hair, eliminate that lipstick smudge, put on a more cheerful face. Improvement will be instantaneous. No training needed.

Here is another possibility: the stewardess makes a quick trip down the aisle, passing out rum-flavored bonbons and explaining, "For those who can't wait till we get the ice out." This breaks the tension, produces an air of cheerfulness, acknowledges the passengers' eagerness for quick service, and says that the ladies are trying their hurried best. Further, it brings the stewardess into friendly personal contact with the passenger and reduces the likelihood of her being pressured and abused. She, in turn, is less likely to irritate other passengers.

From the manufacturing point of view, these two modest proposals represent the substitution of tools (or, as I prefer, technology) for motivation. Mirrors are a tool for getting self-motivated, automatic results in the stewardesses' appearance and personal behavior. Bonbons are a tool for creating a benign interpersonal ambiance that reduces both the likelihood of customer irritation and the reciprocal and contagious stewardess irritation of others. They are small measures, but so is a company president's plant tour.

In each case there is considerable presumption of solid benefits. Yet to get these benefits one must think, as the factory engineer thinks, about what the problems are and what the desired output is, about how to redesign the process and how to install new tools that do the job more automatically, and, whenever people are involved, about how to "control" their personal behavior and channel their choices.

Hard and Soft Technologies

There are numerous examples of strictly "hard" technologies (i.e., pieces of equipment) which are used as substitutes for people—coffee vending machines for waitresses, automatic check-cashing machines for bank tellers, self-operated travel-insurance policy machines for clerks. Although these devices represent a manufacturing approach to service, and while their principles can be extended to other fields, even greater promise lies in the application of "soft" technologies (i.e., technological systems). McDonald's is an example of a soft technology. So are mutual funds. Other examples are all around us, if we just think of them in the right way. Take the life insurance industry:

A life insurance salesman is said to be in a service industry. Yet what does he really do? He researches the prospect's needs by talking with him, designs several policy models for him, and "consumer-use tests" these models by seeking his reactions. Then he redesigns the final model and delivers it for sale to the customer. This is the ultimate example of manufacturing in the field. The factory is in the customer's living room, and the producer is the insurance agent, whom we incorrectly think of as being largely a salesman. Once we think of him as a manufacturer, however, we begin to think of how best to design and manufacture the product rather than how best to sell it.

The agent, for example, could be provided with a booklet of overlay sheets showing the insurance plans of people who are similar to the customer. This gives the customer a more credible and informed basis for making a choice. In time, the agent could be further supported by similar information stored in telephone-access computers.

In short, we begin to think of building a system that will allow the agent to produce his product efficiently and effectively by serving the customer's needs instead of by performing a manipulative selling job.

Manufacturers Outside the Factory

The type of thinking just described applies not only to service industries but also to manufacturing industries. When the computer hardware manufacturer provides installation and maintenance services, debugging dry-runs, software programs, and operator training as part of his hardware sales program, he acknowledges that his "product" consists of considerably more than what he made in the factory. What is done in the field is just as important to the customer as the manufactured equipment itself. Indeed, without these services there would generally be no sale.

The problem in so many cases is that customer service is not viewed by manufacturers as an integral part of what the customer buys, but as something peripheral to landing the sale. However, when it is explicitly accepted as integral to the product itself and, as a consequence, gets the same kind of dedicated attention as the manufacture of the hardware gets, the results can be spectacular. For example:

■ In the greeting card industry, some manufacturer-provided retail display cases have built-in inventory replenishment and reordering features. In effect, these features replace a company salesman with the willing efforts of department managers or store owners. The motivation of the latter to reorder is created by the visible imminence of stockouts, which is achieved with a special color-coded card that shows up as the stock gets low. Order numbers and envelopes are included for reordering. In earlier days a salesman had to call, take inventory, arrange the stock, and write orders. Stockouts were common.

The old process was called customer service and selling. The new process has no name, and probably has never been viewed as constituting a technological substitute for people. But it is. An efficient, automatic, capital-intensive system, supplemented occasionally by people, has replaced an inefficient and unreliable people-intensive system.

■ In a more complex situation, the A. O. Smith Company has introduced the same kind of preplanning, routinizing, people-conserving activity. This company makes, among other things, grain storage silos that must be locally sold, installed, serviced, and financed. There are numerous types of silos with a great variety of accessories for loading, withdrawing, and automatically mixing livestock feed. The selling is carried out by local distributor-erectors and is a lengthy, difficult, sophisticated operation.

Instead of depending solely on the effective training of distributors, who are spread widely in isolated places, A. O. Smith has developed a series of sophisticated, colorful, and interchangeable design-module planning books. These can be easily employed by a distributor to help a farmer decide what he may need, its cost, and its financing requirements. Easy-to-read tables, broken down by the size of farm, numbers and types of animals, and purpose of animals (cattle for meat or cows for milk), show recommended combinations of silo sizes and equipment for maximum effectiveness.

The system is so thorough, so easy to use and understand, and so effective in its selling capability that distributors use it with great eagerness. As a consequence, A. O. Smith, while sitting in Milwaukee, in effect controls every sales presentation made by every one of its far-flung distributors. Instead of constantly sending costly company representatives out to retrain, cajole, wine and dine, and possibly antagonize distributors, the supplier sends out a tool that distributors *want* to utilize in their own self-interest.

Product-line Pragmatics

Thinking of service as an integral part of what is sold can also result in alteration of the product itself—and with dramatic results. In 1961, the Building Controls and Components Group of Honeywell, Inc., the nation's largest producer of heating and air conditioning thermostats and control devices, did a major part of its business in replacement controls (the aftermarket). These were sold through heating and air conditioning distributors, who then supplied plumbers and other installation and repair specialists.

At that time, Honeywell's product line consisted of nearly 18,000 separate catalog parts and pieces. The company had nearly 5,000 distributor accounts, none of which could carry a full line of these items economically, and therefore it maintained nearly 100 fully stocked field warehouses that offered immediate delivery to distributors. The result was that, in a large proportion of cases, distributors sold parts to plumbers that they did not themselves have in stock. They either sent plumbers to nearby Honeywell warehouses for pickup or picked up parts themselves and delivered them directly to the plumbers. The costs to Honeywell of carrying these inventories were enormous, but were considered a normal expense of doing business.

Then Honeywell made a daring move—it announced its new Tradeline Policy. It would close all warehouses. All parts would have to be stocked by the distributors. The original equipment, however, had been redesigned into 300 standard, interchangeable parts. These were interchangeable not only for most Honeywell controls but also for those of its major competitors. Moreover, each package was clearly imprinted to show exactly which Honeywell and competing products were repairable with the contents.

By closing its own warehouses, Honeywell obviously shifted the inventory carrying costs to its distributors. But instead of imposing new burdens on them, the new product lines, with their interchangeability features, enabled the distributors to carry substantially lower inventories, particularly by cutting down the need for competitive product lines which the distributors could nonetheless continue to service. Thus they were able to offer faster service at lower costs to their customers than before.

But not all distributors were easily persuaded of this possibility, and some dropped the line. Those who were persuaded ultimately proved their wisdom by the enormous expansion of their sales. Honeywell's replacement market share almost doubled, and its original equipment share rose by nearly 50 percent. Whereas previously nearly 90 percent of Honeywell's replacement sales were scattered among 4,000 distributors, within ten years after Tradeline's introduction the same proportion (of a doubled volume) was concentrated among only about 900 distributors. Honeywell's cost of servicing these fewer customers was substantially less, its trade inventory carrying costs were cut to zero, and the quality of its distributor services was so substantially improved that only 900 of its distributors captured a larger national market share than did the nearly 4,000 less efficient and more costly distributors.

Again, we see a people-intensive marketing problem being solved by the careful and scrupulous application of manufacturing attitudes. Motivation, hard work, personalization, training, and merchandising incentives were replaced with systematic programming, comprehensive planning, attention to detail, and particularly with imaginative concern for the problems and needs of customers (in this case, the company's distributors).

Stopgaps: complexity . . .

Exaggeration is not without its merits, especially in love and war. But in business one guards against it with zeal, especially when one tries to persuade oneself. The judicious application of the manufacturing mentality may help the service industries and the customer-service activities of others. Yet this does not necessarily mean the more technology, the better.

Entrepreneurial roadsides are littered with the wrecks of efforts to install Cadillac technologies for people who cannot yet handle the Model T. This point is illustrated by the failure of two exceedingly well-financed joint ventures of highly successful technology companies. These joint ventures attempted to provide computerized medical diagnostic services for doctors and hospitals. The companies developed console hookups to central diagnostic computers, so that everybody could stop sending off samples to pathology laboratories and agonizingly poring through medical texts to diagnose the patients' symptoms.

The ventures failed because of hospital and doctor resistance, not for want of superior or reliable products. The customer was compelled suddenly to make an enormous change in his accustomed ways of doing things, and to employ a strange and somewhat formidable piece of equipment that required special training in its use and in the interpretation of its output.

Interactive teaching machines are meeting a similar fate. The learning results they achieve are uniformly spectacular. The need for improved learning is a visible reality. The demand for greater individualization of teaching is widespread. But the equipment has not sold because technologists have created systems employing equipment that is at the cutting edge of technological progress. The teachers and school systems that must use them are far behind, and already feel badly bruised by their failure to comprehend even simple new technologies. For them, the new Cadillac technologies do not solve problems. They create problems.

... compromise

On the other hand, failure to exploit technological possibilities can be equally destructive. When a major petroleum company with nearly 30,000 retail outlets in the United States was persuaded to pioneer a revolutionary automobile repair and servicing system, compromises of the original plan ensured the system's failure.

The theory was to build a gigantic service and repair system that could handle heavy volumes of continuous activity by using specialized diagnostic and repair equipment. With this equipment (rather than a harried and overworked man at a gas station) pinpointing the exact problems, cars could be shuttled off to specific stations in the repair center. Experts would work only on one kind of problem and section of a car, with newly designed fast-action tools. Oil changes would be made in assembly-line fashion by low-paid workers, electrical work would be performed by high-paid technicians doing only that, and a post-diagnostic checkup would be made to guarantee success.

Since profitability would require high volume, the center would have to draw on a vast population area. To facilitate this, the original proposal called for a specially constructed building at a center-city, old warehouse location—the land would be cheaper, the building would be equally accessible throughout the entire metropolitan area, the service center's technological elegance and see-through windows for customers would offset any run-down neighborhood disadvantages, and volume business would come from planned customer decisions rather than random off-street traffic.

The original concept also called for overnight pickup and delivery service; thus a car could be repaired at night while its owners slept, rather than during the day when he would need it. And because the required promotion of this service would tend to alienate the company's franchised service station dealers, perhaps driving them into the hands of competitors, it was recommended that the first center be installed in a major city where the company had no stations.

This sounds like an excellent manufacturing approach to a service situation; but the company made three fatal compromises:

1. It decided to place the center in a costly high-traffic suburban location, on the grounds that "if the experiment fails, at least the building will be in a location that has an alternative use." The results were an awkward location, a land-acquisition cost five times higher than the original center-city location, and, therefore, a vastly inflated break-even point for the service center.

2. It decided not to offer overnight service, on the grounds that "we'd better crawl before we walk. And besides, we don't think people will leave their cars overnight in a strange and distant garage." The fact that the results would be guaranteed by a reputable, nationally known petroleum company operating an obviously sophisticated new type of consumer service facility was not persuasive to the corporate decision makers.

3. It decided to put the first center in a city occupied by its own franchised dealers, on the grounds that "we know it better." To offset the problem of not being able to advertise aggressively for business, the company offered its dealers a commission to send their repair jobs to the center. The dealers did this, but only with jobs they could not, or did not want to, do themselves. As a result, the traffic at the big, expensive center was miserably low.

Companies that take a manufacturing approach to service problems are likely to fail if (1) they compromise technological possibilities at the conception and design stage, or (2) they allow technological complexity to contaminate the operating stage. The substitution of technology and systems for people and serendipity is complex in its conception and design; only in its operation, as at McDonald's, is it simple.

It is the simplicity of mutual funds that, after all, accounts for their success. But the concept is in fact much more complex than that of selling individual stocks through a single customer-man sitting at a desk. Mutual funds are the financial community's equivalent of McDonald's. They are a piece of technology that not only simplifies life for both the seller and the buyer but also creates many more buyers and makes production more profitable.

Mass merchandising is similar. It substitutes a wide selection and fast, efficient self-service for a narrow selection and slow, incompetent sales clerk service. The mass merchandising retail store (e.g., general merchandise supermarket) is a new technology, incorporating into retailing precisely the thinking that goes into the assembly line, except that the customer does his own assembling.

Why Things Go Wrong

The significance of all this is that a "product" is quite different from what it is generally assumed to be. As previously mentioned, when asked once what he did, Charles Revson made this well-known comment: "In the factory we make cosmetics, in the store we sell hope." He defined the product in terms of what the consumer wanted, not in terms of what the manufacturer made. McDonald's obviously does the same—not just hamburgers but also speed, cleanliness, reassurance, cheerfulness, and predictable consistency. Honeywell defined it not in terms of replacement parts but, rather, in terms of those needs of its distributors which, if met, would result in substantially larger proportions of patronage for Honeywell. Thus a product is not something people buy, but a tool they use— a tool to solve their problems or to achieve their intentions.

So many things go wrong because companies fail to adequately define what they sell. Companies in so-called "service industries" generally think of themselves as offering services rather than manufacturing products; hence they fail to think and act as comprehensively as do manufacturing companies concerned with the efficient, low-cost production of customer-satisfying products.

Moreover, manufacturing companies themselves do not generally think of customer service as an integral part of *their* products. It is an afterthought to be handled by the marketing department.

The marketing department, in turn, thinks of itself as providing customer services. There is a hidden and unintentional implication of giving something away for free. One is doing something extra as a favor. When this is the underlying communication to one's own organization, the result is about what one would expect—casual, discretionary attitudes and little attention to detail, and certainly no attention to the possibilities of substituting systems and preplanning for people and pure effort. Hence products are designed that cannot be easily installed, repaired, or modified. (Motorola's "works-in-a-box" television set, which has been promoted so successfully on the basis of its easy replacement and repairability is an outstanding example of the sales-getting potential of proper care in design and manufacturing.)

Chill Winds from Ice Cream

An excellent example of the confusion between what a company "makes" and what a customer "buys" is provided by a producer of private-label ice cream products for supermarket chains. Since supermarkets need to create low-price impressions in order to attract and hold customers, selling successfully to them means getting down to rock-bottom prices. The company (call it the Edwards Company) became extraordinarily good at producing a wide line of ice cream products at rock-bottom costs. It grew rapidly while others went bankrupt. It covered ten states with direct deliveries to stores out of its factory and factory warehouse, but continued growth eventually required establishing plant distribution and marketing centers elsewhere. The result was disaster, even though the company manufactured just as efficiently in the new locations as it did in the old.

Under the direct and constant supervision of the president in the original Edwards location, an exceedingly efficient telephone ordering and delivery system had been working to meet the supermarkets' rather stringent requirement. Because of limited storage and display space, they required several-times-a-week delivery at specified, uncrowded store hours. To make up for low volume in slow periods, they needed regular specials as well as holiday and summer specials. Over time, these needs had become so automatically but efficiently supplied from the original Edwards factory location that this delivery service became routinized and therefore taken for granted.

In building the new plant, the president and his compact management team focused on getting manufacturing costs down to rock bottom. After all, that is what made the sale—low prices. Not being very conscious of the fact that they had created in the original location an enormously customer-satisfying, efficient, automatic ordering and delivery system, they did not know exactly what to look for in evaluating how well they were working out these "service" details at the new plant, distribution, and marketing centers.

In short, they did not know what their product really was (why Edwards had become so successful) and they failed to expand Edwards' success. Service was not considered an integral part of the company's product. It was viewed merely as "something else" you do in the business. Accordingly, service received inadequate attention, and that became the cause of the Edwards Company's failure.

CONCLUSION

Rarely is customer service discretionary. It is a requisite of getting and holding business, just like the generic product itself. Moreover, if customer service is consciously treated as "manufacturing in the field," it will get the same kind of detailed attention that manufacturing gets. It will be carefully planned, controlled, automated where possible, audited for quality control, and regularly reviewed for performance improvement and customer reaction. More important, the same kinds of technological, labor-saving, and systems approaches that now thrive in manufacturing operations will begin to get a chance to thrive in customer service and service industries.

Once service-industry executives and the creators of customer-service programs begin seriously to think of themselves as actually manufacturing a product, they will begin to think like product manufacturers. They will ask: What technologies and systems are employable here? How can things be designed so we can use machines instead of people, systems instead of serendipity? Instead of thinking about better and more training of their customer-service representatives, insurance agents, branch bank managers, or salesmen "out there," they will think about how to eliminate or supplement them.

If we continue to approach service as something done by individuals rather than by machines or systems, we will continue to suffer from two distortions in thinking:

1. Service will be viewed as something residual to the ultimate reality —to a tangible product, to a specific competence (like evaluating loans, writing insurance policies, giving medical aid, preparing on-premises foods). Hence it will have residual respectability, receive attention, and be left, somehow, for residual performers.

2. Service will be treated as purely a human task that must inevitably be diagnosed and performed by a single individual working alone with no help, or, at best, with the rudimentary help of training and a variety of human-engineering motivators. It will never get the kind of manufacturing-type thinking that goes into tangible products.

Until we think of service in more positive and encompassing terms, until it is enthusiastically viewed as manufacturing in the field, receptive to the same kinds of technological approaches that are used in the factory, the results are likely to be just as costly and idiosyncratic as the results of the lonely journeyman carving things laboriously by hand at home.

SECTION TWO

Innovation and Organization

Chapter Four

Creativity Is Not Enough

"CREATIVITY" IS NOT the miraculous road to business growth and affluence that it is so abundantly claimed to be. And for the line manager particularly, it can be a millstone rather than a milestone.

The Great Illusion

The trouble with much of the advice business gets today about the need to be more vigorously creative is that its advocates often fail to distinguish between creativity and innovation. Creativity thinks up new things. Innovation does new things. The difference speaks for itself. Yet the fluent advisers to business seldom make the distinction. They tend to rate ideas more by their novelty than by their practicability.

The operating realities of life are sobering and generally not at all glamorous. A new idea, particularly in the complex infrastructures of today's business organizations, can be creative in the abstract but destructive in actuality. Often instead of helping a company, a tantalizing new idea can seriously hinder it.

Take two artists. One tells you about an idea for a great painting, but does not paint it. The other has the same idea, and paints it. You could easily say that the second man is a great creative artist. But could you say the same thing of the first man? Obviously not. He is a talker, not a painter.

That is precisely the problem with so much of today's pithy praise of creativity in business—with the unending flow of speeches, books, articles, and "creativity workshops" whose purpose is to produce more imaginative and creative managers and companies. Too often they mistake the idea for a great painting with the great painting itself. They mistake brilliant talk for constructive action.

Anybody who knows anything about organizations knows how hard it is to get things done, let alone to introduce new ways of doing things, no matter how promising they seem. A powerful new idea can kick around unused in a company for years, not because its merits are not recognized but because nobody has assumed the responsibility for converting it from words into action. What is lacking is not creativity in the idea-creating sense but innovation in the action-producing sense. The ideas are not being put to work. There is no center of entrepreneurial energy.

Understanding Innovation

One of the most repetitious and most erroneous explanations for the scarcity of significant innovation in business is that businessmen are not adequately creative and that they are enslaved by the incubus of conformity. It is all too often alleged that American business would be a lot better off if industry were simply more creative, if it would hire more creative people and give them the chance to show their fructifying stuff.

But anybody who looks carefully around in any modern business organization and speaks freely and candidly with the people in it will discover something very interesting, namely, that there is really no shortage of creativity or of creative people in American business. The shortage is of innovators. The major problem is that so-called "creative" people often (though certainly not always) pass on to *others* the responsibility for getting down to brass tacks. They have plenty of ideas but little business-like follow-through. They themselves are the bottleneck. They make none of the right kind of effort to help their ideas get a hearing and a try.

Ideation is relatively abundant. It is its implementation that is scarce.

Many people who are full of ideas simply do not understand how an organization must operate to get things done, especially dramatically new things. All too often there is the peculiar underlying assumption that creativity automatically leads to actual innovation. In the crippled logic of this line of thinking, "ideation" (or "creativity," if you emphasize the idea-producing aspect of that term) and "innovation" are treated as synonyms. This kind of thinking is a particular disease of advocates of "brainstorming," who often treat their approach as some sort of ultimate business liberator.[1]

"Ideation" and "innovation" are not synonyms. The former deals with the generation of ideas; the latter, with their implementation. It is the absence of a constant awareness of this distinction that is responsible for some of the corporate standpattism we see today. Nor is it obligatory that an innovation be *successfully* implemented to qualify as an innovation. The object of the innovation is success, but to require in advance that there be no doubt of its success would disable its chance of ever getting tried.

The fact that you can put a dozen inexperienced people into a room and conduct a brainstorming session that produces exciting new ideas shows how little relative importance ideas themselves actually have. Almost anybody with the intelligence of the average businessman can produce them, given a halfway decent environment and stimulus. The scarce people are those who have the know-how, energy, daring, and staying power to implement ideas.

Whatever the goals of a business may be, it must make money. To do that it must get things done. But having ideas is seldom equivalent to getting things done in the business or organizational sense. Ideas do not implement themselves—neither in business nor in art, science, philosophy, politics, love, or war. People implement ideas.

A Form of Irresponsibility

Since business is a uniquely "get-things-done" institution, creativity without action-oriented follow-through is a uniquely barren form of individual behavior. Actually, in a sense, it is even irresponsible. This is so because (1) the creative man who tosses out ideas and does nothing to help them get implemented is shirking any responsibility for one of the prime requisites of the business, namely, action, and (2) by avoiding follow-through he is behaving in an organizationally intolerable—or, at best, sloppy—fashion. The trouble with much creativity today is that many of the people with the ideas have the peculiar notion that their jobs are finished when they suggest them; that it is up to somebody else to work out the dirty details and then implement the proposals.

Typically, the more creative the man, the less responsibility he takes for action. The reason for this is that the generation of ideas and concepts

---

[1] See, for instance, Alex F. Osborn, *Applied Imagination: Principles and Procedures of Creative Thinking,* Charles Scribner's Sons, New York, 1953.

is often his sole talent, his solitary stock-in-trade. He seldom has the energy or staying power, or indeed the interest, to work with the grubby details that require attention for putting his ideas to work.

Anybody can verify this for himself. You need only look around in your own company and pick out the two or three most original idea men in the vicinity. How many of their ideas can you say they have ever vigorously and systematically followed through with detailed plans and proposals for their implementation, or even with only some modest ball-park suggestions of the risks, the costs, the manpower requisites, the time budgets, and the possible payouts?

The usual situation is that idea men constantly pepper everybody with proposals and memorandums that are just brief enough to get attention, to intrigue, and to sustain interest—but too short to include any responsible suggestions regarding how the whole thing is to be implemented and what's at stake. In some instances it must actually be inferred that they use novel ideas for their disruptive or their self-promotional values.

One student of management succession questions whether ideas are always put forth seriously. He suggests that often an idea may simply be a tactical device to attract attention to the person who generated it so that he will come first to mind when promotions are made. Hence ideas are a form of "public relations" within the organization.[2]

It should be pointed out, however, that something favorable can be said about the relationship of irresponsibility to ideation. The effective executive often exhibits what might be called "controlled momentary irresponsibility." He recognizes that this attitude is necessary for the free play of imagination. But what distinguishes him is his ability to alternate appropriately between attitudes of irresponsibility and those of responsibility. He doesn't hold to the former for long—only long enough to make himself more productive.

The Psychology of "Idea Men"

The fact that a consistently highly creative person is generally irresponsible in the sense that we have used this term is in part predictable from what is known about the freewheeling fantasies of very young children. They are extremely creative, as any kindergarten teacher will testify. They have a naïve curiosity that stumps parents with questions like, "Why can you see through glass?" "Why is there a hole in a doughnut?" "Why is the grass green?" It is this questioning attitude that produces in them so much

[2] See Bernard Levenson, "Bureaucratic Succession," in Amitai Etzioni (ed.), *Complex Organizations: A Sociological Reader*, Rinehart & Company, Inc., New York, 1961, pp. 362–375.

creative freshness. Significantly, the unique posture of their lives is their almost total irresponsibility from blame, work, and the other routine necessities of organized society. Even the law absolves them from responsibility for their actions. But all sources testify to their creativity, even biblical mythology, with its assertion about wisdom issuing from "the mouths of babes." Respectable scientific sources have compared the integrative mechanism of adult creativity with the childhood thought process that "manifests itself during the pre-school period—possibly as early as the appearance of three-word sentences...."[3]

Clinical psychologists have also illustrated the operating irresponsibility of creative individuals in Rorschach and stroboscopic tests. For example, one analyst says, "Those who took to the Rorschach like ducks to water, who fantasied and projected freely, even too freely in some cases, or who could permit themselves to tamper with the form of the blot as given, gave us our broadest ranges of movement."[4] In short, they were the least "form-bound," the least inhibited by the facts of their experience, and hence let their minds explore new, untried, and novel alternatives to existing ways of doing things.

The significance of this finding for the analysis of organizations is pointed up by the observation of another psychologist that "the theoreticians on the other hand do not mind living dangerously."[5] The reason is obvious. A theoretician is not immediately responsible for action. He is perfectly content to "live dangerously" because he does so only on the conceptual level, where he cannot get hurt. To assume any responsibility for implementation is to risk dangerous actions, and that can be painfully uncomfortable. The safe solution is to steer clear of implementation and all the dirty work it implies.

The Advice Business

It is to be expected, therefore, that today's most ardent advocates of creativity in business tend to be professional writers, consultants, professors, and often advertising agency executives. Not surprisingly, few of them have any continuing, day-to-day responsibility for the difficult task of im-

---

[3] See Stanley Stark, "Mills, Mannheim, and the Psychology of Knowledge," University of Illinois, Urbana, 1960, p. 15. (Mimeographed.)

[4] G. S. Klein, "The Personal World through Perception," in R. R. Blake and G. V. Ramsey (eds.), *Perception: An Approach to Personality*, The Ronald Press Company, New York, 1951, p. 343. For further research evidence and commentary on the "creative personality," see Morris I. Stein and Shirley J. Heinze, *Creativity and the Individual*, The Free Press of Glencoe, Inc., New York, 1960.

[5] Herbert Feigl, "Philosophical Embarrassments of Psychology," *American Psychologist*, March, 1959, p. 126.

plementing powerful new-business ideas of a complex nature in the ordinary type of business organization. Few of them have ever had any responsibility for doing work in the conventional kind of complex operating organization. They are not really practicing businessmen in the usual sense. They are literary businessmen. They are the doctors who say, "Do as I say, not as I do," reminiscent of the classic injunction of the boxer's manager, "Get in there and fight. They can't hurt us."

The fact that these individuals are also so often outspoken about the alleged virulence of conformity in modern business is not surprising. They can talk this way because they themselves have seldom had the nerve to expose themselves for any substantial length of time to the rigorous discipline of an organization whose principal task is not talk but action, not ideas but work.

Impressive sermons are delivered gravely proclaiming the virtues of creativity and the vices of conformity. But so often the authors of these sermons, too, are "outsiders" to the central sector of the business community. The best-known asserters that American industry is some sort of vast quagmire of quivering conformity—the men who have turned the claim into a tiresome cliché—are people like William H. Whyte, Jr., author of *The Organization Man*,[6] who is a professional writer; Sloan Wilson, author of *The Man in the Gray Flannel Suit*,[7] who was a college English professor when he wrote the book; and C. Northcote Parkinson (more on him later), also a professor.

It is of course inevitable that it is writers, and not business practitioners, who write mostly about business. My purpose is not to condemn them, or to condemn consultants or professors. American business appears generally to benefit from their existence. But it is harmful when the abused executive fails to consider that the very role of these men absolves them from managerial responsibility. Still, it is hard to accept uncritically the doleful prophesy that so many United States companies are hypnotically following one another in a deadly march of confining conformity. It is hard to accept the tantalizing suggestion offered by outsiders that business's salvation lies in a massive infusion of creativity and that from this will follow an automatic flow of profit-building innovation. Perhaps the source of these suggestions should occasionally be kept in mind.

The Chronic Complainers

As I have said, "ideation" is not a synonym for "innovation," "conformity" is not its simple antonym, and innovation is not the automatic conse-

---

[6] Simon & Schuster, Inc., New York, 1956
[7] Simon & Schuster, Inc., New York, 1955.

quence of creative thinking. Indeed, what some people call conformity in business is less related to the lack of abstract creativity than to the lack of responsible action, whether it be the implementation of new or old ideas.

The proof of this is that in most business organizations, the most continually creative men in the echelons below the executive level are men who are actively discontent with the here and now. They are the creative men, but they are also generally known as corporate malcontents. They tend to complain constantly about the standpat senility of the management, about its refusal to see the obvious facts of its own massive inertia. They complain about management refusing to do the things that have been suggested to it for years. They often complain that management does not even want creative ideas, that ideas rock the boat (which they do), and that management is interested more in having a smoothly running (or is it smoothly ruining) organization than in having a rapidly forward-vaulting business.

In short, they talk about the company being a festering sore of deadly conformity, full of decaying vegetables who systematically oppose new ideas with old ideologies. And then, of course, they frequently quote their patron saint, William H. Whyte, Jr., with all his misinformed moralizing and conjectural evidence about what goes on inside an operating organization. (Whyte's fanciful notions of such operations were later demolished by the badly underpublicized but careful studies of the veteran student of social organization, W. Lloyd Warner, in his *Corporation in the Emergent American Society*.[8])

Why Doors Are Closed

The reason the creative malcontent speaks this way is that so often the people to whom he addresses his flow of ideas do, indeed, after awhile, ignore him and tell him to go away. They shut their doors to his endless entreaties; they refuse to hear his ideas any longer. Why? There is a plausible explanation.

The reason the executive so often rejects new ideas is that he is a busy man whose chief day-in, day-out task is to handle an ongoing stream of pressing problems. He receives an unending flow of questions on which actions must be taken. Constantly he is forced to deal with problems to which solutions are more or less urgent but for which answers are far from self-evident. It may seem splendid to a subordinate to supply his boss with a lot of brilliant new ideas to help him in his job. But advocates

[8] Harper & Row, Publishers, Incorporated, New York, 1962; see pp. 47–64.

of creativity must once and for all understand the pressing facts of the executive's life: Every time an idea is submitted to him, it creates more problems for him—and he already has enough.

Professor Raymond A. Bauer of Harvard has pointed out an instructive example from another field of activity. He notes that many congressmen and senators have the opportunity to have a political science "intern" assigned to "help" them. However, some congressmen and senators refuse this help on the grounds that these interns generate so many ideas that they disrupt the legislator's regular business.

Similarly, Dr. E. Paul Torrence of the University of Minnesota found that teachers of highly creative children said they were less desirable to have in the classroom. They were measurably less studious and less hard-working than highly intelligent students. They predictably departed in unpredictable ways from the expectations and order the teachers apparently felt required to institutionalize.[9] Jonathan Kozol has written about quite similar problems in Boston's black ghetto schools.[10]

Making Ideas Useful

Innovation is necessary in business, but it begins with an idea—with somebody's proposal. How can the man with a new idea also be responsible in the organizational sense? At least two "ideas" may be helpful:

1. *He must work with the existing situation.* Since the executive is already constantly bombarded with problems, there is little wonder that after awhile he shuns more new ideas to solve problems he did not even know existed. He needs to get things done, not just more advice about what things to do or how to do them. The "idea man" has to learn to accept this as a fact of life. He has to act accordingly.

2. *When the creative man suggests an idea, the responsible procedure is to include at least some minimal indication of what it involves in terms of concrete activities, costs, risks, manpower, time, and perhaps even specific people who ought to carry it through.* That is the essence of responsible behavior, because it makes it easier for the executive to evaluate the idea while anticipating and dealing with the problems that will invariably come quickly to his mind. That is the way creative thinking will more likely be converted into innovation.

It will be argued, of course, that to saddle the creative individual with the responsibility of spelling out the details of implementation will curb

[9] See Arthur O. England, "Creativity: An Unwelcome Talent?" *Personnel Journal,* September, 1964, pp. 458–461.

[10] Jonathan Kozol, *Death at an Early Age,* Houghton Mifflin Company, Boston, 1967.

or even throttle his unique talent. This may be true. But this could be salutary, both for him and for the company. Ideas are useless unless used. The proof of their value is their implementation. Until then they are in limbo. If the executive's job pressures mean that an idea seldom gets a good hearing unless it is responsibly presented, then the unthrottled and irresponsible creative man is useless to the company. If an insistence on some responsibility for implementation throttles him, he may produce fewer ideas, but their chances of getting a judicious hearing and therefore of being followed through are greatly improved. The company will benefit by trying the ideas, and the creative man will benefit by getting the satisfaction of knowing he is being listened to. He will not have to be a malcontent any more.

Deciding Factors

This is not to suggest that every idea needs a thoroughly documented study before it is mentioned to anyone. Far from it. What is needed will vary from case to case depending on four factors:

1. *The position or rank of the idea originator in the organization.* How "responsible" a man needs to act for an idea to get a hearing clearly depends on his rank. The powerful chief executive officer can simply instruct subordinates to take and develop one of his ideas. That is enough to give it a hearing and perhaps even implementation. To that extent talk *is* virtually action. Similarly, a department head can do the same thing in his domain. But when the ideas flow in the opposite direction—upward instead of downward—they are unlikely to "flow" unless they are supported by the kind of follow-through I have been urging.

2. *The complexity of the idea.* The more complex and involved the implications of an idea, and the more change and rearrangement it may require within the organization or in its present way of doing things, then obviously the greater the need to cover the required ground in some responsible fashion when the proposal is presented.

This is not to suggest that the "how to" questions need to be covered as thoroughly and carefully as would be required by, say, a large corporation's executive committee when it finally decides whether to implement or drop the suggestion. Such a requirement would be so confiningly rigid that it might dry up all ideas. Their originators simply would not have the time, competence, or staff to go to that much effort. But a great deal more effort is needed than is now customary.

3. *The nature of the industry.* How much supporting detail a subordinate should submit along with his idea often depends on the industry involved and the intent of the idea.

One reason why there is such a high premium put on "creativity" in advertising is that the first requisite of an ad is to get attention. Hence creativity frequently revolves around the matter of trying to achieve visual or auditory impact such that the ad stands out above the constantly expanding stream of advertising noise to which the badgered consumer is subjected. To this extent, in the advertising industry being creative is quite a different thing, by and large, from what it is, say, in the steel industry. Putting an eye patch on the man in the Hathaway shirt is "no sooner said than done." The idea is virtually synonymous with its implementation. But in the steel industry an idea, say, to change the discount structure to encourage users of cold-rolled sheet steel to place bigger but fewer orders is so full of possible complications and problems that talk is far from being action, or even a program for action. To get even a sympathetic first hearing, such an idea needs to be accompanied by a good deal of factual and logical support.

4. *The attitude and job of the person to whom the idea is submitted.* Everybody knows that some bosses are more receptive to new ideas than others. Some are more receptive to extreme novelty than others. The extent of their known receptiveness will in part determine the elaborateness of support a suggested new idea requires at its original stage.

But, equally important, it is essential to recognize that the greater the pressures of day-to-day operating responsibilities on the executive, the more resistant he is likely to be to new ideas. If the operating burden happens to fall on him, his job is to make the present setup work smoothly and well. A new idea requires change, and change upsets the smooth (or perhaps faltering) regularity of the present operation on whose effectiveness he is being judged and on which his career future depends. He has very good reason to be extremely careful about a new proposal. He needs lots of good risk-reducing reasons before he will look at one very carefully.

What his actual requirements are will also depend on the attitudes of his superiors to risk–taking and mistakes. In one large American company the two most senior officers several years ago had a unique quality of enormous receptivity to novelty—sometimes the wilder the proposal, the better. The result was that new ideas, no matter how vaguely started or extreme, got quick and sympathetic hearings throughout all levels of the company. But this was a rare organization.

The chairman at that time was about forty years old. He became president when he was twenty-eight, having been selected by his predecessor as the obvious heir apparent when he was about twenty-four. He vaulted quickly from one top job to another, never really having to spend very much time "making good" in the conventional sense in a difficult day-to-day operating job at a low level. Virtually his entire career was one of high-level responsibility where his ideas could be passed down to a corps of subordinates for detailed examination and evaluation. These experiences taught him the value of wild ideation without his having to risk his rise to the top by seeming to suggest irresponsible projects.

The present president of this same company came in as a vice-president, also at twenty-eight, and directly from an advertising agency. His career experiences were similar to the chairman's.

It was relatively easy for both of these men to be permissive. They never really had to risk their climb up the hierarchical ladder by seeming to shoot wild. They always had teams of subordinates to check their ideas and willing superiors to listen to them. Anybody who has not had this history or conditioning will find it extremely hard to change once he gets very far up the corporate pecking order.

A permissive, open, risk-taking environment cannot be created simply by the good intentions of the top management. The reason is that either high-level executives who have got to their top posts by a lifetime of judiciously guarded executive behavior are incapable of changing their habits, or, if their habits are changed, their subordinates will not believe they really mean it. And in lots of small ways these subordinates will have their doubts affirmed by the unintentional signals of their bosses.

Need for Discipline

Writers on the subject of creativity and innovation invariably emphasize the essential primacy of the creative impulse itself. Almost as an after-thought they talk about the necessity of teaching people to sell their ideas and of stimulating executives to listen to the ideas of subordinates and peers. Then they often go on casually to make some unctuous statement about the importance of creating a permissive organizational climate for creative people. They rarely try to look at the executive's job and suggest how the creative genius might alter *his* behavior to suit the boss's require-ments. It is always the boss who is being told to mend his ways. The reason for their siding with the creative man is that the outside critics are generally as hostile to the very idea of the "organization" as the inside creative men themselves. Both actively dislike organizations, but they seldom know exactly why.

Most likely the reason is that organization and creativity do not seem to go together. Organization and conformity do. Writers, critics, and other professionally creative people tend to be autonomous men, preferring to live by their personal wits. For them, to live in a highly structured organizational environment is a form of oppressive imprisonment. Hence, their advocacy of a "permissive environment" for creativity in an organization is often a veiled attack on the idea of the organization itself. This quickly becomes clear when one recognizes this inescapable fact: One of the collateral purposes of an organization *is* to be inhospitable to a great and constant flow of ideas and creativity. Whether we are talking about the United States Steel Corporation or the United Steel Workers of America, the United States Army or the Salvation Army, the U.S.A. or the U.S.S.R., the purpose of organization is to achieve the kind and degree of order and conformity necessary to do a particular job. The organization exists to restrict and channel the range of individual actions and behavior into a predictable and knowable routine. Without organization there would be chaos and decay. Organization exists in order to create that amount and kind of inflexibility that are necessary to get the most pressingly intended job done efficiently and on time.

Creativity and innovation disturb that order. Organization tends to be inhospitable to creativity and innovation, though without creativity and innovation the organization would eventually perish. That is why small, one-man shops are so often more animated and "innovationary" than large ones. They have virtually no organization (precisely because they are one-man shops) and often are run by self-willed autocrats who act on impulse.

Organizations are created to achieve order. They have policies, procedures, and formal or powerfully informal (unspoken) rules. The job for which the organization exists could not possibly get done without these rules, procedures, and policies. And these produce the so-called "conformity" that is so blithely deprecated by the critics of the organization and life inside it.

Parkinson's Flaw

It is not surprising that C. Northcote Parkinson and his "Parkinson's laws" enjoy such an admiring following among teachers, writers, consultants, and professional social critics. Most of these people have carefully chosen as their own professions work that keeps them as far as modern society lets anyone get from the rigorous taskmaster of the organization. Most of them lead a more-or-less one-man, self-employed existence in which there are few make-or-break postmortems of their activities. They live in autonomous isolation. Many of them have avoided life in the organization because they are incapable of submitting to its rigid discipline. Parkinson has provided them a way to laugh at the majority, at those who *do* submit to the organization, and at the same time to feel superior rather than oppressed, as minorities usually do.

It is not surprising (indeed it is quite expected) that Parkinson himself was anything but an organization man—that he was a teacher of history, a painter, and, of all things, a historian on warfare in the Eastern seas. This is about as far as you can get from the modern land-bound organization.

Parkinson's writings finally brought him into such continuing contact with business that he finally decided to go into business himself. In doing so he proved the truth of all that I have been saying: The business his notoriety ultimately led him to enter was, of course, the consulting business!

Parkinson is very entertaining. The executive who cannot laugh along with him is probably too paranoid to be trusted with a responsible job. But most of today's blithe cartoonists of the organization would be impoverished for material were they not blessed with an enormous ignorance of the facts of organizational life. Let me put it as emphatically as possible. A company cannot function as an anarchy. It must be organized, it must be routinized, it must be planned in some way in the various phases of its operations. That is why we have so many organizations of so many different kinds. And to the extent that planning and control are needed, we get rigidity, order, and therefore some amount of conformity. No organization can have everybody running off uncoordinated in several different directions at once. There must be rules, standards, and directions.

Where there are enough rules, there will be damn fool rules. These can be mercilessly cartooned. But some rules that look foolish to an expert on ancient naval history would seem far from foolish to him if he bothered to understand the problems of the business, or the government, or whatever group the particular organization is designed to deal with.

CONCLUSION

All this raises a seemingly frightening question: If conformity and rigidity are necessary requisites of organization, and if these in turn help stifle creativity, and furthermore if the creative man might indeed be stifled if he is required to spell out the details needed to convert his ideas into effective innovations, does all this mean that modern organizations have evolved into such involuted monsters of administration that they must suffer the fearful fate of the dinosaur—too big and unwieldy to survive?

The answer is *no*. First, it is questionable whether the creative impulse will automatically dry up if the idea man is required to take some responsibility for follow-through. The people who so resolutely proclaim their own creative energies will scarcely assert that they need a hothouse for its flowering. Second, the large organization has some important attributes that actually facilitate innovation. Its capacity to distribute risk over its broad economic base and among the many individuals involved in implementing newness is enormous. Its resources and capacities make it both economically and, for the individuals involved, personally easier to break untried ground.

What often misleads people is the false assumption that to make big operating changes also requires making big organizational changes. Yet it is precisely one of the great virtues of a big organization that, in the short run at least, its momentum is irreversible and its organizational structure is, for all practical purposes, nearly impenetrable. A vast machinery exists to get a certain job done. That job must continue to get the toughest kind of serious attention, no matter how exotically revolutionary a big operating or policy change may be. The boat can and may have to be rocked, but one virtue of a big boat is that it takes an awful lot to rock it. Certain people or departments in the boat may feel the rocking more than others, and to that extent strive to avoid the incidents that produce it. But the built-in stabilizers of bigness and of group decision making can be used as powerful influences in *encouraging* people to risk these incidents.

Adding Flexibility

Finally, the large organization has alternatives to the alleged "conservatizing" consequences of bigness. The relatively rigid organization *can* build into its own processes certain flexibilities that would provide fructifying opportunities for the creative but irresponsible individual. Some of these alternatives were discussed earlier.

Some of them, however, have created their own organizational problems, some of them not terribly reassuring. The fact is that the problems and needs of companies differ. To this extent they have to find their own special ways of dealing with the issues discussed in this chapter. The important point is to be conscious of the possible need and value of finding ways to make creativity yield more innovation.

Some companies have greater need for such measures than others. As pointed out earlier, the need hinges in part on the nature of the industry. Certainly it is easier to convert creativity into innovation in the advertising business than it is in an operating company, with its elaborate production processes, long channels of distribution, and complex administrative setup.

For those critics of, and advisers to, industry who repeatedly call for more creativity in business, it is well to try first to understand the profound distinction between creativity and innovation, and then perhaps to spend a little more time calling on creative individuals to take added responsibility for implementation. The fructifying potentials of creativity vary enormously with the particular industry, with the climate in the organization, with the organizational level of the idea man, and with the kinds of day-in, day-out problems, pressures, and responsibilities of the man to whom he addresses his ideas. Without clearly appreciating these facts, those who declare that a company will somehow grow and prosper merely by having more creative people make a fetish of their own illusions.

Chapter Five

Thinking Big Is Not Enough

AMERICANS ARE NOTED for their preference for scale. Magnitude is a measure of meaning. The bigger the better. "Think Big" is the distinctive and perennial American slogan. A few years ago it was only kooks, impecunious student couples, and two-car suburbanites in high personal-property tax towns who were presumed to be attracted by Volkswagen's peculiarly European slogan: "Think Small." Volkswagen's slogan worked not because it competed with America's think-big attitudes but because it actually complemented and reinforced them. It was not a challenge to American values. Its ambitions were actually a playful affirmation of what really counts, namely, bigness.

The Volkswagen slogan had an appropriately minority suggestion of miniatureness and quaintness. It is not only because of its silhouette that the car is called "The Bug." A bug is small, close to the ground, even cute. If it isn't careful, it might get overrun and flattened. In the American rhetoric, to qualify as cute something must be viewed as only temporarily small—a cute baby, a cute kitten. In short, it does not merit serious adult attention except as a fetching or exceptional curiosity. It is not quite finished, not quite mature, not really legitimate in any practical way. When the young married couple starts facing the serious business of life, the cute little Volkswagen will obviously have to give way in favor of a solidly adult Detroit chariot. Or so it seemed.

America thinks big. Nobody has the slightest doubt that to be big is to be great. Only the unschooled child says that it's a "great big house" or a "great big airplane." No well-acculturated American adult would utter such an obvious redundancy, except occasionally to speak of Texas millionaires.

Bigness is a dream that continues to animate American life and shape its business ethic. Yet, powerful forces operate to suggest that business success will increasingly require an unaccustomed parallel capacity to think small. It is a necessity imposed on American business by the rising tendency of both industrial and household consumers to be more discriminating in what they buy. The day of the universal brand is rapidly yielding to consumer demands for specialty brands and tailored products uniquely suited to the particular discriminate functions or styles of life that people are learning to value and assert. This imposes on American business the necessity for a way of thinking that is already having a profound impact on organization structure and costs of doing business.

Selectivity and Segmentation

New times are upon us. The traditional idea of the mass market, on which so many American business fortunes were built, is dying a gradual death. It may even be a compulsive death. With fits and starts and occasional dramatic profits, it is still with us, but not, in the traditional sense, for long. It is being replaced by a new kind of market dominated by a new and powerfully different kind of consumer.

The age of the indiscriminate mass consumer is in its twilight. We are rapidly entering an age of the discriminating consumer whose ambition is not to "keep up with the Joneses" but to "keep away from the Joneses." The Joneses are ceasing to be a symbol of democratic affluence. They are becoming a symbol of mass-market anonymity, of deadening uniformity.

For a good many years to come, business success will depend less on an executive's capacity to think big and more on his capacity to think small—more correctly, to think selectively. He must stop thinking of his customers as part of some massively homogeneous market. He must start thinking of them as numerous small islands of distinctiveness, each of which requires its own unique strategies in product policy, in promotional strategy, in pricing, in distribution methods, and in direct-selling techniques.

An aggressively think-small attitude produced such enormous successes as Pepperidge Farm bread, Caedmon records, Early American cake mixes, compact cars and sporty personal cars, personal calculators, and even M&M candy. Enormous opportunity and profit await the company that begins more aggressively to think small. And this applies most urgently to America's largest corporations, who seem so often to be so firmly married to the think-big formulas that produced such unmatched greatness in the past. For them, an unbending think-big attitude may be the surest road to ruin.

In a world of systems selling and broadly encompassing definitions of what an industry is, it is time we look again at the details of how the world now works.

From Small Beginnings . . .

Every business started as a small business. Big companies did not suddenly erupt from the primeval rocks on some glorious spring morning to the inspirational accompaniment of Beethoven's "Ode to Joy." Even John D. Rockefeller started as a peddler with a horse. Eugene Ferkauf of Korvette sold discount luggage out of an obscure one-room second-floor loft. J. Eric Jonsson and Patrick E. Haggerty of Texas Instruments had a little geophysical operation that became interested in transistors. Appropriately to their Dallas origins they bet a lot on a little item. Charles Lubin ran an obscure little neighborhood bakery on Chicago's north side, which later achieved fame and fiscal eminence as Sara Lee cakes and pastries.

Each of these men became a corporate hero, appropriately celebrated for his pioneering wisdom and entrepreneurial energy. Each no doubt deserves both his plaudits and his millions. Standard Oil is huge; Korvette is big and, for reasons not central to this exposition, now transmuted into the less casually controlled orbit of another enterprise. Texas Instruments is enormous in both size and profits; and Sara Lee, though willingly gobbled up in the great merger movement, is willingly gobbled up by the rest of us in proportions greater than we would like but with resistance less than we can muster.

The trouble with heroes is that their admirers endow them with such a powerfully brilliant glow that we are blinded to the more significant facts of their achievements. One thing is significantly identical about the heroes we have mentioned: Each made a revolution, and yet each made it in an industry to which he was a stranger and which was occupied by others of greater experience, larger fiscal resources, and more connections. Rockefeller was a vegetable peddler when others had already waxed rich in oil. Ferkauf was, in the accepted parlance of the trade, a mere schnook compared with the experienced might of Federated Department Stores and Allied Stores. Compared with RCA, Philco, General Electric, and their heavily capitalized and innovation-minded brethren, Texas Instruments was a phantom outsider. And Mr. Lubin was so far outside the commercial baking industry that he probably could not have qualified as a journeyman baker in the mass-production factories of Consolidated or Ward.

The Pathology of Revolution

Revolutions are seldom made by insiders. A few exceptions prove the point that business revolutions are made by outsiders.[1] Typically also they are made not by successful giants but by small generally undercapitalized and inexperienced outsiders.

One of the most remarkable recent examples is ocean-cargo containerization. This revolution, which is still only in its infancy, did not emanate from the shipping giants—American Export Isbrandtsen Lines, or United States Lines, or Grace Line, or Cunard, or Matson, or Moore-McCormack. It was launched and led by Malcolm McLean, then president of McLean Trucking Co. He had none of the constipating sentimentality that leads one to refer to a ship as a "she." He viewed ships as a giant bridge for his trucks. So in 1956, with four old tankers, he launched Sea/Land, now the leader in ocean-cargo containerization.

Other examples of big new industries and big new ways of doing things that emanated from the small beginnings of outsiders are almost endless: tape recorders and magnetic tape, motels, paperback books, television program production, frozen foods, vinyl tile, auto rentals, polarized glass, aluminum die casting, affinity-group flying, helicopters, all-purpose credit cards, supermarkets, plastic bearings, single-handle faucets, rockets, chemical hair setters, hair coloring, "instant" photo developing, fast-service gasoline stations, paper "cans," electrostatic copying. For the hopeful men of large corporations who annually approve large R & D budgets, large test-market budgets, and large new-business budgets, the list is too long for comfort.

Seeing Is Not Believing

The fact that so many of these developments sprang from obscure sources outside the industries that they so enormously affected is not without significance. The pattern has been repetitive enough to suggest a lesson, even a law of nature.

For people inclined to derive lessons or laws, the explanation is not as obvious as it seems. A rash and incorrect observation would be that large firms suffer from a special kind of commercial constipation. They may do an existing job well, even with awesome muscle and efficiency.

[1] Some notable commercial exceptions are Herbert Mayes, who revolutionized the women's service magazines; Du Pont in the plastics field; and CBS in the distribution of recorded music.

But they do not seem to do entirely new jobs well. Either they don't have the competence to create powerful new innovations in their own fields, or they don't have the inclination to make change, at least not change that will greatly affect the secure viability of existing product lines or investments. Hence, the Hollywood movie companies resisted television either because they lacked the vision to comprehend its potentials or because they comprehended the potentials only too well. In the former case, they would have pooh-poohed television as a crude and inferior medium of no promise. In the latter, they would have refused to get into television because this would have contributed to the even more rapid decline of the movies, with all the destruction of assets this implied.

The historic facts are that the big Hollywood movie moguls did indeed pooh-pooh the fledgling television industry, even as late as the early 1950s. The reason was remarkably human. They looked at television with all the care with which men of their temperament and style of doing business were capable. They saw in the TV set a huge ugly box from which emanated a tiny light, frequently distorted and inclined to ungovernable gyrations, producing vulgar apparitions of grunting wrestlers and roller-derby toughs. The occasional dramatic shows were hopelessly amateurish. Slammed doors sent cardboard walls into tremors that threatened total collapse, boom microphones habitually fell on the actors, prop shadows loomed suddenly across the faces of harassed comics, and property men were constantly caught receding from the fragile and unconvincing scenery. Kinescoped prerecorded performances were more polished but technically shoddy. All this made for feeble viewing.

The movie moguls had a different idea of what the public wanted. They built their industry on the solidly sound premise that the public needed an escape—not from the reality of life, but from the confinement of home—to get out of the house and make a solemn occasion of the regular pilgrimage to a neo-Gothic emporium of elaborately vulgar decor and overuniformed ticket takers. Television required people to stay home, and they were fed up with home. Besides, the economics and technology of television would never be able to produce programs of sufficient professionalism to hold an audience. The movies, by contrast, were seen as a robust American institution of immortal proportions. They were here to stay.

Hollywood's analysis of television's limitations and of the public's inclinations was predictable, if inaccurate. Hollywood looked out the window at the newly emerging world. The window turned out to be a mirror, revealing not the reality of what was out there, but the illusions that were congenial to the observers. With enormous investments in sound stages, in long-term star-system contracts, and in chains of movie houses, it was in a sense natural for the moviemakers to see only the reasons why television would fail. Television's success would be Hollywood's destruction. Obviously, television would never thrive.

That only a generation earlier the Hollywood moguls had themselves been the equivalent of television's youthful entrepreneurs was beside the point. To the cynical chorus of New York's legitimate-theater entrepreneurs, they had started Hollywood with flimsy equipment, desperately terrible scripts, and awful reproduction. Now, still gloating in the recent history of their successfully defiant opposition to Broadway's catcalls, they said about television precisely what Broadway had so condescendingly said about them less than a generation before.

Television began in the late 1940s and the early 1950s. It was a time still dominated by men who knew the economic stagnation of the 1930s, who by temperament were now more inclined to preserve what they had than to reach out to capitalize on what was possible, and who more commonly ignored or rationalized changing conditions in the world rather than face up to them.

What was true then is not commonly true now. Today even the largest, the most bureaucratic, and the most hidebound companies recognize the hazards of their perceptions' being distorted by their present commitments. They know the need to face the realities of the competitive world through clearly two-way windows. They know that obsolescence is the reigning rule of commercial life, and that if they don't participate in its creation, they will suffer the consequences of its revolutionary creation by others.

It is surprising, therefore, to witness the continued emanation of so many business revolutions from sources outside the industries in which they occur. If the large, well-capitalized, big R & D corporations are attuned to the necessity of creating competitive newness and if they spend so much money in its quest, why is the quest not more productive?

It is in fact more productive than it appears to be. Not all revolutions make headlines, certainly not in the visible public press. Indeed some revolutions are not even evident to their makers, as is certainly true of the Detroit revolution that now enables each customer almost to design his own mass-produced car.

But the general rule still holds: The major dramatic revolutions and innovations of the commercial world continue to come in disproportionate magnitudes from smallish and superficially inadequate capitalized sources. The reason the large companies lag in this area is clearly not for want of inclination, effort, or money. It is not even that large organizations are necessarily less flexible and therefore less capable of quick maneuver and adaptation.

The Lag in Largeness

Two extraordinarily simple reasons explain why the larger companies have lagged: Large organizations are seldom organized and operated to do the job, and large companies tend to think wrongly for the purpose. They generally think big, not small.

The large organization is large because it has a large and complex task. It is sensibly structured for a simple purpose: to routinize the accomplishment and control of an essentially repetitive task. The purposeful mastery of routine is the central purpose and predominant fact of organization. The manufacturing job must get done efficiently, and the more routine the process can be made, the less costly it generally is. The same applies to accounting, to distribution, and in fact to every single aspect of the operation. Everybody in the company has an explicit task of clearly defined and limited proportions. The first priority is getting that task done smoothly and efficiently. The whole planning and control system is based on this priority, with its procedure of budgets, targets, regular reviews, and performance evaluations.

That is as it should be. But the resulting organization is not one that is congenial to innovations of anything but the most marginal sorts. The problem is not to change this organization, but to augment it. The problem is to create within the large organization the entrepreneurial equivalent of smallness: to create centers of entrepreneurial initiative that are structurally separate from the organization's major domain or sphere and method of operation—a place where men can, in effect, try to create and run autonomous small businesses of their own.[2]

The second reason for the failure of large corporations to produce as many commercial revolutions as smaller companies—entirely new products, new services, new ways of marketing—is that big corporations do not think small. They think big.

Of course, the large corporation thinks small in selected sectors of its operations. It thinks small at the section level in its plant, counting the productivity of each pieceworker. It thinks small at the sales level, looking for relatively modest increments of sales from each salesman. It thinks small in cost control and return-on-investment improvement. But when it comes to the creation of new products, the search for new markets, or the production of new investment opportunities, it thinks big, and not without cause. The Mobil Oil Corporation, with a cash flow in excess of $1 mil-

---

[2] For a full discussion of what must and can be done in this regard, see Chap. 7, Disorganizing for Innovation.

lion every day of the year including Sundays and holidays, can hardly be expected to turn gleeful cartwheels at a proposal for a new-business opportunity calling for only a $1-million investment.

But there is more to resistance to newness than the fact that big companies need big outlets for big money. Part of it is the American ideological preference for size. The think-big syndrome is vigorously at work. It is a seductively captivating syndrome for every person involved. It marks him as a man with the kind of vision that made America great and helped make the large corporation the behemoth it is today. And it is reinforced by the obvious facts of the corporation's logistics. A suggestion at one of the giant baking corporations in 1954 that it begin to produce and sell a Sara Lee type of cake can be imagined as getting the following response: "Young man, do you realize what the size of that market is? It's peanuts, that's what. We're organized to exploit mass markets and that's what we shoot for. We don't use flour grain by the carload. We use it by the trainload. Our sales organization can't fuss with dribs and drabs. We need mass-market ideas. So keep your eye on the ball and don't fool with chicken feed."

One Man's Meat

For Charles Lubin, the minuscule market for Sara Lee products was not chicken feed. It was enormous—or at least promising. When it matured into large-enough proportions, the expected happened. Sara Lee became big enough and was available at a high-enough price-earnings ratio to be a good buy for a competitor of the baking companies. The same has happened to Pepperidge Farm, to Basic Systems, to Spencer Gifts, to Playskool, to Diner's Club, to Bomar, to Oklahoma Oil, and to many others who helped change the commercial environments they entered with such modest beginnings, and often uninformed optimism.

A lot of new industries originate in pure ignorance. Ignorance and incompetence, sustained only by blind enthusiasm, are the pathology of business failure. One out of many succeeds. The fact that success is so rare and originates out of such a welter of unbusinesslike attitudes and practices does not justify the conclusion that all success is serendipitous, accidental, or without food for learning.

What we learn is, again, that all big businesses and big industries started small; that large markets do not suddenly, or at least not very often, materialize full-blown. They start small and grow big. Even such a massive and costly new business as Comsat will one day be viewed as having started awfully small.

The significance of an industry's bigness is not its size but how its size developed. To understand growth and capitalize on opportunity it is useful to look at the business world not in terms of what consumers do, but in terms of how they get to the point of doing it. While markets expand because more people or companies buy a product, what is more relevant to recognize is that more people buy because more of them have learned to think of that product as an appropriate, a useful, and a legitimate item of consumption.

The Learning Curve of Markets

In their rise from anonymity to bigness, markets generally trace a trajectory similar to what educators call a "learning curve." A student makes slow initial progress on a new subject. Then he picks up speed, bursts ahead, and finally levels or tops out. Markets behave similarly. Nothing illustrates the point better than the rise of the compact car in the late 1950s and early 1960s. Prior to that time, it is no exaggeration to say that the small car was not a legitimate commodity in the value system of the American motorist. As we previously noted, the size of one's car was a measure of one's personal success. To be seen driving a small car was to admit to either small (and therefore inadequate) ambitions or small achievements. It was a mark either of failure or of aberrant behavior worthy only of kooks, college professors, or professional malcontents.

The aggressive missionary style of George Romney's head-on attack on the "fuel-guzzling dinosaurs" of Detroit helped the American Motors Corporation break the traditional symbolic meaning of the car as a measure of social and economic achievement. The campaign came at a felicitous moment, just as Americans began behaving less as car owners and more as car users. What began to matter was the personal, not the social, utility of the car; not what it meant as a symbol of achievement, but what it meant as a practical tool of daily life.

Americans were beginning at that time to discover other means of publicly displaying their economic and social achievement—mid-winter tropical vacations, skiing, vacations in Rome, expressively casual clothes, possession of hi-fi equipment. The car began gradually to take a back seat. Indeed, with Romney's vigorous assist, it became a matter of pride not to own a flashy big car. Since events march on, especially when it comes to American cars, and newer vogues and values arise from the old, by the early 1960s the user preference for the compact stripped-down utility car was transmuted into a preference for the compact sports-oriented personal car. The Mustang and then the Cougar, the Firebird, and the Camaro achieved rapid success. They were cars from whose possession one derived not a special sense of prideful ownership, but a special sense of personal participation in its use. That accounts for the heightened appeal of the four-speed floor stick shift and bucket seats. The bucket seat imparts a sense of personal distinction and control—your own personal driver's seat, like that of the racing driver or the airplane pilot, unshared by a passive passenger. It is a private seat of power that cradles and holds the driver in a position that enables him better to control and direct the car. The stick shift reinforces this sense of control, suggesting the driver's personal mastery over the use of power via a more active participation in the car's operation than with the automatic shift. These and other features were responsive to the motorist's new perception of himself as a car user, a car driver, not a car owner.

Compact-car sales grew steadily after a slow start to over 600,000 in 1959, at which point they suddenly skyrocketed to 1,622,000 in 1960. What is significant about the steady growth after the mid-1950s is not that each year more people bought compact cars, but that with each passing year fewer people felt that any stigma was attached to their possession. Increasingly people unlearned the old standards and meanings of cars and learned the legitimacy of the new silhouette. Learning to accept and value the new value system preceded the acquisition of the new type of automobile. Once the level of acceptance produced a generalized legitimacy for the compact car, sales suddenly shot skyward.

No different process characterized the growth of computer usage, air travel, numerically controlled machine tools, mutual funds, and oxygenization in steel production. The process is a consumer learning curve. That explains why a product or a process or a service can have enough merit to rise from a 1 percent acceptance in 1960 to an 80 percent acceptance in 1970, but not to an 80 percent acceptance in 1961. While there are technical and purchase-cycle reasons for delays, none of these are sufficient to explain them adequately.

The ultimate explanation is not even that we are creatures of habit or that we resist the uncertainties of change. The ultimate explanation is that man is a learning creature. He does not suddenly discover the utility and value of something new. He learns gradually to accept its legitimacy as well as appreciate its utility. That is why most executives faced with a proposal to do something new generally respond with the question, "Who's doing it now?" They are interested in two things—reducing the risk of buying (or innovating) by looking at the experiences of those who have already bought or tried what is being proposed, and they want to make sure that the action they are asked to take will not reflect adversely on their good judgment. They want to be sure that it is a legitimate act, that they will not be thought foolish or kooky. Just as there are consumption leaders and influentials in the use of hair coloring and Christmas cruises, so there are consumption leaders and influentials in corporate matters—whether we are talking about using industrial robots, new forms of corporate organization, the use of linear programming, or containerization.

Influentials versus Leaders

The leader, however, is not always the influential. Studies by Prof. Paul Lazarsfeld and others make a useful distinction. Leaders are first triers, but first triers seldom influence many others to become first triers. First triers too generally are isolates, misfits, or impractical dreamers. If they are dreamers, their purchase is a signal to most others that the product is offbeat and not sufficiently legitimate for the solid citizen. If they are isolates, they have insufficient contacts to make their influence felt. The effective leader is the influential consumer—the individual or company whose first steps carry authority and therefore produce a following. When Du Pont adopts a new way of achieving dimensional effectiveness in plastics, it carries a lot more authority than Widget Chemical Industries would.

The process of learning is a process of discovering by repeated exposure that the object in question is indeed a legitimate category of use or consumption—that its consumption, use, or possession not only is useful but also carries no risks of peer-group disapproval. That explains why new things that have languished for years in the shadow of failure, attracting all the time only the slightest patronage, suddenly take off after breaking through what appears to be a crust or lid of resistance. Takeoff follows the acceptance by powerful influentials who represent the crust that must be punctured. They are, in effect, the teachers of the masses. The implicit recognition of this fact explains the use of respectable and admired people and companies for product testimonials. The acceptance by respectable people or companies of something new carries with it a powerful supporting sanction. This reduces the perceived risk for those who have withheld action by making the product respectable, visible, and acceptable. The consumer has learned not just of the product's existence, but more importantly that it is respectable and probably works.

This learning-curve view of the commercial pathology of newness is a worthwhile concept for the contemplation of large companies habituated to thinking big. Since all genuine newness starts small, since all newness is likely to remain small for some time, and since consumers are not likely to respond favorably to market research inquiries on dramatic newness before that newness has been properly legitimized, it is clear that the markets for dramatically new things will at the outset or in advance of their availability always seem small.

This helps explain why small new companies started some of the revolutions we have cited. It is not their greater daring or flexibility. It is that they are satisfied with small volume and are organized to handle it. As a giant retailing mogul explained his success to a magazine reporter: "Restraint and modesty, not greed. I buy for a penny and sell for two cents. I'm satisfied with one percent."

Patience vesus Profits

The large firm that is satisfied to pursue only relatively large market opportunities but also is not content with being simply an imitator or follower must therefore ask itself a new kind of question when exploring such opportunities. Before it asks itself about the probable size of the market for a new product or service or process, it should first ask about the probability of its achieving early legitimization. The latter is a cause of the former. To look only at the presently evident market size is likely to result in an underestimate of the market potential because the complex mechanics of the consumer learning curve are not taken into account.

The computer is a perfect example. Once the barrier was penetrated, not only did the market for present applications skyrocket, but the process of the market becoming accustomed to its use and being comfortable with its retinue of mathematicians and programmers finally created a hugely permissive environment that resulted in huge new waves of uses and demand. Simultaneously both bigger room-sized and smaller desk-sized uses developed.

Office reproduction equipment has gone through the same explosive cycle. So have television, hair preparations, numerically controlled machine tools, supermarkets, motels, portable dictating machines, curtain-wall construction, paperback books, plastics, and much earlier in our century automobiles and radios.

The idea of the consumer learning curve tells us that the large company that uses relatively large markets as a criterion for its entry into dramatically new or different areas is faced with a special requirement. It must first try to assess in perhaps unaccustomed ways the probability of the item's achieving a legitimizing breakthrough—of its ever becoming respectable enough to produce a large market. Then it must determine how long this will take and whether it will be prepared to wait that long. Deciding whether it can wait that long is almost as important as determining whether the breakthrough is likely. Unless this determination is made, the project may be abandoned during the agonizing early stage of the consumer learning curve.

Staying power is a problem not only for the small, undercapitalized firm but also for new projects in large firms. For the small firm it is a matter of money. For the large one it is a matter of patience. It is well to try to know in advance what kind of money and time demands are involved.

The large company is of course better able to finance a slow process of product acceptance than the small one. But a properly run large firm will not usually permit its possession of money to underwrite delays beyond what had been expected or predicted. Size has certain virtues and advantages, and these should be employed. Otherwise there is no operational merit to being big. It is only when plans and controls are poor and management is indecisive that bigness will permit delays to drag out projects beyond what seems sensible. And yet it was precisely this kind of hesitation that produced for one large cigarette company one of its most profitable successes. The company launched a filter brand that in time proved a failure by the company's volume standards. Incapable of making a firm decision to kill it off, and busy with other matters, the management permitted the new brand to remain on the market for over a year after the facts of its failure were clear. At the end of that year sales began a perceptible climb. Today this is one of the company's most profitable big brands.

The lesson is not always to give a new product more time. It is to make better advance judgments regarding how much time will be needed.

The Pathology of Legitimization

This gets us to our second point concerning what the learning curve requires of the large company that is oriented toward large markets. It requires a new way of viewing consumer dynamics and suggests new ideas about introducing new products. It requires looking at the pattern of legitimization, the pattern by which products, life-styles, services, or commercial institutions (like, say, mutual funds, condominiums, or drive-in theaters) progress from the disapproved underworld of commerce to the public's approved plaudits.

In part this requires finding and influencing the consumer leaders who influence others. It requires understanding how influentials reach and influence their "constituents," and understanding how the acceptability of newness is diffused throughout the population. Lazarsfeld has found that the process by which people are influenced for or against products varies greatly between product categories, even products of superficial similarity. Even among the same groups or categories of consumers, the influentials for new breakfast foods were found to be different from the influentials for clothing. The influentials for daytime dresses were different from those for cocktail dresses. Among doctors, the influentials for adoptions of new drugs for mild cases of nervous tension were found to be different from those for drugs for serious mental disturbances. For nervous tension, the influential is usually the highly social, circulating, golf-playing doctor. For serious mental disturbances, where more is at stake and the risks are greater, the influential is likely to be the hospital resident who plays neither at golf nor at AMA meetings.

We have suggested that every custom started with a broken precedent. Precedents often become customs; small markets often become big. Youthful markets, like youthful ideas, take time to mature. Instant bigness prevails neither in nature nor in commerce. The pattern by which growth precedes size, and size precedes maturity, imposes a think-small necessity on large companies oriented toward thinking big. But there is another and equally compelling reason for this necessity. This is the gradual decline of the traditional mass market. Markets are becoming increasingly fragmented into distinctive consumer subsegments. The age of the minimarket is replacing that of the mass market. This applies as well to industrial as to consumer goods and services.

A visible and highly indicative example of this is the proliferating availability in the United States of a rising variety of domestic and foreign-made cars. The automobile market can no longer usefully be divided into three broad categories according to price lines—low, medium, and high. Accessory packages and special design features are now the more common ways consumers distinguish between cars. People want sports cars, high-performance cars, new suspension- and handling-feature cars, family station wagons, and special compact-feature cars. Today's theme is not the price line but the customer-satisfying line. It is by their preferences for specific features that people most meaningfully segment themselves into customer groups, not by their preferences for price. Each group is different enough in some way from the other to justify not only a different car, but also some difference in marketing approach.

In low-priced consumer goods, this is equally true. The dessert-food market is not just Junket, Jell-O, ice cream, and pie. The standard version of Jell-O itself comes not just in "six delicious flavors" but in almost two dozen. And just as there has been a blurring of automobile price lines, so also has there been a blurring in dessert products. Not many years past, in simpler days, Jell-O was perceived as representing a particular segment of the dessert market—the gelatin segment. We see now that a distinct gelatin segment never really existed. There was a fast-preparation, homemade segment for which gelatin and packaged puddings were practically the sole qualifiers. Technology has now provided other fast desserts, like frozen cakes and refrigerator-baked cold preparations, and we see that the old segment was really not gelatin but speed. This market has expanded enormously in recent years. Like the auto market, the expansion has been accompanied by a large expansion in the number of options available to the consumer. Though the total market is now much larger, the segment available to any brand is relatively smaller. In some cases it is absolutely smaller. It is not the mass market that counts; it is its segments.

Similar things are happening everywhere. The product mix of Republic Steel has never been simple. The salesman always carried in his pocket a bulging little specification book listing all terms and prices. As customer requirements have become more specialized, this handy little book has been transmuted into the proportions of the Moscow street directory. And it is as incomprehensible as that directory, even to the technically literate but unaided reader.

Learning to See
What's Happening

The everyday preoccupations of executive life in the large corporation often make it difficult to focus early enough in the development of new market phenomena on the fine distinctions that characterize these phenomena. Even the alert manager can easily miss the significance to his own business of many symptoms he encounters daily. For example, he daily encounters a flow of bills his wife has run up at local stores. If he looks carefully, he is likely to discover that his wife is shopping at some unaccustomed places. While she may be doing a lot of one-stop department store shopping, she is also spending a lot more at a variety of seemingly obscure boutiques. He may also notice but not grasp the significance of the fact that she is now bringing to the dinner table, for better or worse, a greater variety of unusual dishes, and with greater frequency. And he himself, the chief provider and traditional head of the household, if he stops to notice, will see that he is drifting into some unexpected consumption patterns. If he doesn't already have one, he probably has more than once eyed a dandy imported sports car. Chances are he is also accumulating an unaccustomed variety of multicolored sports jackets and blazers, that he has at least one especially colorful pair of golfing slacks, and that his liquor cabinet is becoming congested with strangely shaped bottles of cordials, brandies, and aperitifs. If he examines carefully what he and his wife talked about in planning last year's vacations, he is apt to notice that they talked not so much about "getting away from it all," in which case almost any place would do, but about getting *to* certain special places. Was it to be a golfing vacation, a swimming vacation, a touring vacation, or a cruise? And if a cruise, was it to be the Greek Islands or the Caribbean Islands? And what about those cruises whose special-interest appeals are on board the ships themselves, such as bridge-playing cruises, gourmet-food cruises, and even tennis-clinic cruises?

Back at the office, the pattern is not especially different. The higher he is on the organization chart, the greater a consumer he is of staff experts and staff reports. The staff is bigger than it used to be and, more significantly, different. It is not the staff, but a variety of staffs, each with its own narrow, if not narrowly oriented, specialty. He doesn't have just a finance group; he has finance and control. He doesn't just have a marketing group; he has advertising, sales promotion, distributor relations, operations research, sales analysis, and market research. And among the market researchers he has not just the head counters but also the head shrinkers. If he doesn't actually have them, he hires them as consultants or for specific projects.

Not only is the content of his surroundings, both at home and at the office, more fragmented into distinguishably separate forms, but so is the process. At the office, tasks are increasingly viewed as consisting of parts and pieces, each best helped along by experts and specialists. A company does not have a cash-flow problem. It has a series of problems that produce a cash-flow consequence. Outside the shop the executive does not have a wardrobe problem; he has a series of problems that have a wardrobe consequence. He leads different lives—an eight-to-five, Monday-through-Friday life, for which a particular way of adorning himself seems appropriate; a whole series of weekend lives, from golf, to fishing, to boating, to football-game attendance, to afternoon cocktail parties, to evening dinner parties, to gardening, to lying around the house, all of which have special wardrobes and distributive consumption styles. Gone are the bad old days when the same suit of clothes was fully appropriate for all those. Gone are the dreary days when, regardless of one's fiscal condition, the suit for a Saturday afternoon cocktail party on the lawn was perfectly suitable for Sunday morning in church. Sartorial correctness now requires the adornment to vary with the function. Masculine dress, like corporate staff composition, follows function. And we don't think twice about it. Besides, life is more interesting that way.

The Segmented Society

What is happening is clear enough. We are abandoning in many ways the style of thinking that characterized less sophisticated days. These were the days of mass-market thinking, when fine distinctions were sacrificed to the beautiful economics of mass production, and careful discrimination to the easy generalizations of the entrepreneurial mind.

One of the most visible embryonic examples of our abandonment of the mass-market idea is the way in which business advertises its products. Thus, *Time* magazine has found a profitable market among advertisers for fragmented editions of its publications. The most understandable of these fragmentations are regional. In 1961 it ran 243 pages of regional ads— that is, advertisements which appeared in copies going only to specific geographic regions—say, Southern California or New England. By 1967 it was running 1,841 regional pages, and by 1974 many more. In 1962 it had 405 advertising pages for specific metropolitan markets, compared with 3,157 such pages only five years later. This increasing regional segmentation of advertisers' efforts has even spawned a new kind of advertising agency. Smith & Dorian, Inc., is a network of centrally directed local agencies with emphasis on specialized local impact for national clients. Its billings rose from $1 to $13 million during the first two years of its existence.

Everybody knows, of course, that there are profound differences in consumption habits throughout America's vast continent. Low-calorie foods sell better in Los Angeles than Atlanta, baked beans better in Boston than Chicago. But the extent and subtlety of these differences are seldom fully appreciated, and the reasons for them even less. Thus, milk flavorings and sweeteners enjoy an acceptance in New York City far out of proportion to its population. The best guess is that New York City parents are generally more permissive with their children, perhaps because of their own underprivileged childhoods.

Wesson Oil, a cottonseed product, is extremely strong in cotton-producing areas of the South. But in the North and Middle West, where the big cash crop is corn, Wesson loses its crown to Mazola, a corn product. On the other hand, Corn Products Co. makes its Karo Syrup in two viscosities, solely because Pennsylvanians, perhaps because of the effect of Dutch cooking, prefer a thicker syrup than the rest of the country. Nearly twice as many homes in icy St. Paul have home freezers as those in more temperate Indianapolis. Rotary lawn mowers sell much better than reel mowers in Duluth, while the reverse is true in Fresno. In cigarettes, brand A had 22 percent of its sales in the Northeastern market, and only 8 percent in the South Central market; but 28 percent of brand B's sales were in the South Central and only 14 percent in the Northeastern states. And in the home appliance field, even after correcting for the effect of different historical and distribution conditions, brand A had 26 percent of its sales in the North Central states versus 5 percent in the South. But brand B's sales were 31 percent in the South and 25 percent in the North Central area. For years regional sales managers have been complaining, "But my market is different." More and more his bosses are getting the idea that maybe this is a fact, not an excuse.

Perhaps today's most vigorously discussed form of consumer segmentation is racial. Does "the" black consumer consume differently from "the" white consumer? I have already suggested that there is no such thing as "the" consumer, but still overall averages can help us focus on the fact of segments themselves. A study by Carl M. Larson and John S. Wright of the University of Illinois is instructive. They made pantry surveys of households—looked at what was on the kitchen shelves. Among black households, for example, 86 percent had Open Pit barbecue sauce on hand, while 68 percent of white households on the same income levels had it. Aunt Jemima cornmeal was in 23 percent of the white households but in only 3 percent of the black homes, although 94 percent of the black households had Quaker cornmeal, compared with 62 percent of white households. For Holsum bread the percentages were about the same. This was also true for Jewel pork sausage, Hills Bros. coffee, and Kelloggs' cereals. Other interesting results:

Brand	% Black	% White
Riceland rice	76	35
Pillsbury flour	69	33
Red Cross spaghetti	84	31
Parker House sausage	49	0
Oscar Mayer sausage	16	47

The results suggest something about differences in consumption patterns, but also about differences in reactions to products and brands that project certain kinds of images. Precisely because the results are averages, they give few actionable clues except that we must learn more before we act— we have to divide the results down into finer categories of consumers within both the white and the black samples.

Racial and regional differences or market segments are important but probably less significant than other differences. *Time,* for example, also has "demographic" editions—ten to college students, nine to educators, and thirteen to doctors. In 1963, it carried only nine demographic advertising pages; by 1967, it carried 229. In short, *Time* advertisers cared enough about the distinctive character of certain of their prospects that by 1967 they took twenty-five times as many advertising pages targeted to specific, limited demographic groups as they did in 1963.

Modern Man Is Multiple

As sellers we have come to understand that a man is not a consumer—he is many consumers, even within the same general category of product, like clothing. A housewife doesn't just produce a meal for the table; she produces many meals to solve many problems. Sometimes she is a gourmet cook, working long hours in her laboratory with herbs, spices, grinders, ovens, crusts, creams, sauces, and timers. At other times, when the rush is on or the moon is out of phase, she is a heater-upper—not an opener of drab tin cans (that has an unfortunate old connotation), but a tearer-opener of exotic frozen packages (which have a more legitimate connotation).

Even when she works at being Julia Child, she is also being a tearer-opener. She devotes elaborate care to the few items she makes from scratch, and supplements these with quick convenience accessories from the supermarket freezer. She is at the very same hour for the very same meal both a gourmet cook and a thoroughly modern convenience-foods Millie. She defies categorization. She is, like her husband, many things at the same time. She must be viewed not as a market segment, but as many segments at different times as well as at the same time. Each segment must be viewed according to the problems she is trying to solve in particular instances, not just according to her income, education, family size, or other demographic characteristics. It is not enough to say, for example, that she buys hosiery. For some functions it will be the old standby—15-denier, 30-mesh South Pacific brown. For another function it will be a fishnet in a wild shade of purple. For a cocktail party it may indeed be the $1.55 South Pacific. For supermarket shopping the next afternoon, almost any 59-cent brand will do.

Not surprisingly, the giant corporation with a complex balance sheet devised for the comprehension of only a few, and a technology too involved even for M.I.T. professors, behaves quite like Millie. The president's stationery, not just his limousine, is more splendid than the purchasing agent's. The lubricating oil for cutting titanium is more carefully specified than the oil for cutting low-grade steel. Looking at the purchasing process for titanium cutting oils does not tell an aspiring seller of commodity lubricants that he should not call on this prospect. Whether he is a prospect is determined not by looking at what he does in general, such as fashioning parts from metal, but by looking at the various metals he cuts and at the amount of precision each requires.

To recognize these facts about how the world works, although seemingly obvious when presented in this fashion, compels the abandonment of former formulas. It is the values, the needs, and the behavior of people and companies that count, not a quick view of what in a general way they do. These are the things that give the marketplace its distinction. These are what dictate the posture of those who would convert others into customers. Even if Millie successfully imitates Julia, that does not qualify her for treatment exclusively as a gourmet cook. She also makes hamburgers and heats frozen pizza. To sell to her, the seller must understand her better. She is as much a customer for bay leaves as for ground round, as much for cocktail dresses as for casual car coats. A fabricator of metal parts is as much a customer for tins of siliconized specialty lubricants as for drums of commodity oils.

Selling to Segments

All this suggests the clear necessity to look at the details, not just the SIC numbers. As functions become increasingly specialized, and as tasks become increasingly particularized according to technology and to the objectives and skills of the people involved, successful selling increasingly requires the rule of "Think Small." Where think-small attitudes prevail, the results can be startling.

Take the case of IBM's computer sales operations. IBM's sales offices are organized on local and regional bases. But in addition, it has offices organized along industry lines. In New York, one office consists of specialists in the banking field. They go to banking industry seminars, not to computer seminars. They know banking as well as their customers know it. A Miami group specializes in women's sportswear. A North Carolina group specializes in furniture. A Southern California group specializes in the aerospace industry. None of these salesmen need to ask the prospect what his problems are. They know the problems because their orientations and entire professional lives are hooked into the industries they service.

The advance of technology increasingly makes possible an accelerating shift of national sales organizations from the traditional geographic system to the industry-specialist system. The jet airplane helps make Chicago as accessible to a New York–based salesman as it is to the Chicago sales office. As cathode-tube telephones come into use and mature into general acceptance, the direct, face-to-face meeting that the jet airplane now facilitates will be accelerated in both speed and frequency. The industry sales specialist will therefore come into even greater ascendance, especially where the industry is geographically dispersed. It will make attention to the unique details of the prospect's industry more easily and effectively possible because the salesman will be a quickly available, face-to-face specialist in that industry. In many cases, companies that do not organize and orient themselves in this way will be in trouble.

The reader can look at his own personal financial affairs to see what this trouble can mean. He invests in the stock market and watches regularly what the market did today. But none of the daily changes in the averages really interest him. He is interested in the specific stocks he owns or might own. In searching for what he might own, he knows that there is no such thing as "the" market. There is a series of submarkets, from blue chips to low grades, from service firms to heavy capital goods manufacturers; and within each of these, there is a wide range of performance situations. The Dow Jones averages are interesting, but not for him especially helpful. The investment adviser who talks exclusively in general market terms, or even only of industry categories, is not likely to keep anybody's patronage for long. He will be in trouble, the same kind of trouble as the company that fails in its own affairs to focus on the detailed specifics of its market.

In his own firm, the business manager, whether he is looking at organizational problems, deciding about new fields to enter or new products or services to launch, or deciding on how to plan, direct, or audit the sales effort, must be as diligently concerned with the specifics of market segments as he is with segments of the stock market. He cannot afford not to think small.

Organizational Implications

The organizational implications are particularly impressive. Take the case of the steel industry's loss of such a large share of the industrial and commercial window-frame market to aluminum. When aluminum's inroads began, it is easy to imagine the following dialogue within a major steel company between Harry, the steel salesman, and George, the general sales manager:

> HARRY: George, we've got to do something about the window-frame market. Those aluminum guys are moving in fast and stirring up a lot of business.
>
> GEORGE: Look, Harry, I'm glad you're concerned about how we're doing. But let's keep our eye on the real nut of this business. We make zillions of tons of steel a year. The window business is a lousy point zero zero zero zero percent of our volume, and . . .
>
> HARRY: But, George, don't you see that . . .
>
> GEORGE: Don't "don't-you-see" me, Harry. The boss is on my tail to work

down all that heavy stuff in the warehouses. The mills are down to fifty-five percent. Prices are going to hell. Imports are killing us. And you come in here with this story about chicken feed. Even if we'd triple its sales, we wouldn't move enough to notice it on our freight bills. I appreciate your interest, Harry, don't get me wrong. But face facts. We've got to keep our eye on the main ball, not on this penny-ante stuff. Come in here with some big ingot orders, get us some big sheet business. That's what we need.

HARRY: [*Exits, deflated and frustrated.*]

Had this steel company's sales department been organized along industry lines instead—even along major mill-product lines—somebody would have been in charge of the commercial and industrial construction business. Had this end of the business in turn been further subdivided so that Harry was responsible for, say, industrial and commercial fenestration, the dialogue would have been predictably different. Harry would have been conscious of one inescapable fact—that commercial and industrial fenestration was 100 percent of his business. Performance in that responsibility would have been the entire basis upon which he was being judged. At stake would have been *his* mortgage, *his* station wagon, *his* children's shoes, *his* Doberman's horsemeat. Harry would not have exited peaceably. He would have fought for his life, for programs and actions to repel aluminum's inroads. And George would not so cavalierly have shifted the ground to his bulging warehouse of I beams and flat cold-rolled.

Most American steel manufacturers have now come to understand the urgent need for creating smaller centers of market responsibility in their organizations. Estimates put steel's losses to substitute materials—aluminum, plastics, and various forms of reinforced concrete—at over 2.5 million tons a year. That is not crippling for an industry that pours around 150 million tons a year. But increasingly the 2.5 million tons represent the work of young product designers who are coming of age with the realization that steel does not exhaust their options.

The result is a revolution in America's steel industry. U.S. Steel Corporation now has a construction marketing section with such special programs as "power styling" for the electrical industry. The program studies the electrical industry in detail and as a consequence develops design and product concepts rather than waiting for the industry to do so itself, perhaps with other materials. In one recent year, U.S. Steel sought out over fifty utility companies to present to them eighty-five new steel-using concepts, including such slightly exotic ones as a utility pole that incorporates a sheltered bus stop; a substation raised on stilts, with a view-of-the-city restaurant underneath; and a futuristic wireless power transmission system using laser beams.

In short, steel looks to the future by creating opportunities for itself in much the same way as accounted for the enormous thrust and growth of companies like Reynolds Aluminum. It tries to create customers, not just fill orders, and it does not shrink from such seemingly minuscule efforts as, for example, creating a stainless steel threshhold for residential use. Although U.S. Steel actually organized a market development effort as early as 1938, it was not until quite recently, when people recognized the need to think small, or at least to think in terms of very specific applications activities, that the effort got strong support and began to pay off.

This specialization of effort is now beginning to pervade the entire steel industry. For example, Bethlehem Steel Corp., the industry's No. 2 producer, now has applications engineers assigned not only to specific products, like enameled steel, but also to the appliance industry users of such steel.

Creating customers is not just a matter of creating new or improved applications. You also create a customer when you keep from losing him. The window-frame dialogue between Harry and George would be almost impossible at U.S. Steel today. Besides being organized for more attention to specific markets, U.S. Steel also has a program of "order analysis"—the seller's equivalent of purchasing's "value analysis." This means that U.S. Steel takes official notice of changes in customer steel usage, and indeed works with customers to improve their steel-using products. As a consequence, in one case U.S. Steel suggested to a venerable buyer a higher-strength steel that saved the customer $13 per ton. In another case, better gear steels saved a customer $28 per ton in extra charges.

There is no inconsistency between thinking big and thinking small. Each has its special place. But the attractions of thinking big are so seductive that the company intent on genuinely effective growth—even on mere survival—must constantly guard against its contaminating presence. To think big is to be marked as a "man of vision." There is something attractively masculine about men with strongly held big ideas who go after the big account, the big deal, the commercial jugular vein. It is an eminently American posture.

Because of the attractions of thinking big, because thinking big has often gotten remarkably big results, it cannot therefore be permitted to obscure the uncompromisable fact that in the end it is not customers who buy a product or service, but _the_ customer. _The_ customer comes in many different guises. Steel customers are at least as diverse as steel-using industries, and within these industries there are major differences in problems, resources, objectives, and steel-buying decision-makers. The necessity of focusing carefully on these differences, both in the products that are produced and the ways in which they are sold, as well as in how the sales effort is organized, controlled, and audited, ultimately vindicates the virtue of a think-small posture in everyday business operations.

The concept of market segments is of course no longer novel. It is even becoming somewhat fashionable. But where it is actively employed it is used mostly as a guide for modifying and differentiating existing products and services, not as a way of thinking about the overall strategy of corporate growth and development. It is this latter use of the concept that needs a great deal more attention, particularly in the large enterprise. Without that focus for the concept's use, the large enterprise will continue to sit at the sidelines and watch a disproportionate share of the big new commercial innovations being made by the small new upstarts.

Chapter Six

New Products: Allurements and Illusions

NOTHING TYPIFIES American business rhetoric so much these days as the necessity of constantly creating new products. Second only to this is the spectral preoccupation with the alleged high mortality of newness. It is repetitively said with utmost gravity that nine out of ten new products fail. Yet the evidence for this persistent assertion is skimpy. The classifications and standards that produce the assertion are sloppy. The facts more commonly are quite the opposite. Once products are actually issued and offered to the market, success is surprisingly common. What actually causes these one-out-of-ten commentaries is not what happens in the market, but what happens before the market.

Not a great many products that get serious ongoing R & D attention survive the standards of that attention. And the large corporation in particular, which by definition is likely to consider a large number of new things, is ipso facto likely to reject a large number. But there is a problem. The large corporation has unique organizational difficulties in producing newness. The results are costly, pervasive, and not entirely necessary.

The frustration and disappointments that large companies have repeatedly experienced in their quest for internal growth and expansion through new products have been so massive in so many cases that some have begun to lose faith, even though the rhetoric goes on. They have lost faith not only in the worthwhileness of the effort but, even worse, also in their abilities to do the job. They are beginning to think that maybe new-product development and exploitation are uniquely a "small, young-company business," just as computers, for example, are thought of as a "young man's business."

Distortions in the Mirror

Their disillusionment in themselves is magnified by the almost totally false picture they have about what is happening in other companies. They falsely believe that others are infinitely more successful in creating and launching newness. This belief is sedulously nurtured by the expanding emphasis in the business press on the importance and prevalence of new business developments, new products, new packaging, new services, and so forth. The more dramatically and effectively the business press focuses on the new things being done by others, the more thoroughly its readers from big corporations become convinced that there is something basically wrong with their own companies and themselves. All they know is that while others are seemingly vaulting forward with great entrepreneurial zest, they themselves are crawling like snails. And when they do decide to move, all they see within their own shops is an inexplicable and irritating slowness, characterized by endlessly unproductive meetings, a constant array of new design problems and people problems, forever-unfinished product and consumer research, repeated false starts, a procession of disappointments in trusted and otherwise get-things-done executives, and, of course, overspent budgets.

The usual "solution" is to call in a doctor—a business consultant, preferably a consulting firm with unimpeachable credentials. Six months later its voluminous report and recommendations usually result in a corporate reorganization. The marketing department will get a new market development group and a new or bigger commercial research department. Product R & D will be divided into two (or even three) separate groups—a sales service group, a product development group, and a basic research group. Most dramatic of all, a holding-company structure will be established whereby autonomous operating companies are created under a super-headquarters corporate parent.

In the process, new jobs are created; titles are changed and shuffled; walls are ripped apart and rearranged into new offices; vigorous younger men are plucked out of remote field installations and ceremoniously installed in the new headquarters offices; new, sophisticated control systems are established; and finally, in an atmosphere of triumph and expectation, top management settles back to await productive and profitable outpourings from its new organization.

Within two years the consultants are back. This time their assignment is not, as you might expect from what occurred, to find out what went wrong, why the glowing promise of yesteryear failed miserably to materialize, but to recommend what is now needed to make the system work. If the theory, the idea, and the organizational setup of the new system made sense two years ago to the people who installed and budgeted it, they will of course now believe that it still makes sense. The point is to make it work, so that new ideas, new products, and growing profits do indeed issue from it.

The usual conclusion drawn from this second round of costly consultancy is either that the company tried, under the new system, to do too many new things too fast, with the result that nothing actually got done, or that the wrong people were put in charge of some of the new jobs. What is needed is therefore greater discrimination in the selection of the new-product tasks to be undertaken or a reshuffle of certain executives, and probably some of both.

But two years later the consultants are back once again. By now there are some new faces in the top management. They will have decided that while the new-product effort was itself a useful experiment, its cost was intolerable, and that what is needed is to pay more attention to the here and now, to get down to the solid brass tacks of making the present products more profitable. The consultants now, as part of their assignment, have been asked to prepare a plan to trim down the whole new-product and innovation effort.

Meanwhile the business press continues full of breathless articles about the magnificent successes of companies with new products, new packages, new customer-service departments, new sales techniques, new discoveries in consumer research methods, and so forth. To the ordinary observer, everybody seems to be going full blast, doing new things as if run by a perpetual-motion machine—everybody save the hapless enterprise for which the observer works. The grass indeed looks greener across the street.

The Other Grass Is Not Greener

Yet the fact is, at least among the larger corporations, that the amount of new-product animation and achievement in "other companies" is largely illusory. There is very little dramatic new-product newness—even routine newness—regardless of company size. Compared with the number of companies in the United States, their fiscal resources, and the number of people involved in product and market development work, very few new things are actually happening. Most newness is old wine in new bottles.

The envious and frustrated big-corporation executive should consider how he gets his facts about the activities of other companies. He gets them less from what he sees on the market than from what he reads in the business press. And what he reads is a systematic distortion.

Journalism is, after all, journalistic. Thus it not only confines itself to the high spots of events, but actually creates high spots where none exist. It is, for example, an old story in the newspaper business, and particularly in relation to the "police beat," where most journalists get their start and on-the-job training, that when things get dull and news is scarce, you create a "crime wave." The procedure has a prescribed textbook routine. You simply assemble the statistics of all the petty crimes in town for the last two weeks and then write a front-page article that begins with some dramatic lead such as, "A hungry and ferocious lion nightly stalks the streets of Center City. His fierce fangs and sharp claws strike with indiscriminate violence in unexpected quarters. He spreads fear and apprehension in an otherwise peaceful community. Officially, on the police blotter of Center City, that lion is called 'crime.' A rising wave of criminality engulfs the city. Last night, for example, two armed men. . . ."

The business press today presents us with its own equivalent of a crime wave. It is a new-products wave. The journalistic process of making the story dramatic and arresting has led to systematic oversimplification and exaggeration. The usual publications greatly oversimplify how new things get done. They generally exaggerate the smoothness, the simplicity, the speed, and the vigor with which they were done. And they exaggerate the quantity and quality of the achievements.

Cosmeticizing History

The trouble with history is that it is written by the winners. The trouble with trade-press articles about new-product successes and the achievements of big-corporation top executives is that the reporters get their facts from the reportees—the people they write about. The resulting distortions are even greater than if the winners themselves had written the articles. Every man has within his fragile pride some trace of modesty and restraint. He will not write flattering lies about himself. But in conversation with others he will not hesitate to imply achievements that his journalistic listener is expected to translate and embellish into Texas-sized exaggerations. In most cases the facts that are given to a reporter by the reportee are in some intentional or accidental fashion distorted and incomplete. Only the rare chief executive is psychologically so secure that he will confide to the interviewing reporter that he moved up the corporate ladder chiefly through the sponsorship of his predecessor, in whose shadow he followed for twenty years largely because of his ability to keep other meddlesome subordinates from bothering his boss. Only the rare chief will say that he got his job because the executive committee couldn't decide between two other men who were the prime contenders. And, regarding the historical details of a successful new product, the larger the corporation, the fewer the details the top marketing vice-president is likely to know. He will tell the interviewer what he can, glowing with pride that he has been singled out for print. He can hardly be blamed for pretending to know all the details when he knows only the few that reached his busy desk, or for wanting to tell a story of heroism and efficiency, rather than one of blundering and mismanagement. At best he will tell the interviewer that "there were a couple of production details that had us guessing for a little while about a year ago," but he won't fill in the details—largely because he doesn't know them. The fact that these "details" at one point stopped all progress on the project for three months; that they caused the treasurer to withhold all the project's operating funds for two weeks; that there were endlessly unproductive all-afternoon meetings between the engineers, the project manager, the market research people, and the cutting-tool supplier; that the marketing vice-president himself spent three whole days during one memorable week trying to get (unsuccessfully) to the bottom of the mess; that one perfectly able man resigned from the company on the verge of exhaustion; that one hapless victim had his career advancement in the company forever blocked because he was in charge of delays over which he had little control; and that a supplier salesman was fired—none of these details got into the final story that the journalist heard. All he got was an unintentional *post hoc* smoothing of the true maze of history.

The stories the business reporter generally gets make the innovating company and the responsible executive look an awful lot better than they really are. The retrospective rewrite has begun. Now the reporter and the editor add their own special talents to the facts they have. The business editor knows that his readers are executives who like to think of themselves as movers and doers and who like to think that other corporations get things done because they also are run by movers and doers. Hence, the editor understandably requires that articles in his journal emphasize the "true" causes of business success—which are men, not machines; executives, not procedures. What he requires in his new-product success stories is not the drama of a well-oiled company, not an efficient taskforce, not a powerful committee, not an exceptionally able bureaucracy, but a hero—a single, bare-chested mover and doer. Even the story of General Motors, which is uniquely the success of procedures and methods, committees and reviews, coordination and compromise—even that story is always told in terms of heroic men. After all, men read the stories, not committees and procedures. The reporter understandably satisfies his editor by overfulfilling the editor's expectations, by painting his heroes in the most fetchingly charismatic terms consistent with credibility. The company is made to look like an army of tigers commanded by none other than Prometheus himself.

When the finely filtered printed story finally reaches the hapless executive on the other side of the fence, he reads it with a curious mixture of admiration, envy, and flagellating dismay. Why, he wonders, can't *we* do things that way? Why do we stumble, delay, procrastinate, and so systematically foul up? Why can't we be like others? Well, he thinks, maybe it's not "we." Maybe it's "me." I've never been able in any job I've had to get things and people moving the way that fellow in the article did. I've gotten ahead, I suppose, by most standards. But, damnit, I've never gotten anything really dramatically new done. I've certainly not gotten it done fast and smoothly. And so he loses faith in himself, although he hides it beneath a carefully cultivated facade of self-assurance.

It takes an especially self-confident or insensitive executive not to feel like a loser in the face of the rising abundance of such articles in the business press. The result is inevitable, tragic, and unfair. The articles imply a standard and a goal that are purely fictional and patently impossible. Like the envious, middle-aged James Bond admirer who can never match his hero's amorous exploits, the self-doubting reader cannot win because he is trying to make truth live up to fiction. Truth can match fiction in all things save two—love and the uses of personal power. In practice, perhaps the former is merely an aspect of the latter. Hence, the one solitary area in which truth, or reality, cannot match fiction is precisely the one that concerns the executive so much—the exercise of power.

Illusions of Executive Power

Few complex organizations, no matter how authoritarian, can effectively give even their top officials enough power over their subordinates to get things done as rapidly and as effectively as they would like. When forced to depend on others, man is forced to tolerate most of the things that make others different from him. The larger and more complex the organization, the more people there are on whom the leader is forced to depend. Hence, the more he is forced to compromise. The interaction of many different subordinates with many different personalities requires them to make a great many compromises among themselves, let alone compromises between them as a group and the leader as an individual. The process of reaching these compromises is a process of search and discovery; of fighting and persuading; of pushing and pulling and aggravation; and of mollification of tempers, nerves, feelings, pride, insecurities, and ambitions. It is a process of teaching, persuading, soothing, and sometimes bullying and firing.

Reaching a conclusion or a solution in the large, complex organization is not an identifiable or prophetic event. It does not happen suddenly, like pregnancy. It is a process, and the process is seldom a smooth curve, moving like a train coming predictably out of the horizon on railroad tracks laid perfectly parallel by rational engineers. People are important, and occasionally there are heroes. But there are few heroic events. There is only persistence, energy, compromise, and understanding. Lyndon B. Johnson's Presidency was uniquely devoid of heroes, and yet it was more productive of major legislation than any Presidency since Jackson's, save perhaps that of Franklin D. Roosevelt, who had the special advantage of a terrible economic depression to smooth his path. The Johnson administration was productive in spite of the fact that the government and the White House are constantly watched by swarms of reporters and critics, whose presence produces caution, compromise, delay, and frustration.

Interestingly, the Johnson administration had some of the same qualities of silent and effective anonymity as General Motors. General Motors makes fewer headlines than Charles Bludhorn. But the headlines it makes are predictable in both timing and content. They are merely the stories of quarterly earnings records. Yet, in spite of its profit records, what General Motors is perhaps best known for is its administrative style. Significantly, what Mr. Johnson was perhaps best known for was *his* administrative style, characterized by Isaiah's slightly saccharine motto, "Let us reason together."[1]

NEW ROADS TO NEWNESS

There is a tremendously high cost to the exaggeration of the extent to which new things are being done in the large American business firm and to the ease and simplicity with which they are done. The net result is that there is hardly a large-company high executive who does not feel frustrated and disillusioned with what he and his company have been able to get done. The danger is that some will prematurely give up trying to be more

---

[1] See Theodore Levitt, "The Johnson Treatment," *Harvard Business Review,* January–February, 1967.

aggressively entrepreneurial—thinking that regardless of what it is they try to do, it will flounder and fail, or at best cost more than seems worthwhile. The extent to which this may have already begun to happen is reflected in three things that have gained attention and momentum:

1. The increasing corporate reliance, in spite of antitrust risks, on growth through acquisition rather than internal expansion

2. The rise of joint ventures between the large company and the embryonic new company, rather than the more venerable pattern of joint ventures between large companies

3. The increasing interest among corporate presidents in reverse dilution of equity as a means of showing earnings-per-share growth.

While the large corporation is generally highly sensitive to the Antitrust Division's unrelenting concern about mergers and acquisitions, there is obviously enough play in the Division's interpretations to justify the *Wall Street Journal*'s having an almost daily merger-acquisition roundup. Some companies, which for various reasons have shunned mergers and acquisitions, have decided that they suffer from certain limitations in creating particular types of new ventures. Yet they feel the need to get into them. As a result, companies like Corning Glass and Du Pont have invested in small specialty companies whose products they will either use or jointly market.

In these quasi joint ventures the small company generally retains control of the operation. In the words of one large-company executive, the reason is "that we've learned that the talent and skills needed to create some of these new businesses are different from the talent and skills needed to operate a big company like ours. We just don't know how to do things the way some of these little guys do. So we decided to help them with money and technical support, but to let them run things their way. We've seen other big companies absorb some of these little fellows, but nobody was happy with the result. It didn't work. You can absorb a smaller company if it has reached a certain size and a certain professionalism in its management. But you cannot very effectively absorb a really small outfit that is in the process of building a business and is being run day to day in all details by the guy who's building it. If you want what he's got, you've got to let him do things largely his way. And he has to do it outside your system. When he gets big and professional enough, maybe then we can talk merger. But until then it doesn't enter our minds."

Finally, there has been a good deal of reverse equity dilution. This is the process by which corporations use idle cash, debt, and senior securities to buy and retire some of their own common stock. Even a present-value method has been suggested for determining when this is better than using the same funds for internal growth.[2] But since the potential per-share earnings increment of internal investments is necessarily more speculative than the sure-thing per-share increment of reverse dilution, the appeal of the latter is obviously considerable. This was particularly so in a stock-market climate that emphasized per-share earnings growth rather than routine business stability.

Acquisitions and joint ventures are perfectly respectable ways to grow and to get into new products and new businesses. While all large companies are engaged these days in some sort of new-product activities, the extent to which they are losing confidence in their abilities to create genuine dramatic newness is unfortunate. The fact that they see themselves as having the option of acquiring small new companies that have done themselves what the acquiring companies feel they have trouble doing enables the large companies to feel much more relaxed about what they believe are their limitations in creating certain kinds of newness.

The Benefits of Size

Yet for the large company, among the payouts of its size are its special access to vast capital and technical resources, its unique strength in various distribution channels, and its staying power through adversity. These unique assets should and can be effectively capitalized upon to create new products and new businesses. The question is to know how.

But perhaps it is more important for large companies to accept more fully at the outset that a good many of the frustrations and reversals they have suffered in the past are, in fact, par for the course. These are, to a very considerable extent, normal. Once large companies recognize this, they are less likely to have expectations and standards whose fulfillment is almost impossible. Perhaps the first thing to know is that "other companies" are not nearly as dynamic or ingenious or efficient as surface evidence suggests, that in spite of appearances they are probably not much different from "your" company.

But there are special things a large company can and must do to facilitate dramatic newness. First, it should be seen that really dramatic newness is not likely to emanate from the operating departments of large corporations. Their departments are too busy doing their day-to-day jobs and meeting profit plans. They cannot spare the kind of time and attention necessary to produce dramatic breakthroughs in product development and marketing methods. Moreover, efforts to do existing things in new ways are likely to be viewed as potential threats by the people who are in charge

---

[2] Charles D. Ellis, "Repurchase Stock to Revitalize Equity," *Harvard Business Review*, July–August, 1965.

and who have mastered the existing ways of doing things. Hence the more dramatically different a new idea is, the greater the chances that it will be resisted. People will resist not because they are opposed to progress, but because they are human beings. Most people resist the unknown. When they have heavy responsibilities for the profitable operation of a given setup whose ins and outs they have spent years learning to master, to suggest suddenly that they should also foster a lot of new things that might significantly change the entire character of their routine and responsibilities is to make a suggestion not likely to get much support.

Opposition to unsettling newness in organizations is a problem unique to organizations whose primary purpose is to secure the efficiency of routine tasks. The intrusion of new and uncertain tasks jeopardizes the manager's ability to achieve the results for which he is being evaluated daily. It is not surprising, therefore, that opposition to dramatic newness is not unique to the kinds of business organizations with which we are all familiar. Nikita Khrushchev once criticized Soviet managerial opposition to innovation with these remarks:

> In our country, some bureaucrats are so used to the old nag that they do not want to change over to a good race horse, for fear he might tear away on the turn and even spill them out of the sleigh! Therefore such people will hold on to the old nag's tail with both hands and teeth.[3]

It is not so much that Soviet bureaucrats are all that wedded to the past as that they are judged and paid on the basis of how effectively they secure efficiency today. Joseph Berliner's perceptive study of Soviet managers shows how similar U.S.S.R. and U.S.A. practices are. He points out that bonuses for the fulfillment of operating targets are key motivators.[4] Hence, operating managers often systematically oppose, even without being aware of the fact that this is indeed what they are doing, product development tasks whose payouts are long term and uncertain. David Granick sums up the result in terms fully understandable to the American manager: "Bonuses, promotions, and emotions all follow one another too quickly to allow any but the most secure or idealistic Soviet manager to give full weight to the long-run implications of his decision."[5]

[3] Quoted from *Pravda*, July 2, 1959, by Barry M. Richman, "Managerial Opposition to Product-innovation in Soviet Union Industry," *California Management Review*, Winter, 1963, p. 15.

[4] Joseph Berliner, *Factory and Manager in the U.S.S.R.*, Harvard University Press, Cambridge, Mass., 1957.

[5] David Granick, "Soviet American Comparisons," *Comparisons of the U.S. and Soviet Economies*, part I, Joint Economic Committee, Washington, D.C., 1960, p. 145. See also David Granick, *The Red Executive*, Doubleday & Company, Inc., Garden City, N.Y., 1960.

The necessity imposed on operating managers to keep their efforts focused on efficiency today creates an understandable, though seldom acknowledged or intended, resistance to newness by the operating departments. That in part explains why R & D is generally given its own organizational slot. But it also explains why there continues to be so much debate as to where it should be slotted—in manufacturing, in marketing, or in a separate staff compartment.

The Marketing R & D Department

Because of all this I urged some years ago the necessity of a variant on the usual R & D activity in the form of a marketing R & D department.[6] It would have only one responsibility—to conceive and launch dramatic customer-getting newness, particularly but not exclusively newness in marketing methods, procedures, and programs. This department would report directly to the marketing vice-president and, in addition, have close, informal access to the chief executive.

The reasoning for this proposal was that creating newness in marketing is even more vicarious and problematic than it is in products. Ideas for new marketing methods have a disabling intangibility. Management cannot be presented, as in the case of a new product, with a reassuringly tangible custom-made model of what is proposed. Its working parts cannot be touched or operated or tried out at home. The market for the proposed newness cannot be easily researched or measured. New marketing methods, especially when they depart dramatically from those of the present, can imply a direct challenge to one of the company's major assets —namely, the institutions and procedures by which it sells. All these factors tend to generate resistance to change in basic marketing practices. I felt the need for an organizational mechanism that would be enormously hospitable to suggested marketing changes in the large corporation—a mechanism that would operate somewhat outside the normal marketing structure of the company. Hence the marketing R & D department.

For several years departments of this kind have been operating in a number of large firms. They have not been notably successful. The troubles they've had exist in all R & D, whether preoccupied primarily with products or procedures or institutions. These have generally stemmed from the following situations:

1. They have tried to do too many things at once, indiscriminately giving seriously time-consuming attention to too many projects.

[6] Theodore Levitt, *Innovation in Marketing*, McGraw-Hill Book Company, New York, 1962.

2. They have diluted their task by undertaking projects that were routine and tactical, rather than genuinely innovative and strategic. They have handled projects that should have been handled by the operating departments, thus undermining the marketing development department's sense of mission and its entrepreneurial zest.

3. They have become overorganized, trying to make entrepreneurial efforts conform to the administrative routines of large corporations. They have tried to conform to organizational structures and management styles geared to optimizing present products and present procedures, not to facilitating change.

4. The standards by which their proposals were judged were wrong. These were standards developed for evaluating the efficiency of a going concern and for investing in existing types of activities and practices. Proposals for highly speculative new things were required either to furnish data that did not exist or to demonstrate rates of return that were unattainable until the projects had been operating for a longer period of time than the usual corporate financial standards permitted.

5. Finally, too many high-level operating executives got involved in the act. They were routinely consulted regarding the advisability of project proposals, thus negating the very reason for establishing the department outside the direct responsibilities of the operating executives.

As a result of all this, marketing development departments got very little done and soon seemed enormously wasteful. But even worse was what happened to the people who worked in and ran these departments. Increasingly they felt that top management would not support in practice what they had preached in the preliminaries. Increasingly they felt hemmed in by the application of standards and rules that were designed to run a business, not to create a business. Their frustration usually produced intemperance. They committed the ultimate sin—the sin of seeming to be not only publicly critical of their superiors but, even worse, also disloyal. Since, therefore, the new departments produced nothing, except perhaps discontent and trouble, they very logically did not deserve to survive. So they have been eliminated. The form of this euthanasia has not always been an outright or dramatic death sentence, but the result has always been the same.

It is now reasonably clear that the administrative logic of the large corporation makes my notion of this kind of marketing development department unsuitable for such a corporation. No amount of good intention or skillful leadership is likely to overcome, or correct for long, the restrictive and dysfunctional practices and standards described above. The large organization, whether run for profit or not, is organized and operated largely to do an extremely complex repetitive job. Most of its assets, most of its people, and most of its procedures exist to do old things well. And it generally succeeds splendidly. It does its job with a degree of zest and flexibility that is, in spite of the problems listed above, quite remarkable. It even does lots of new things, and it does them well, stumbling only on the big dramatic new projects.

Just as the disillusioned executive often permits trade-press oversimplifications to set for himself an unrealistic standard of innovationist achievement, so abstract absolute expectations can set unrealistic standards about what a business should generally be accomplishing. The fact that lots of new things may need doing, that lots of customer needs remain underfulfilled, and that the technology exists for doing lots more than we are doing is no automatic evidence that large American corporations are doing an inadequate job. Even a brief visit to other industrialized nations and their larger firms confirms very quickly that the large American corporation is more productive, more energetic, more innovationist, and more efficient than we sometimes give it credit for being.[7]

The Evidence

But the honest and informed observer is forced to conclude that when it comes to creating really dramatic newness, the large corporation has not visibly distinguished itself. While it is important for each large company to see that the incidence and smoothness of other companies' new-product and new-method outpourings are exaggerated, it is also important to see what has not been done by the large corporation:

1. Hilton or Statler did not create the motel revolution. It was small, undercapitalized local entrepreneurs who had no previous experience in the lodging business.

2. Neither Ward Baking nor National Biscuit nor Bond created the frozen cake revolution. It was a small local baker in Chicago, Sara Lee.

3. Similarly, it was not Ward or Bond that created the revolution of quality in white packaged bread. That was done by two tiny companies absolutely new to the baking business, Pepperidge Farm and Arnold's.

4. It was not RCA or General Electric that created the mass market for

[7] See Richman, *loc. cit.;* Granick, *op. cit.;* David Granick, *The European Executive,* Doubleday & Company, Inc., Garden City, N.Y., 1962; Berliner, *op. cit.;* James C. Abeggler, *The Japanese Factory,* The Free Press of Glencoe, Inc., New York, 1958; Robert Guillain, *The Japanese Challenge,* J. B. Lippincott Co., New York and Philadelphia, 1970, translated from the French by Patrick O'Brian; and M. Y. Yoshino, *Japan's Managerial System,* M.I.T. Press, Cambridge, Mass., 1968.

transistors. It was a remote and tiny company in the geophysical business, now famous as Texas Instruments.

5. Armstrong Cork and Congoleum-Nairn did not make the vinyl tile revolution in floor care. It was a totally unknown company, Delaware Floor Products.

6. Metro-Goldwyn-Mayer and Paramount did not create the feature TV series, which made television an entertainment success. It was entirely new companies like Four-Star, Revue, and Desilu.

7. General Foods and Campbell Soups did not create the new convenience foods revolution. It was completely new companies like Swanson's.

8. Neither General Motors nor Exxon developed the first mass-production-efficiency, twenty-four-hour automotive repair and maintenance center. It was the small Canadian Tire Co. of Toronto.

9. Federated Department Stores and Allied Stores did not develop the mass-merchandising, one-floor suburban shopping revolution. It was people never before in the retailing business, like Two Guys From Harrison.

10. Nor, finally, in the 1930s was it the A & P or Jewel or Kroger chains that created the supermarket. It was undercapitalized upstarts like King Kullen on Long Island and Big Bear in Ohio.

In short, when it comes to really big things, it is significant that so few emanate from the most experienced, the best-capitalized, the best-managed, or the biggest companies. Lots of reasons explain this interesting fact. The most important reason is that the larger a company becomes, the more effectively it will be organized, operated, and motivated to carry out relatively routine rather than relatively new tasks. The large organization as a consequence develops a managerial style that is not particularly amenable to activities that conflict with its central continuing purpose.

Its central continuing purpose is perceived as getting today's ongoing job done. Today's job deals with massive matters. This, as we have seen in Chapter Five, produces a disposition against their opposite—small matters. Largeness is geared to getting large jobs done on a vast scale. Yet things that are dramatically new tend, by their very nature, to be small scale. Certainly at the beginning they are small, especially in comparison with what the large company is accustomed and organized to do. In the consumption of new materials, the large company thinks in terms of tons per hour, the small one in terms of tons per year. In the uses of people, the large one thinks in terms of creating and staffing divisions, the small one in terms of giving somebody an additional task. In the managerial process, the large organization thinks in terms of an orderly and appropriate chain of command, the small one in terms of the boss keeping in touch over lunch. Regarding capital requirements, the large corporation thinks of millions, the small one of as little as possible.

When a company has a cash flow of $1 million per day, including Sundays, holidays, and February 29, its top executives will have little patience with "small" projects with modest capital requirements. Not only will they be disinclined to "think small"—as at the outset Pepperidge Farm did, as Texas Instruments did, as Two Guys did, as Swanson's did, and even as Holiday Inns did—but they will be incapable of thinking small. People who successfully fight their way to the top echelons of giant organizations learned many years before that what counts is to think big.

Yet it is well for these same executives to remember, as Soviet officials are now discovering, that the administrative and budgetary machinery uniquely identified with successful large corporations is decentralization— breaking the large corporate organism up into small decentralized and discrete profit centers. Smallness does have its virtues.

It is precisely because the large corporation does in practice recognize the administrative virtues of smallness that it is appropriate to suggest a way in which it can sponsor and pursue within its own organization dramatic new-business activities through smallness. That is the subject of the next chapter.

Chapter Seven

Disorganizing for Innovation

ALL ORGANIZATIONS are hierarchical. At each level people serve under those above them. An organization is therefore a structured institution. If it is not structured, it is a mob. Mobs do not get things done; they destroy things. As predictably as the winter solstice we are periodically treated to elegantly reasoned suggestions that organizations can be democratized like Quaker prayer meetings. This is a utopian denial of why organizations exist. They exist, as Peter Drucker has so effectively argued, to get specific results. Results are not accidental. Neither are they the spontaneous or democratic evocations of like-minded men dedicated to a common cause. They come from purposeful direction, defined and set into motion by men of purpose and with standards appropriate to the task.

The purpose of the large organization is to achieve its larger purpose. This, as we have seen, is to achieve the smoothly efficient exercise of its day-to-day activities—to run the plant, direct the sales organization, manage the finances, control the effort. If these tasks could be accomplished without the organizing presence of the organization itself, there would be no organization. Men do not willingly subject themselves to rules, procedures, bosses, and time clocks. They do it because the results they seek would otherwise be unattained. Leon Trotsky's brief romantic flirtation with the idea of a nonhierarchical army during the Russian civil war did not fail for want of sincerity, effort, time, or inspirational support. It failed for want of practicality. To win a war takes more than clarity of objective, unanimity of purpose, or correctness of strategy. It takes hierarchical direction.

Organizational effectiveness is not a matter of devising policies by consensus or getting the willing support of the people needed to execute the policies that have been laid down.

People who advocate organizational democracy generally do it because of sentiment or ideology, not because of what they know is best. But they suffer from the warped notion that democracy must always and at all levels be participative rather than merely representative—in short, that everything must be done by referendum lest it fall from democracy's grace.

Yet the realities of life tell us that organizations whose leaders have been democratically elected are no less democratic for telling their members to do what they are told. The leadership need not seek the permission of its constituency for every deed it expects the constituency to perform. There is no presumption that leaders who are democratically selected must govern by democratic consensus or referendum.

"Give Us This Day Our Daily Bread"

Every organization has a creed—silent, powerful, and consolidating. All organizational creeds have in common the implicit acceptance of their own legitimacy. There is a purpose for which everybody works. Rules, procedures, and standards define what is to be done, and how. Those who persistently dissent must ultimately depart. Even when dissenters ascend to power, they do not change the rules or the procedures or the standards so much as they change the directions to which these are applied. Allegiance to the daily task remains the predominant and inevitable focus.

Within this powerfully constraining context, to focus as well on trying to get powerful innovations—to do entirely new and therefore disruptive things—is an especially difficult and fragile undertaking. The accepted procedure for creating newness under these circumstances is to establish within the operating organization entirely separate centers of initiative especially created for such purposes. The R & D department and the long-range planning department are such centers. They are implicit recognitions that an organization that exists to get today's job done cannot also do tomorrow's job very well. Tomorrow's job needs a new structural entity, a diminutive autonomous organization of its own.

As we have seen, when tomorrow's job involves attempts to create entirely new businesses, entirely new products, entirely new markets, or entirely new operating methods of more than trivial dimensions, there develops an almost inescapable clash with the prevailing organizational creed. Anyone who tends to doubt this needs only examine his own organizational experience. Whether in a corporation or a country club or a church, an intense struggle predictably surrounds efforts to do drastically new or different things. One may ponder why these struggles are always so abrasive, and why the leaders of abortive efforts to make change always pay such a heavy personal price.

The establishment of separate centers of initiative for creating innovation or for handling activities that are not directly concerned with operations (i.e., staff) is a sensible, though not always effective, way of legitimizing the activities that generally seem to people in operating departments to be outside the central operating purpose of the organization. It is a palliative that has its purposes.

Time and acculturation have tended to legitimize long-range planning and R & D, especially since neither has had a too direct, visible, or upsetting impact on today's operations. When, however, as is now the fashion, R & D is looked on as a central and well-financed function, and its output is viewed as something that requires even more financing and effort, the old legitimacy is strained. The laboratory's output is sought to be quickly translated into commercial success. Today's typical expectation from R & D's outputs is rapid increments of massive revenue. We are no longer patient with marginal additions building steadily into solid businesses over time. An impatient managerial world, oriented to price-earnings ratios, expiring stock options, and rapid hierarchical advancement, wants swift results of visible and leverageable dimensions.

But it can seldom have these without great expense. The usual organizational result is ambivalence and conflict. Expenses hurt the price-earnings ratio, and that hurts everything. This accounts for the severity of top-management reactions to failures to move costly new projects along as rapidly as is hoped. On the one hand, new things are unsettling to begin with. For top management to have supported them was to have created problems with operating management. To have gotten for these problems nothing but delays and unpredicted expenses is a double insult. A good many top executives have therefore concluded that the solution is to let other companies do the innovating, while getting for one's own company a favored price-earnings ratio and for oneself an attractive stock-option package by making highly leveraged acquisitions of smaller companies that have successfully done what one's own company has decided not to do itself.

The Power of Bigness

The irony of all this is that the large company is in an especially strong position to support, create, and commercialize powerful new innovations. It is far better qualified than the small firm. It has more talent to do the job, more money to support it, greater ability to sustain losses during its early commercial stage, and generally a good reputation with which to give the innovation an appealing public credibility. It will be a very great loss indeed if new-product activity and internally generated new-business development among large companies become increasingly confined to those which do them only as a last resort, not because they genuinely want to but because they feel unavoidably compelled to. Among larger companies there is increasing evidence that it is not entrepreneurial zeal that sustains new-product and new-business innovation, but fear of antitrust prohibition of acquisitions in cognate fields.

The large corporation is much more capable of effective innovation than is commonly supposed. It can do it with a degree of ease and smoothness much greater than has been generally experienced. The trouble is not its excessive size or insufficient know-how or limited will. The trouble lies in the method. The miniature organizational unit on the order of the R & D department or a marketing R & D department or a new-products department is not so promising as was once supposed. The inevitable tendency of such departments is bureaucracy and rigidity. It is remarkable how quickly they come to look and act exactly like the larger parent organization—which created them so that they might be and remain different.

Repeated failure tells us that hortatory pronouncements about the need for these departments to be run and evaluated differently from the way operating departments are run and evaluated are not enough. This counsel will continue to fail as long as the basic organizational principle of the larger corporation is retained in the microcosmic form of the R & D or development department. This is the not-so-ancient but oh-so-sacred principle of matching authority with responsibility in a decentralized structure characterized by thorough planning and tight budgeting.

New Methods for New Purposes

For the special purpose of creating important newness, the conventional organizing principle of the modern corporation must be finally and forcefully jettisoned. We shall see presently why the traditional system, which works so superbly for traditional tasks, is so terribly unworkable for new tasks.

Many suggestions have been made, of course, for new formulas to handle newness. Du Pont's New Venture Management system in its development department has received a good deal of attention,[1] as have such ideas as the Risk Manager that exists in various companies,[2] 3M's New Business Development Division project approach, and Owens-Corning Fiberglass's Advanced Development system.[3] All have one common ingredient—a self-conscious attempt to turn managers into entrepreneurs. Each assigns a proposed new project to a man who gets wide latitude for its execution, with the implicit promise of major managerial responsibilities if he succeeds.

It is of course a terribly good idea. The only trouble is that it doesn't work—for while the structure is fine, the process is not. Only at 3M is the process really unique. The 3M experience shows that taking men out of line organizations and divorcing them fully from their authority is enormously helpful. But even this is not enough. It is not from the authority of an organization that venture managers must be removed; it is from its culture. To establish a venture system inside a development department that has been organized for precisely this purpose, as Du Pont and others have done, merely duplicates the organization's culture in a new but equally restraining setting. The restraining artifacts of this culture are plans, budgets, completed staff work, and, above all, bosses trained in the traditional habits and values of that culture.

When we look at the history of great commercial successes of genuinely dramatic import and proportions, we see certain instructively common attributes. When Vladimir Zworykin, the father of television, demonstrated the first crude and enormously bulky TV system to his top management at RCA, the unimpressed reaction of one severely practical and highly successful executive was typical: "Why don't you take that guy off that foolishness and put him on something useful?"—like cutting costs on radio receivers, for example. It was only when RCA's single-minded chief, with managerial habits now widely considered of the old school, got wind of the discovery that Zworykin received unqualified backing to move onward with the project.

This is a perfect example of a high-risk, high-cost project's having succeeded only because traditional organizational decision-making standards were abandoned. The decision was made intuitively by a strong-

---

[1] Russell W. Peterson, "New Venture Management in a Large Company," *Harvard Business Review,* May–June, 1967; Mack Hanna, "Corporate Growth Through Venture Management," *Harvard Business Review,* January–February, 1969.

[2] Robert Levy, "The Go-go World of the Risk Manager," *Dun's Review,* November, 1967.

[3] "The Corporate Venture Team," *Sales Management,* Jan. 15, 1967.

minded and secure chief executive who heard of the project almost accidentally and made a decision without benefit of staff analysis and evaluation. The same unorthodox process characterized other dramatic product coups, such as xerography; dramatic marketing methods, such as the supermarket, conceived by King Cullen while he was with the old Kroger Company, which rejected it so summarily that Cullen quit to start his own company; and extraordinary services, such as car leasing, originally the lingering child of General Motors but successful only after released to independent ownership and perseverance.

Faith versus System

The essential ingredient that is missing in the well-intentioned venture-team systems of the companies that are increasingly going in this direction is not entrepreneurship. It is entrepreneurial faith. The venture-team system has the right general idea, but not the right environment. The system generally supposes that if you put a strong young man in charge of a project and let him develop the concept, assemble the people and plant to get it moving, give him enormous freedom to run things, and promise him the chance of a lifetime—if you do all this, you will have created the best possible combination for getting the best possible results. And the system has produced some notable successes: at Du Pont, Crolyn, the remarkable magnetic tape that doubles the information-packing capacity per square inch; at Owens-Corning, seamless fiber glass for underground oil-storage tanks; at Union Carbide, Surfel, the widely accepted feltlike synthetic.

Two things are special about these recent examples. One is that each started with the development of a product, not a market. In the words of Eugene Clay, while head of Owens-Corning's advanced development department, "Once a product leaves here, I wipe it out of my mind." Significantly, it leaves the department before the market is developed, thereafter to enter the minds of others who harvest the predictable headaches that market development entails.

The second significant factor is that because these were strictly *product* development ventures, the development process itself was more linear and predictable, and therefore more easily manageable, than if they had been *business* development projects. While supervisory management is never happy about reverses and delays in product development, it is generally more tolerant of delays in product development than in business development or new marketing ventures. Product failures or delays are more convincingly reinstated in the corporate graces than similar failures or delays in such projects as market development. The reason is simply that products are more tangible than projects. The ultimate uses and benefits of a new product are fairly demonstrable. The existence of a profitable market for such a product is not. You can make a working model of the product. It can be manipulated and modified. If things go wrong you can demonstrate with a new model how to put them right. Not so with market or business development. There are no tangible models that can be presented to the men in whose decisions reside the fate of such intangible projects. All you can present is a verbal "model" of what is proposed—a description or explanation that does nothing more than make a promise. By contrast, the model of a product makes an impact. It produces a result.

All this means is that it is less risky to support the development of new products than the development of their markets. Once the latter fails, it is much more difficult to make a convincing argument for another try than if a new product fails to perform technically as promised. You can tangibly demonstrate a revised working model of the product, thus giving strong support to your plea for a second chance. No such strength adheres to pleas for a second try at developing a market.

The Du Pont, Owens-Corning, and Union Carbide ventures dealt with product development in their first stages. It was at these stages that management support was easiest to get. Management was able to employ more-or-less accustomed rules to making go, no-go decisions. Does the gadget work or not? Is it chemically feasible? Can it be manufactured in quantity? But when it came to evaluating the potential methods and progress of market development, the old decision-making rules did not easily apply. What was a long-enough period to develop the market for something so new and different? Would the trade be willing to pay a high-enough price? To what extent were the delays and false starts the fault of the project manager or the normal consequence of the situation? To what extent does the availability of a new product or service affect the demand for it, rather than the traditional question, which tries to suit the product to the demand? How much do we spend to find out? When we are finished, how sure are we that we've tried it long enough or done the job right?

In the usual course of running a business, these questions or problems are uncommon. That is because the usual course of business is preoccupied with doing a better job of what is already being done, not with doing entirely different things. The usual task is largely managerial, not entrepreneurial. Managers are careful calculators of reasonable pros and cons, men reliable for their level-headed probity and balance. While they may have great wisdom, self-assurance, and energy, these talents are not likely to apply to dramatic and highly risky new ventures. Their talents apply to an existing situation.

Megalomania in the Marketplace

Entrepreneurship is the name we give to activities that are just on the verge of rashness and indiscretion. The entrepreneurial spirit is a euphemism for commercial megalomania, where the man is driven less by demonstrable good sense than by an almost irrational faith or confidence in his superior vision and energy. He supports ventures whose virtues and consequences are infinitely less predictable, less measurable, less demonstrable than what other people are comfortable with or persuaded about. We have already referred to the case of Xerox launching its 914 copier. The 914 was planned in 1955 and 1956. With traditional managerial diligence, Xerox called on the nation's three most reputable consulting firms to make separate independent studies as to market opportunities and potential. Two said the 914 would be a definite commercial failure and advised against it. The third saw some glimmering chance, but felt the total market was an optimistic 8,000 placements. The cumulative total would be attained only in the sixth year after initial launching. Its most pessimistic, and presumably most realistic, forecast was a cumulated 3,000 placements in six years. Joseph Wilson, Xerox's president, refused to believe the results. He and his associates saw in these forecasts a familiar pattern—formalized projections based on symmetrically static notions about consumer behavior. The forecasts gave only the barest consideration to the idea of a consumer learning curve—the idea that people would learn to want copies of written materials once quality copies became easily available. With faith in the force of the product's own capacity to produce visibility and activate a latent need, Xerox went boldly ahead. The 914 was launched finally in 1961. Placements began in 1962, and within three years over 80,000 units were in place.

We shall examine later in this book the unique dynamics and pitfalls of predicting the future in matters as new and uncertain as this. At the moment, we are interested in management style. Xerox's style in the case of the 914 derived from a vision. Without a vision of what was possible, management would have been limited to the style represented by the consulting reports. But there was even more involved at Xerox than a vision. The 914 action represents the confident daring of an organization which, for all practical purposes, was commanded in all major areas by a single and powerful individual, Joseph Wilson—a man accustomed to the persevering and confident opposition of nay-sayers. Equally helpful was the fact of his having almost complete power in his company to pursue his own personal vision, free from strong Wall Street and stockholder considerations, which often dampen enterprise elsewhere.

Industrial heroes of this sort do not always end their lives heroically, as Henry Ford and Will Durant proved so ignominiously. But the excessively calculated avoidance of ignominy is also the story of commerical constipation. Entrepreneurship is not consistent with certainty. It requires faith, fortified by energy, daring, and luck. The conventional standards of corporate planning and budgetary controls do not facilitate this style. While they are very important and workable for most operations, they tend to hobble genuine entrepreneurship. They must therefore be relegated to a less rigorously applicable part when the objective is the creation of dramatic newness.

The Role of Cunning and Concealment

When the culture of an organization requires that the methods of running a going operation also be used to govern decisions about newly proposed operations, it may take a courageous act of entrepreneurship just to overcome the constraints of these methods. An interesting example of this occurred in connection with the launching of a new product for the consumer market by a subsidiary division of a large, integrated oil company. The division managers had correctly concluded that the ideal time for the product's launching was September—which marked the beginning of the major consumer buying period and the resumption of large-audience television viewing and was also the time when the manufacturing facilities would be ready, under the normally planned circumstances.

But by the previous December, the division general manager concluded that a successful launch required a four-month acceleration of the timetable. He would have to launch the product in May, when the television audience was shrinking, when usage would be declining, and long before equipment suppliers expected to be ready. His conclusion was based strictly on the way in which the parent corporation's executive committee made decisions. The launch would cost $4.8 million out of pocket. It would take at least two months for any revenue to appear. Since the corporation was on an October fiscal year, and did not capitalize development costs, a September launch would represent a $4.8-million expense with no offsetting revenue. The result would be depressed earnings.

He had observed the executive committee's operations carefully and concluded that except for oil explorations its decisions were heavily influenced by year-to-year profit-and-loss considerations. He concluded that a proposed $4.8-million September expenditure would have little chance of approval. A November introduction, he was sure, would get approval, but it would also demoralize the division and especially the eager team of highly able men who had worked so diligently on the project over such a long period. Because he expected to launch other new products later and felt he might lose some of the men if the present product were delayed, he opted for a May introduction, driving his men to even more accelerated effort. A May expenditure of $4.8 million would be less efficient, but it would produce $2-million revenue by the end of October, thus reducing the negative cash flow for the fiscal year to $2.8 million. Hopefully the executive committee's uneasiness would be reduced equivalently.

He was right. The product was a rousing success. He successfully outfoxed the conventional canons of fiscal legitimacy by violating its central rule of efficiency. He became a celebrated hero to the austere men of practical affairs he outmaneuvered with such practical cunning.

In the large organization, cunning and concealment characterize successful innovations with remarkable frequency. The reason is based on the character of large organizations. Herbert A. Shepard has pointed out that "Innovative ideas are most likely to occur to persons who have some familiarity with the situation to which the ideas apply. Hence, most novel ideas are likely to be generated at some distance from the power center of the organization. Since new ideas are disturbances, they are efficiently screened out of the stream of upward communication. But because power is centralized at the top, top support for [a powerful] idea is almost a necessity if it is to move toward becoming an innovation."[4] Hence a variety of strategies will emerge out of the restraints imposed by the system. Concealment is the most common. Routine examples at the lower levels are known to almost everyone:

1. A machine operator develops a device to simplify his work but conceals it from the industrial engineers when they come around to set performance standards for his job.

2. A salesman uses methods and procedures that raise his effectiveness but are systematically hidden from his superiors lest they become standardized throughout the sales organization and thus raise the expected normal level of performance.

3. A local shop conspiracy permits the circulation of an innovation—say, a jig to help perform a frequent operation—among a few friends, who act as sentinels for one another to avoid being found out.

What goes on below also goes on above, though the objective is generally expansive rather than restrictive. As in the case of the early launching of the oil company's consumer product, the objective is to liberate

---

[4] Herbert A. Shepard, "Innovation-resisting and Innovation-producing Organizations," *Journal of Business,* October, 1967, p. 47.

a proposed innovation from the organization's restrictions rather than to restrict its availability to the innovator:

1. The vice-president of one company speaks of "holding an umbrella" over certain subordinates so that they are free to innovate and are protected from the scrutiny and standards he himself imposes so rigidly on the rest of his organization.

2. Another speaks of "surrounding the president with a moving framework" so that new organizational developments can occur without being easily detected during their formidable early stages.

3. An entire laboratory has conspired for five years to conceal the activities of a small group working (ultimately successfully) on an important weapons system in continuous violation of the project's cancellation. Not only have the group's activities been concealed, but also its salaries, expenses, and facilities.

4. One-third of the sales of two very large American corporations are in areas that the boards of directors had explicitly decided not to enter, only to discover that fast-moving men at the lower levels had quickly negotiated obligatory contracts to do the work.

5. A manufacturing vice-president conceals a successful experiment in union-management relations at a single plant until its efficiency is proved.

The risks of such concealment can be very great indeed, but that, presumably, is part of entrepreneurship. When such entrepreneurship is not complemented by cunning, it can be disastrous for the innovator. The manufacturing vice-president might easily have gotten sacked after revealing his successful departure from company rules. To assure that his idea, even after successfully proved in microcosm, becomes a widely accepted innovation in his organization, it is not sufficient for the concealing innovator to have the courage to "bet my job and reputation on it." He must take steps to assure the maintenance and advancement of his own influence.

Thus, the lower-level people who negotiated the contract in anticipation of the board of directors' ruling against the project consciously made themselves so indispensable to its successful execution that they had to be retained. Similarly, a group of engineers designed a radically new process plant that they arranged to have evaluated by a distinguished consultant. His blessing lent authority and produced management approval.

As a final example, a man in charge of manufacturing several product lines in a large corporation developed a plan to alter radically the financial, marketing, engineering, and production organization behind one of the lines that he felt was getting into serious competitive troubles. But he was aware that such a change would be resisted at higher levels. He therefore waited for two years until things got so bad that top management was forced to consider whether the line should be dropped. At this point of crisis he produced his plan and got quick approval.

UNDERSTANDING THE LARGE ORGANIZATION

James Q. Wilson of Harvard University's Government Department has made a profound observation about the unique problems of large organizations. He suggests that the very factors that increase the probability that organizational participants will devise and present innovative proposals are precisely those which decrease the probability that the organization will adopt them.[5] Wilson refers mainly to ideas that represent "a fundamental change in a 'significant' number of tasks."

He suggests that the factors which increase the probability of powerful new ideas are closely related to the diversity of an organization's incentive and task structures. Incentive structures tend to be more diverse in large organizations that employ a more diverse group of people—not just plant employees and salesmen and a few accountants, but a wide range of men whose loyalties (and hence incentives) are not just to their employers but also to their professions and their professional peers in other employments. Engineers have professional ties, not just company ties. So do marketing managers, seriously professional financial functionaries, market researchers, industrial engineers, and even the general managers who increasingly see themselves as members of a profession. Their incentives are therefore to make a visible mark professionally, not just organizationally. The more such men there are in an organization, the greater the probability that new ideas will be suggested.

The diversity of "task structures" also expands in the larger organization. One mechanical engineer may work on tasks quite different from those of a companion at the next desk with whom he shared a room at the same university. He is likely to develop expertise and ideas quite different from those of his colleague. The greater the diversity of task structure, the more varied the knowledge of the men who perform the tasks and hence the greater the probability of new ideas.

When diversity of task is coupled with diversity of incentives, Wilson argues, there will be a very high probability that such an organization's members will conceive and propose more ideas capable of major new impact. But since an organization with great task diversity is also very

---

[5] James Q. Wilson, "Innovation in Organization: Notes Toward a Theory," in James D. Thompson (ed.), *Approaches to Organization Design*, The University of Pittsburgh Press, Pittsburgh, 1966, pp. 193–218.

large and therefore has a highly structured and bureaucratic chain of command, Wilson maintains that a relatively small proportion of the ideas will be adopted and converted into major innovations. Organizational size and structure tend to smother in operation the very thing that size so uniquely produces in fact—powerful new ideas.

As we have already seen, the large organization seems implicitly to understand this fact and has therefore created devices designed to facilitate the translation of ideas into innovations. The R & D department is such a device, as are the market development departments, venture teams, and risks managers. These organizational arrangements work reasonably well for many purposes. But there is considerable evidence that when it comes to the implementation of highly novel, highly risky, or highly upsetting proposals, they work not well at all. The trouble is related to the fact that these departments do not offer a sufficiently facilitating environment. The culture is wrong.

As long as venture teams, risk managers, or project groups are specifically slotted into organizational departments subjected to the same standards of review and evaluation to which the rest of the corporation is subjected, the teams, managers, and groups will be evaluated and expected to operate exactly like the rest of the corporation. A change in structure without a change in procedure is an empty ceremony. It is the failure to see this that accounts for so much disappointment with the meager results of these new organizational forms.

It is almost inescapable, like a law of nature, that the special department especially created to do special new things will eventually be sucked into the bureaucratic vortex of the parent company which created the department precisely so that it might be liberated from conventionality and bureaucracy. The development department must have a budget and performance goals. The bigger the budget, the more rigidly the goals will have to be administered. Repeated overspending or underperformance will not long be tolerated, even if it can be demonstrated that the underlying causes were inescapable and temporary. Since the organization exists to get things done, it judges and promotes men on their demonstrated ability to achieve this purpose. Understandably it has a higher opinion of men who succeed at low-risk tasks than of men who just miss at high-risk tasks. It is not without significance that the adage "Nothing ventured, nothing gained" originated in preindustrial society, before organizations had as clearly purposeful functions as they do today.

No department manager who aspires to advanced rank will be so foolish as repeatedly to try to explain to his superiors why delays and overspending were inescapable, even when they were. Men in high places learn very quickly that the man in charge requires a resoundingly good explanation for anything that goes wrong. Men who aspire to high places learn very quickly that it is better to avoid high-leverage projects that might go wrong than to take them on with the knowledge that if things do go wrong, good reasons will be available to explain why. The result is that once things start going wrong, the knowledgeable and ambitious department manager will, if he can, scrap the project rather than risk a perpetual series of stop-gaps and surgeries for which excuses must constantly be concocted. He will risk less and be viewed more favorably by his superiors if he engages in prompt euthanasia rather than repeated surgery. The conventional standards by which executives and departments are judged leave him no choice but to make wanton cutbacks. In time he learns the overriding virtue of initiating no projects whose daring is too great, whose time horizon is too distant, whose output is too uncertain, whose payoff is more risky than he can explain to men whose interests are highly fiscal, highly short term, and predictable.

Not that the executive committee is exclusively oriented toward the short term. It is not; but one needs only to look at the typical composition of corporate five- and ten-year plans to appreciate the enormously restricted definition of long-term legitimacy. Rare is the plan that is little more than an elaborate series of cash-flow extrapolations of present operations. Serendipity is no part of the calculation, nor should it be. But neither is part of the calculation an occasional encouragement of untested or as yet unfound newness. The only newness likely to be tolerated outside of, say, an unexpected new plant or division office is for planned acquisitions or the launching of peripheral newness in the form of slight product modifications, redesigned packages, or entirely new products which, however, are resolutely part of an already widely accepted family of products. All else is off limits, even though progress may depend on it. There are exceptions, but it may be put down as a general rule that the large, established organization waits on the small, new organization to inaugurate dramatic, high-risk newness. But while it is a rule of experience, it is not a law of nature. The large organization is capable of doing far better.

The 3M Process

One American corporation of size handles the creation of dramatic newness in a uniquely proved fashion. The company is 3M. It believes genuinely in the idea of creating not just new products but totally new (to it) businesses. Its New Business Ventures Division has the special charter of working only on projects that are not in the legitimate province of existing divisions. Anything cognate to their present activities is off limits to the

New Business Ventures Division. Hence, this department is forced into total newness.

But that in itself would be insufficient to overcome what we have seen are the conservatising consequences of applying conventional corporate canons of budgeting and auditing. At 3M, new-venture projects have a fiscal life entirely different from that of the rest of the corporation. The system is enormously simple. The division has a budget, but literally no full-time new-project managers. New-project managers are men from the rest of this sprawling corporation who have submitted proposals that have gotten the division's blessing. This is the first step in 3M's remarkable process.

This first step is not particularly sophisticated. There is only one real guidepost to help decide what should be blessed at the outset and what not. This is that the idea preferably produce a patentable product or process. There are no criteria or guidelines such as potential size of market or development costs. The result is a highly permissive attitude toward what can be done. It is, for some purposes, an ideal system. It opens the possibility that with an especially permissive, audacious, or inspired division chief, a lot of deviate ideas will be welcomed. But there are hazards. There remains lots of room for the restrictive influence of traditional ideas around the company. The wrong kind of department chief may see virtue only in what he has experienced, and never in anything that is provocatively new. But the fact that the department is prohibited from working in areas cognate to the company's numerous other operations helps assure a felicitous measure of liberality in assessing new proposals.

Once a project is accepted, its proposer is transferred to the New Business Ventures Division, where he heads the projects and gets free rein to select his team. He receives a one-year budget, and it is from this point on that 3M's process departs even more fundamentally from anything others do. Whether the project leader's budget is renewed for a second year and what the size of the new budget will be are considerably less a function of the expected size of the market or its forecasted profitability than of the actual tangible progress the project has made during its preceding year. If the project leader has displayed energy, imagination, and managerial capability and has made a measure of solid progress, he is more likely to get his requested budget than if he has merely documented the potential of what he is doing. If he does the latter, he is likely to get no budget, even when the outlook seems otherwise enormously promising.

Hence, 3M makes new-project budget decisions primarily on the demonstrated capability and achievements of the project leader rather than simply on the virtues of the project. After the first year, it is the man, not his idea, that 3M largely supports. While men still need to judge the man, over the years the division has developed a highly facilitating ethos of its own. It is the ethos of entrepreneurship, characterized by a cheerful self-confidence in the superior merit of its special mission.

So successful are its results and so successful have some of its project managers been in becoming heads of the divisions that their projects spawned, that men throughout the company now eagerly seek new-business ideas to take to the New Business Ventures Division so that they may try for the golden ring. Their eagerness is spurred, moreover, by the comforting knowledge that failure is not disabling to their careers. Men in charge of projects that fail either to work or to get repeated budget support return to former divisions, not generally as labeled failures but more usually as envied heroes. They are viewed as men who have succeeded in getting the rare chance to try something for which few are chosen and with which even fewer will have the luck to succeed. It is like surviving Bataan, only fun.

It cannot be said that 3M's system is necessarily suitable for all corporations, or indeed that it is good enough even for 3M. What is important about it, however, is more than what is quickly apparent:

1. It works because it has operated and been allowed to work for a long time. It is part of the corporate culture—the institutionalization of entrepreneurial faith. The method had to be allowed to operate a long time before it achieved the status of corporate legitimacy, and it had to have at least one dramatic early success. This produced a condition wherein men now eagerly seek a "chance of a lifetime" without lifetime injury to their career chances at 3M.

2. The budgetary decision-making process after the first year is almost naïvely simple and inspired. All evaluation focuses on the effective progress of the man in charge of the task, not any longer on the supposed virtues of the task itself. If he fails, the project generally fails. There will be no budget.

3. As a consequence of this method of making project budget decisions, the New Business Ventures Division's own budget becomes to a considerable extent a function of the budgetary decisions regarding individual projects in the division, rather than having the projects depend on how much has been allocated to the division. This substantially reduces the usual organizational pressures that typically impose a company's more conventional standards of performance and evaluation on new projects. In the usual cases, new projects are, perhaps often unintention-

ally, evaluated within the context of the supervising department's need to operate according to the same general standards as operating departments. The pervasiveness of this problem is reflected in the plethora of articles and books that constantly search for better ways of evaluating the efficiency and effectiveness of R & D and market development departments. The contents of these publications are even more indicative. They seldom fail to propose standards and machinery that are calculated to appeal to the line manager's need for clear-cut criteria of conventional merit. They are seldom distinguishable from the standards applied to, say, the performance of a regional warehouse in Broken Bow, Nebraska.

The Entrepreneurial Equivalent of Smallness

The 3M system is an organizational effort to install in the large organization the entrepreneurial equivalent of the small organization. Unfortunately, it is not easily duplicated because it is unlikely that any large organization can from scratch adopt and stick with such a highly unorthodox way of new-project decision making. It is one thing to have, in Paul R. Lawrence's felicitous phrase, entrepreneurial enclaves in the large organization. It is quite another to manage them in ways that abandon so completely the ordinary operating standards of the large corporation. If such enclaves are specifically housed in departments designed to foster them, then the usual evaluation standards must be abandoned for these departments as well. That, unfortunately, gets into big money and will generally not be tolerated.

Lawrence and Lorsch have studied the organization of innovation in detail. They too emphasize the importance of something more than simply having the right organization, although they propose organizational approaches for overcoming organizational barriers.[6] They start with the proposition that the idea originator is often not very good at its commercialization or institutionalization. It is a point frequently made and verified even in noncommercial settings.[7] What is needed, according to Lawrence and Lorsch, is an integrator—a separate functionary who integrates the innovationary idea into the ongoing operation it is designed to serve. Two types of integrating procedures are generally employed—separate organizational entities such as technical service departments, market development departments, or new-product departments; or tem-

[6] Paul R. Lawrence and Jay W. Lorsch, *Organization Environment*, Harvard Business School, Bureau of Research, Boston, 1967; also Paul R. Lawrence, "Organizing for Innovation," *Harvard Business School Bulletin*, May–June, 1964, pp. 7–11.

[7] See David Moment, "Role Patterns, Performances, and Satisfaction in Student Projects Groups," unpublished paper, Harvard Business School, Boston, April, 1964.

porary groups such as the task force, the project team, or the cross-functional committee.

Lawrence and Lorsch do not overlook the many unhappy experiences companies have had with these devices. They argue that the litter of failures is the fallout not of bad ideas, but of bad execution. The execution requires a very carefully selected group of men, tailor-made to the distinctive task it has. As at 3M, they argue that if it is not the "man" that counts, certainly it is the "team," and that its composition is a delicate matter of selecting and balancing personalities. The task-oriented operating executive is not accustomed to this kind of delicate selection and needs to develop a great deal more skill at it than he has now.

The merits of these suggestions have been demonstrated. There remains the question of how effectively it is possible always to get the right tailor-made balancing of integrative teams. One thing is clear—if they are to be tailor-made, there must not be a permanently staffed department from which the teams are drawn. While such a department's full-time personnel will presumably be experienced in the integrative process, they will also be acculturated to the processes they know rather than adaptable to processes suitable to the specific task. This kind of tailor-making is therefore an illusion. You may be getting the personalities specifically needed for the team but not the performance specifically needed for the task. Besides, you still get the structured organizational context, which we have seen is almost inescapably restrictive.

Integrators and Instigators

What seems to be called for, therefore, is temporary groups of integrators specifically created for each specific task and drawn from various sectors of the company. The venture team or the task force can be such a unit. The question remains of where to slot the team organizationally. To whom does it report? The answer is not easy. It is far easier to suggest to whom it should not report.

If the central reason for organization is to accomplish an ongoing, routinized task whose administrators are judged by the effectiveness with which they perform it, and if innovation, particularly significant innovation, creates upsetting uncertainties, there is an automatic presumption against having a venture team report to operating management. Should it therefore report to a staff executive? There are strong arguments against it. Staff executives seldom have the full respect and confidence of line executives. They are not viewed as being wise in the ways of the "real" world. Hence, to have staff men make important decisions regarding activities, products, operating practices, or new businesses that will affect the operations for which line executives are responsible is to create a situation calculated to produce the line executive's rejection of what the venture team proposes. Moreover, in the large organization, staff departments are subjected to the same restrictive budgetary pressures and routinized operating standards as the line. Hence they are no more free than the line departments to entertain high-risk ventures. Even an organizational group like the R & D department, whose routine purpose is to create newness while the rest of the company manages a less glamorous routine, cannot escape the overwhelming pressure of the prevailing culture of obedience to routines that are essentially static.

The standard solution is to have the team report to the ultimate organizational integrator himself—the chief executive. This is a tempting way out. It has been justified by rather interesting observations on the character of hierarchical institutions. For instance, operations research originated with the famous "Blackett's Circus" in England during World War II, working on military matters. One of the first books on the subject stressed the importance of having OR teams report directly to the chief executive because it argued that the military organization learns only from the top. Lower levels cannot be allowed to innovate, only execute. Changes in operations at lower levels occur as a result of instructions from higher levels. The more radical the idea, the less likely and indeed the less tolerable is a lower-level decision to use it. It must be initiated at the top. It follows that if a team exists to create radical ideas, it should report to the top. The proposition is plausible. It is also silly and naïve.

To suggest a routine of direct reporting to the top executive exaggerates his wisdom and ignores his utter dependence on the organization beneath him. He cannot know everything that is knowable well enough to be able to make an independent decision of all that must be decided. He needs lieutenants and a staff. The intervention of a staff means the intervention once again of the organization. He needs the advice and consent of his lieutenants, especially on matters likely to affect their operations greatly. If he neither seeks nor gets his lieutenants' consent, they can easily sabotage, perhaps unintentionally, the implementation of the powerful new ideas that he sponsored. On the other hand, the chief executive cannot reject the advice of his staff without seeming to be arbitrary to the point of raising questions about his own suitability for the job. The only way for him to make his rejection rational is to get himself a separate and redundant consenting staff of his personal choice. But since such a staff would almost necessarily be a sycophantic one, he will doubt its reliability and constantly subject himself to doubt about the wisdom of what he is about to do. The result is more likely to be paralysis than action.[8] True, the more centralized the authority, the greater the scope for its independent action. It is also true, however, that the larger the organization, the less centralized the authority. The American Presidency is often said to be the most powerful office in the world, and yet it is useful to contemplate President Kennedy's plaintive response to an advocate of a proposed innovation: "I agree with you, but will the government?"

March and Simon suggest, with Wilson, that diversity in the organization's "subcultures" stimulates proposals but, contrary to Wilson, that centralized authority leads to their acceptance.[9]

Centralized authority is a double-edged sword. It can act terribly fast and with daring, but both for and against ideas; or it can act not at all, leaving no residual claim of redress.

The End of Orderliness

The large organization pays the entrepreneurial penalties for the operational benefits bestowed by its structure. There are no organizational solutions to its search for innovations. That is why the consultants always get called back. They always propose things that have a clean and logical organizational content. But whatever they propose finally fails, or never really works from the outset.

Clean and logical organizational solutions are illusory. All clean and logical solutions fail. The only thing that works is variety and serendipity. Franklin Roosevelt's famous method of drawing directly on constantly new sources of advice and of constantly keeping the Cabinet and senior advisers off balance regarding what he might do and at odds with one another regarding their range of authority is instructive, though perhaps not entirely prescriptive. President Kennedy did much the same thing. The device did not merely accept or tolerate diversity of methods; it generated diversity. It was aggressively agnostic about the virtues of the kind of orderly system that President Eisenhower, for example, favored, and President Nixon institutionalized so rigidly.

No business organization of size that sees the need for development and innovation can afford not to have an orderly arrangement for product planning, R & D, or market development. But neither should it be deceived

---

[8] There is a particularly interesting exposition of the captivity of the chief executive by his organization in J. K. Galbraith, *The New Industrial State,* Houghton Mifflin Company, Boston, 1967, chap. 6.

[9] James G. March and Herbert A. Simon, *Organizations,* John Wiley & Sons, Inc., New York, 1958, pp. 172–210.

into believing that once established, staffed, and budgeted, these are enough in themselves for getting innovation, and particularly dramatic innovation. More is needed. At the upper organizational levels there must be a constant search for, and sponsorship of, unexpected and erratic inputs. There must be a random float of new ideas eagerly sought, varied organizational devices for their implementation, and a cheerful disregard of consistency.

Obviously none of this can be formalized. Formalization requires procedures, and these get rigid, bureaucratized, and exploited. Change and newness must be sanctioned by the symbolically most important and visible functionary in the organization, the chief executive. He must be the ultimate champion of what amounts to serendipitous inputs of change. It has been asked whether ". . . the most important aspect of top management is not formal organizational procedures [to produce newness], but the social tangle which necessitates bringing the product champion into being in the first place."[10] The implication is splendid, but the author ends up creating a formal system of new-product and new-idea champions.

Formalism is the inescapable necessity of organizations. It is, however, also the enemy of radical or high-leverage newness, and often of any kind of useful newness at all. The modern search for ways to get creativity and innovation into organizations descends always into the creation of some formal system or piece of organizational machinery. The reason is clear enough: The prevailing culture of the large organization says that you must "organize for the job." But when it comes to significant newness, that is not the "job" to which the quoted phrase refers. The accustomed job is the routine job; and while the creation of some newness can and must be routinized, dramatic or radical or just plain unaccustomed newness cannot generally be routinized. It requires a break from the culture.

Peter G. Peterson, while president of Bell & Howell Company, observed that "It is ironic that while we, as businessmen, pay lip service to individual initiative, risk-taking and boldness, we are driven by our own passion for security . . . and, in our case, it is the passion to know for sure what can only be estimated at best . . . we must subject to a critical scrutiny our over-reliance on facts and figures, statistics and surveys . . . our passion for statistical security."[11] Peterson correctly declares that the creation of dramatic newness requires escape from the conventional, though not necessarily incorrect, ways of doing things. It is not that facts

[10] Donald A. Schon, "Champions for Radical Inventions," *Harvard Business Review*, March–April, 1963, p. 86

[11] Peter G. Peterson, "Dogma in Marketing," *Vital Speeches of the Day*, Nov. 1, 1964, pp. 43–46.

and figures or organization and order are inappropriate to the main corporate purpose, but that they may be inappropriate to specific purposes. Peterson cites the example of the bridge buff who knows everything objective there is to know about the game—how to make double squeeze plays and end plays, all the complicated percentages, all the elaborate bidding conventions and slam tries. But he always loses. All the bridge champions play the cards with the same degree of well-schooled proficiency. But the winners have the "feel of the table," playing not just the cards but the players; and they play the players better than the losers. It is not entirely by rules but also by intuition and instinct that they play.

The way to encourage dramatic newness, to raise up to the organization's top the exciting ideas that would ordinarily be diluted or buried or rejected far below, is for the chief executive to take special pains to destroy the routine expectations of order and system on matters of major potential significance. This means not that he must establish a system of formal bottom-up direct reportings to himself, but that he must practice a floating and constantly changing style with respect to eliciting, evaluating, encouraging, and doing new things. He has got to create an "anything goes" culture, and to keep it constantly going. There are lots of ways: the powerful but casual lunchtime advocacy of heresy to his staff and his line lieutenants; the sudden, occasional assignment of a restless critic from the lower echelons to his office; the occasional and unexpected intrusion of a dramatic new experiment into an operating department, even against the wishes of the department's head, such that the act seems spontaneous without seeming to reject the more normal consultative process by which such matters are decided; the unexpected temporary assignment of an "indispensable" operations vice-president to a six-week stint to get an offbeat task accomplished; an unannounced all-day meeting of the entire executive group for the purpose of listening to a senior executive from another company discuss how it manages its unorthodox corporation or of having each member of the group discuss the three most exciting things he would like to get done if he had the chance; the occasional making of a difficult, high-risk decision in the presence of key executives with the declaration that "Sometimes we've got to swing on gut feel, or we'll never break loose—and this is one such situation, so let's go."

Symbols for Success

The more routinized and formalized an organization's procedures are the more powerfully symbolic and contradictory must be the actions whose purpose is to legitimize decisions that violate the routine. Only the chief executive can set this pattern into motion. It cannot be done by subordinates. Contraorganizational acts by subordinates will merely confirm the illegitimacy of such acts. It is only after a pattern of legitimacy is established from the top that subordinates, even high-level ones, will feel secure enough to emulate the process.

The emphasis must be on the process, not on the organizational system. If a system is employed, its temporal limitations must be recognized. Hence, it must in a few years be drastically altered or fully replaced before its inevitable bureaucratization creates disillusionment about the virtue of innovation itself.

The promise of organizational solutions is tantalizing and seldom resisted. If it can be kept in mind that organization is the handmaiden of routine rather than of rationalization, then its seductive attractiveness will be more effectively resisted.

Dramatic innovation generally occurs when a prophetic insight is supported by a powerful individual or group. When there is no quick high-level support, lower-level men will fight for their ideas at the risk of their organizational lives. Few organizations have any Admiral Rickovers— men who have the self-willed vanity to risk everything against the opposition of the system and who will persevere to the end, bleeding profusely from their wounds but never relenting. In most cases, they will be fired, which is not really possible in the United States Navy.

The chief executive must recognize the terrible extent to which his every word and deed are watched for meaning and intent by those below him, and the extent to which his momentary departures from customary practices and behavior become signals that guide, direct, inspire, or thwart those below. He is capable of creating a spirit of faith in his organization that will produce results far more magnificent than the pure exercise of primitive muscle. "A corporation, like a state, needs a faith," proclaims one author. "Just as soldiers fight much better for a great cause like Christianity or Liberty or Democracy than for the protection of trading interests, so insurance firms can [get more results from] salesmen who feel they are spreading protection and security and peace of mind among their fellow citizens than ones who simply believe they are being paid to increase the company's return on employed capital and the annual dividends to stockholders."[12]

The faith of America is a faith in the infinity of growth and development, the idea that when we work, we do more than a job: we create constant and beneficent newness. The corporation that seeks to grow by

[12] Antony Jay, *Management and Machiavelli*, Holt, Rinehart and Winston, Inc., New York, 1967, p. 199.

more than the annual rate of population growth must develop a spirit that is congruent with this faith. Words and reorganization will not be enough. It takes deeds, and particularly deeds of dramatic proportion. The most visible source of such deeds is the chief executive—what he does others will see. They will also, and perhaps even more clearly, see what he does not do. Because he is so visible, his style will be contagious throughout his organization.

The essence of how he must behave in his quest to create advancements of quantum proportions lies in the recognition that the world is linear only in little things. Big and unusual things rarely occur in routine ways. Hence, the quest for the unusual requires a departure from routine systems. The chief executive, who presides in the main over a system whose purpose is the management of routine, must therefore augment his ordinary efforts with periodically extraordinary ones. If he wants unusual newness, he must sponsor and legitimize serendipity.

Just as the philosopher should not waste his powers on the creation of systems but attack the question of truth, so the chief business executive should not waste his punch on the exclusive administration of systems. He should attack the problem of change. Truth and change have a powerful similarity. They both deal with a constantly unfinished task. It is the perennial pursuit of this unfinished task to which both the philosopher's and the chief executive's inspiration must be directed.

Innovation and Imitation

Chapter Eight

Exploiting What You Have

A LOT OF EXECUTIVES ARE by now familiar with the idea of the product life cycle. Few seem to do anything about it—to use it to their advantage. This chapter will suggest ways to do just that.

Since the concept has been presented somewhat differently by different authors and for different audiences, it is useful to review it briefly so that every reader will have the same background for the discussion that follows later in this chapter.

HISTORICAL PATTERN

The life story of most successful products is a history of their passing through certain recognizable stages. These are shown in Exhibit 1 (see page 159) and occur in the following order:

STAGE 1 *Market Development.* This is when a new product is first brought to market, before there is a proved demand for it, and often before it has been fully proved out technically in all respects. Sales are low and creep along slowly.

STAGE 2 *Market Growth.* Demand begins to accelerate, and the size of the total market expands rapidly. It might also be called the "takeoff stage."

STAGE 3 *Market Maturity*. Demand levels off and grows, for the most part, only at the replacement and new family-formation rate.

STAGE 4 *Market Decline*. The product begins to lose consumer appeal, and sales drift downward, such as when buggy whips lost out with the advent of automobiles and when silk lost out to nylon.

Three operating questions will quickly occur to the alert executive:

- Given a proposed new product or service, how and to what extent can the shape and duration of each stage be predicted?
- Given an existing product, how can one determine what stage it is in?
- Given all this knowledge, how can it be effectively used?

A brief further elaboration of each stage will be useful before dealing with these questions in detail.

Development Stage

Bringing a new product to market is fraught with unknowns, uncertainties, and frequently unknowable risks. Generally, demand has to be "created" during the product's initial *market development stage*. How long this takes depends on the product's complexity, its degree of newness, its fit into consumer needs, and the presence of competitive substitutes of one form or another. A proved cancer cure would require virtually no market development; it would get immediate massive support. An alleged superior substitute for the lost-wax process of sculpture casting would take lots longer.

While it has been demonstrated time after time that properly customer-oriented new-product development is one of the primary conditions of sales and profit growth, what has been demonstrated even more conclusively are the ravaging costs and frequent fatalities associated with launching new products. Nothing seems to take more time, cost more money, involve more pitfalls, cause more anguish, or break more careers than sincere and well-conceived new-product programs. The fact is that most new products don't have any sort of classical life-cycle curve at all. They have instead from the very outset an infinitely descending curve. The product not only doesn't get off the ground; but also it goes quickly underground—6 feet under.

It is little wonder, therefore, that some disillusioned and badly burned companies have recently adopted a more conservative policy —what I call the "used-apple policy." Instead of aspiring to be the first company to see and seize an opportunity, they systematically avoid being first. They let others take the first bite of the supposedly juicy apple that tantalizes them. They let others do the pioneering. If the idea works, they quickly follow suit. They say, in effect, "We don't have to get the first bite of the apple. The second one is good enough." They are willing to eat from a used apple, but they try to be alert enough to make sure it is only slightly used—that they at least get the second big bite, not the tenth skimpy one.

Growth Stage

The usual characteristic of a successful new product is a gradual rise in its sales curve during the market development stage. At some point in this rise a marked increase in consumer demand occurs and sales take off. The boom is on. This is the beginning of stage 2—the *market growth stage.* At this point potential competitors who have been watching developments during stage 1 jump into the fray. The first ones to get in are generally those with an exceptionally effective used-apple policy. Some enter the market with carbon copies of the originator's product. Others make functional and design improvements. And at this point product and brand differentiation begin to develop.

The ensuing fight for the consumer's patronage poses to the originating producer an entirely new set of problems. Instead of seeking ways of getting consumers to *try the product,* the originator now faces the more compelling problem of getting them to *prefer* his *brand.* This generally requires important changes in marketing strategies and methods. But the policies and tactics now adopted will be neither freely the sole choice of the originating producer, nor as experimental as they might have been during stage 1. The presence of competitors both dictates and limits what can easily be tried—such as, for example, testing what is the best price level or the best channel of distribution.

As the rate of consumer acceptance accelerates, it generally becomes increasingly easy to open new distribution channels and retail outlets. The consequent filling of distribution pipelines generally causes the entire industry's factory sales to rise more rapidly than store sales. This creates an exaggerated impression of profit opportunity, which, in turn, attracts more competitors. Some of these will begin to charge lower prices because of later advances in technology, production shortcuts, the need to take lower margins in order to get distribution, and the like. All this in time inescapably moves the industry to the threshold of a new stage of competition.

Maturity Stage

This new stage is the *market maturity stage.* The first sign of its advent is evidence of market saturation. This means that most existing companies or households that are sales prospects will be owning or using the product. Sales now grow about on a par with population. No more distribution pipelines need be filled. Price competition now becomes intense. Competitive attempts to achieve and hold brand preference now involve making finer and finer differentiations in the product, in customer services, and in the promotional practices and claims made for the product.

Typically, the market maturity stage forces the producer to concentrate on holding his distribution outlets, retaining his shelf space, and, in the end, trying to secure even more intensive distribution. Whereas during the market development stage the originator depended heavily on the positive efforts of his retailers and distributors to help sell his product, retailers and distributors will now frequently have been reduced largely to being merchandise displayers and order takers. In the case of branded products in particular, the originator must now, more than ever, communicate directly with the consumer.

The market maturity stage typically calls for a new kind of emphasis on competing more effectively. The originator is increasingly forced to appeal to the consumer on the basis of price, marginal product differences, or both. Depending on the product, services and deals offered in connection with it are often the clearest and most effective forms of differentiation. Beyond these, there will be attempts to create and promote fine product distinctions through packaging and advertising, and to appeal to special market segments. The market maturity stage can be passed through rapidly, as in the case of most women's fashion fads, or it can persist for generations with per capita consumption neither rising nor falling, as in the case of such staples as men's shoes and industrial fasteners. Or maturity can persist, but in a state of gradual but steady per capita decline, as in the case of beer and steel.

Decline Stage

When market maturity tapers offs and consequently comes to an end, the product enters stage 4—the *market decline stage*. In all cases of maturity and decline the industry is transformed. Few companies are able to weather the competitive storm. As demand declines, the overcapacity that was already apparent during the period of maturity now becomes endemic. Some producers see the handwriting implacably on the wall but feel that with proper management and cunning they will be one of the survivors after the industrywide deluge they so clearly foresee. To hasten their competitors' eclipse directly, or to frighten them into early voluntary withdrawal from the industry, they initiate a variety of aggressively depressive tactics, propose mergers or buy-outs, and generally engage in activities that make life thanklessly burdensome for all firms and make death the inevitable consequence for most of them. A few companies do indeed weather the storm, sustaining life through the constant descent that now clearly characterizes the industry. Production gets concentrated into fewer hands. Prices and margins get depressed. Consumers get bored. The only cases where there is any relief from this boredom and gradual euthanasia are where styling and fashion play some constantly revivifying role.

PREPLANNING IMPORTANCE

Knowing that the lives of successful products and services are generally characterized by something like the pattern illustrated in Exhibit 1 can become the basis for important life-giving policies and practices. One of the greatest values of the life-cycle concept is for managers about to launch a new product. The first step for them is to try to foresee the profile of the proposed product's cycle.

As with so many things in business, and perhaps uniquely in marketing, it is almost impossible to make universally useful suggestions regarding how to manage one's affairs. It is certainly particularly difficult to provide widely useful advice on how to foresee or predict the slope and duration of a product's life. Indeed, it is precisely because so little specific day-to-day guidance is possible in anything, and because no checklist has ever by itself been very useful to anybody for very long, that business management will probably never be a science—always an art—and will pay exceptional rewards to managers with rare talent, enormous energy, iron nerves, and a great capacity for assuming responsibility and bearing accountability.

But this does not mean that useful efforts cannot or should not be made to try to foresee the slope and duration of a new product's life. Not only does time spent in attempting this kind of foresight help assure that a more rational approach is brought to product planning and merchandising, but, as will be shown later, it can also help create valuable lead time for important strategic and tactical moves after the product is brought to market. Specifically, it can be a great help in developing an orderly series of competitive moves, in expanding or stretching out the life of a product, in maintaining a clean product line, and in purposely phasing out dying and costly old products.[1]

Failure Possibilities . . .

As pointed out above, the length and slope of the market development stage depend on the product's complexity, its degree of newness, its fit into customer needs, and the presence of competitive substitutes.

The more unique or distinctive the newness of the product, the longer

[1] See Philip Kotler, "Phasing Out Weak Products," *Harvard Business Review,* March–April, 1965, p. 107.

it generally takes to get it successfully off the ground. The world does not automatically beat a path to the man with the better mousetrap. The world has to be told, coddled, enticed, romanced, and even bribed (as with, for example, coupons, samples, free application aids, and the like). When the product's newness is distinctive and the job it is designed to do is unique, the public will generally be less quick to perceive it as something it clearly needs or wants.

This makes life particularly difficult for the innovator. He will have more than the usual difficulties of identifying those characteristics of his product and those supporting communications themes or devices which imply value to the consumer. As a consequence, the more distinctive the newness, the greater will be the risk of failure. There is likely to be insufficient working capital to sustain a long and frustrating period of market development, and great difficulty in convincing bosses, investors, and bankers that they should put up more money.

In any particular situation the more people who will be involved in making a single purchasing decision for a new product, the more drawn out stage 1 will be. In the highly fragmented construction materials industry, for example, success takes an exceptionally long time to catch hold; and having once caught hold, it tends to hold tenaciously for a long time —often too long. On the other hand, fashion items clearly catch on fastest and last the shortest. Indeed, the facilitating power of fashion and aesthetics is now getting increasing attention in some uncommon places. Machine-tool companies have successfully shortened the market development stage of newly introduced equipment by paying unaccustomed attention to styling and design appearance.

What factors tend to prolong the market development stage and therefore raise the risk of failure? The more complex the product, the more distinctive its newness, the less influenced by fashion, the greater the number of persons influencing a single buying decision, the more costly it is, and the greater the required shift in the customer's usual way of doing things—these are the conditions most likely to slow things up and create problems.

Success Possibilities

The prevalence of many problems in new-product introduction suggests the existence of opportunities to deal with or control the forces that produce the problems. For example, the newer the product, the more important it becomes for the customers to have a favorable first experience with it. Newness creates a certain special visibility for the product, with a certain number of people standing on the sidelines to see how the first customers get on with it. If their first experience is unfavorable in some crucial way, this may have repercussions far out of proportion to the actual extent of the underfulfillment of the customer's expectations. But a favorable first experience or application will, for the same reason, get a lot of disproportionately favorable publicity.

The possibility of exaggerated disillusionment with a poor first experience can raise vital questions regarding the appropriate channels of distribution for a new product. On the one hand, getting the product successfully launched may require having—as in the case of, say, the early days of home washing machines—many retailers who can give consumers considerable help in the product's correct utilization and thus help assure a favorable first experience for those buyers. On the other hand, channels that provide this kind of help (such as small neighborhood appliance stores in the case of washing machines) during the market development stage may not be the ones best able to merchandise the product most successfully later, when help in creating and personally reassuring customers is less important than wide product distribution. To the extent that channel decisions during this first stage sacrifice some of the requirements of the market development stage to some of the requirements of later stages, the rate of the product's acceptance by consumers at the outset may be delayed.

In the market development stage, pricing questions are among the hardest to deal with. Should the developer set an initially high price to recoup his investment quickly—i.e., "skim the cream"—or should he set a low price to discourage potential competition—i.e., aim for "exclusion"? The answer depends on the innovator's estimate of the probable length of the product's life cycle, the degree of patent protection the product is likely to enjoy, the amount of capital needed to get the product off the ground, the elasticity of demand during the early life of the product, and many other factors. The decision that is finally made may affect not just the rate at which the product catches on at the beginning, but even the duration of its total life. Thus some products that are priced too low at the outset (particularly fashion goods, such as the chemise, or sack, years ago) may catch on so quickly that they become short-lived fads. A slower rate of consumer acceptance might often extend their life cycles and raise the total profits they yield.

The actual slope, or rate of the growth stage, depends on some of the same things that determine success or failure in stage 1. But the extent to which patent exclusiveness can play a critical role is sometimes inexplicably forgotten. More frequently than one might predict offhand, holders of strong patent positions fail to recognize either the market-developing virtue of making their patents available to competitors or the market-destroying possibilities of failing to control more effectively their competitors' use of such products.

Generally speaking, the more producers there are of a new product, the more effort goes into developing a market for it. The net result is very likely to be more rapid and steeper growth of the total market. The originator's market share may fall, but his total sales and profits may rise more rapidly. Certainly this has been the case in recent years of color television. RCA's eagerness to make its tubes available to competitors reflects its recognition of the power of numbers over the power of monopoly.

On the other hand, the failure to set and enforce appropriate quality standards in the early days of polystyrene and polyethylene drinking glasses and cups produced such sloppy, inferior goods that it took years to recover the consumer's confidence in plastics and revive the growth pattern.

But to try to see in advance what a product's growth pattern might be is not very useful if one fails to distinguish between the industry pattern and the pattern of the single firm—for its particular brand. The industry's cycle will almost certainly be different from the cycle of individual firms. Moreover, the life cycle of a given product may be different for different companies in the same industry at the same point in time, and it certainly affects different companies in the same industry differently.

ORIGINATOR'S BURDENS

The company with most at stake is the original producer—the company that launches an entirely new product. This company generally bears most of the costs, the tribulations, and certainly the risks of developing both the product and the market.

Competitive Pressure

Once the innovator demonstrates during the market development stage that a solid demand exists, armies of imitators rush in to capitalize on and help create the boom that becomes the market growth, or takeoff, stage. As a result, while exceedingly rapid growth will now characterize the product's total demand, the growth stage of the originating company paradoxically now becomes truncated. It has to share the boom with new competitors. Its own acceleration is diminished, and may actually fail to last as long as the industry's. This occurs not only because there are so many competitors, but, as we noted earlier, also because competitors often come in with product improvements and lower prices. While these developments generally help keep the market expanding, they greatly restrict the originating company's rate of growth and the length of its takeoff stage.

All this can be illustrated by comparing the company sales curve in Exhibit 2 (page 160) with the life-cycle curve of the product in Exhibit 1. During stage 1 in Exhibit 1 there is generally only one company— the originator—even though the whole exhibit represents the entire industry. In stage 1 the originator is the entire industry. But by stage 2 he shares the industry with many competitors. Hence, while Exhibit 1 is an industry curve, its stage 1 represents only a single company's sales.

Exhibit 2 shows the life cycle of the originator's brand—his own sales curve, not that of the industry. It can be seen that between year 1 and year 2 his sales are rising almost as rapidly as the industry's. But after year 2, while industry sales in Exhibit 1 are still in vigorous expansion, the originator's sales curve in Exhibit 2 has begun to slow its ascent. He is now sharing the boom with a great many competitors, some of whom are much better positioned now than he is.

EXHIBIT 1 Product Life Cycle—Entire Industry

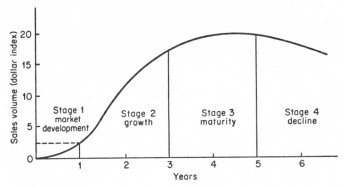

Profit Squeeze

In the process the originator may begin to encounter a serious squeeze on his profit margins. Exhibit 3, which traces the profits per unit of the originator's sales, illustrates this point. During the market development stage his per-unit profits are negative. Sales volume is too low at existing prices. However, during the stage of market growth the acceleration of sales and output will reduce per-unit production costs and therefore dramatically raise per-unit profits. Total profits will rise enormously. It is the presence of such lush profits that both attracts and ultimately destroys competitors.

Consequently, while (1) industry sales may still be rising nicely (as at the year 3 point in Exhibit 1), (2) the originating company's sales may at the same point of time have begun to slow down noticeably (as in Exhibit 2), and (3) at this point, the originator's total profits may still be high because his volume of sales is huge and on a slight upward trend, his profits per unit will often have taken a drastic downward course. Indeed, they will often have done so long before the sales curve flattened. They will have topped out and begun to decline perhaps around the year 2 point (as in Exhibit 3). By the time the originator's sales begin to flatten out (as at the year 3 point in Exhibit 2), unit profits may actually be approaching zero (as in Exhibit 3).

At this point more competitors are in the industry, the rate of industry demand growth has slowed somewhat, and competitors are cutting prices. Some of them do this in order to get business; others do it because their costs are lower thanks to their modern and more productive equipment.

EXHIBIT 2   Product Life Cycle—Originating Company

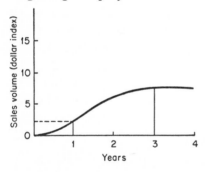

EXHIBIT 3   Unit Profit Contribution Life Cycle—Originating Company

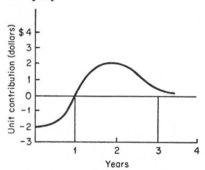

The industry's stage 3—maturity—generally lasts as long as there are no important competitive substitutes (such as, for example, aluminum for steel in "tin" cans), no drastic shifts in influential value systems (such as the end of female modesty in the 1920s and the consequent destruction of the market for veils), no major changes in dominant fashions (such as the hourglass female form and the end of waist cinchers), no changes in the demand for primary products that use the product in question (such as the effect of the decline of new railroad expansion on the demand for railroad ties), and no changes either in the rate of obsolescence of the product or in the character or introductory rate of product modifications.

Maturity can last for a long time, or it can actually never be attained. Fashion goods and fad items sometimes surge to sudden heights, hesitate momentarily at an uneasy peak, and then quickly drop off into total obscurity.

Stage Recognition

The various characteristics of the stages described above will help one to recognize the stage a particular product occupies at any given time. But hindsight will always be more accurate than current sight. Perhaps the best way of seeing one's current stage is to try to foresee the next stage and work backward.

This approach has several virtues. It forces one to look ahead, constantly to try to foresee his future and competitive environment. This will have its own rewards. As Charles F. Kettering, perhaps the last of Detroit's primitive inventors and probably the greatest of all its inventors, was fond of saying, "We should all be concerned about the future because that's where we'll have to spend the rest of our lives." By looking at the future one can better assess the stage of the present.

Looking ahead sometimes gives more perspective to the present than looking at the present alone. Most people know more about the present than is good for them. It is neither healthy nor helpful to know the present too well, for our perception of the present is too often too heavily distorted by the urgent pressures of day-to-day events. The significance of business decisions is that they inescapably deal with the future, with what is to be done, rather than with what has been done. To know where the present is in the continuum of competitive time and events is more important and useful than to know it for itself alone. It therefore often makes more sense to try to know what the future will bring, and when it will bring it, than to try to know in exhaustive detail what the present itself actually contains.

Finally, the value of knowing what stage a product occupies at any given time resides only in the way that fact is used. But its use is always in the future. Hence a prediction of the future environment in which the information will be used is often more functional for the effective capitalization on knowledge about the present than knowledge about the present itself. The utility of present knowledge is limited to its use for decisions about tomorrow.

SEQUENTIAL ACTIONS

The life-cycle concept can be effectively employed in the strategy of both existing and new products. For purposes of continuity and clarity, the remainder of this chapter will describe some of the uses of the concept from the early stages of new-product planning through the later stages of keeping the product profitably alive. The chief discussion will focus on what I call a policy of "life extension" or "market stretching."

To the extent that Exhibits 2 and 3 outline the classical patterns of successful new products, one of the constant aims of the originating producer should be to avoid the severe discipline imposed by an early profit squeeze in the market growth stage, and to avoid the wear and waste so typical of the market maturity stage. Hence the following proposition would seem reasonable: When a company develops a new product or service, it should try to plan at the very outset a series of actions to be employed at various subsequent stages in the product's or service's existence so that its sales and profit curves are constantly sustained rather than following their usual declining slope.

In other words, advance planning should be directed at extending, or stretching out, the life of the product. It is this idea of *planning in advance* of the actual launching of a new product to take specific actions later in its life cycle—actions designed to sustain its growth and profitability—which appears to have great potential as an instrument of long-term product strategy.

Nylon's Life

How this might work for a product can be illustrated by looking at the history of nylon. The way in which nylon's booming sales life has been repeatedly and systematically extended and stretched can serve as a model for other products. What has happened in nylon may not have been purposely planned that way at the outset, but the results are quite as if they had been.

The first nylon end uses were primarily military—parachutes, thread, rope. This was followed by nylon's entry into the circular-knit market and its subsequent domination of the women's hosiery business. Here it developed the kind of steadily rising growth and profit curves that every executive dreams about. After some years these curves began to flatten out. But before they flattened very noticeably, Du Pont had already developed measures designed to revitalize sales and profits. It did several things, each of which is demonstrated graphically in Exhibit 4. This exhibit and the explanation that follows takes some liberties with the actual facts of the nylon situation in order to highlight the points I wish to make. But they take no liberties with the essential requisites of product strategy.

Point A of Exhibit 4 shows the hypothetical point at which the nylon curve (dominated at this point by hosiery) flattened out. If nothing further had been done, the sales curve would have continued along the

EXHIBIT 4 Hypothetical Life Cycle—Nylon

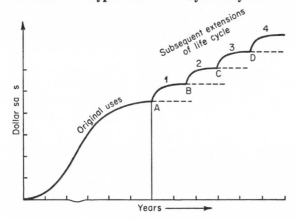

flattened path indicated by the dotted line at point A. This is also the hypothetical point at which the first systematic effort was made to extend the product's life. Du Pont, in effect, took certain "actions" that pushed hosiery sales upward rather than allowing them to continue the path implied by the dotted-line extension of the curve at point A. At point A action 1 pushed an otherwise flat curve upward.

At points B, C, and D still other new sales- and profit-expansion actions (2, 3, 4, and so forth) were taken. What were these actions? Or, more usefully, what was their strategic content? What did they try to do? They involved strategies that tried to expand sales via four different routes:

1. Promoting *more frequent usage* of the product among current users
2. Developing *more varied usage* of the product among current users
3. Creating *new users* for the product by expanding the market
4. Finding *new uses* for the basic material

Frequent Usage. Du Pont studies had shown an increasing trend toward "bareleggedness" among women. This was coincident with the trend toward more casual living and a declining perception among teenagers of what might be called the "social necessity" of wearing stockings. In the light of those findings, one approach to propping up the flattening sales curves might have been to reiterate the social necessity of wearing stockings at all times. That would have been a sales-building action, though obviously difficult and exceedingly costly. But it could clearly have fulfilled the strategy of promoting more frequent usage among current users as a means of extending the product's life.

Varied Usage. For Du Pont, this strategy took the form of an attempt to promote the "fashion smartness" of tinted hose and later of patterned and highly textured hosiery. The idea was to raise each woman's inventory of hosiery by obsolescing the perception of hosiery as a fashion staple that came only in a narrow range of browns and pinks. Hosiery was to be converted from a "neutral" accessory to a central ingredient of fashion with a "suitable" tint and pattern for each outer garment in the lady's wardrobe.

This not only would raise sales by expanding women's hosiery wardrobes and stores' inventories, but also would open the door for annual tint and pattern obsolescence, much the same as there is an annual color obsolescence in outer garments. Beyond that, the use of color and pattern to focus attention on the leg would help arrest the decline of the leg as an element of sex appeal—a trend which some researchers had discerned and which, they claimed, damaged hosiery sales.

New Users. Creating new users for nylon hosiery might conceivably have taken the form of attempting to legitimize the necessity of wearing hosiery among younger teen-agers and sub-teen-agers. Advertising, public relations, and merchandising of youthful social and style leaders would have been called for.

New Uses. For nylon, the development of new uses has had many triumphs—from varied types of hosiery, such as stretch stockings and stretch socks, to new uses for the raw material itself, such as for rugs, tires, bearings, and so forth. Indeed, if there had been no further product innovations designed to create new uses for nylon after the original military, miscellaneous, and circular-knit uses, nylon consumption in 1962 would have reached a saturation level at approximately 50 million pounds annually.

Instead, in 1962 consumption exceeded 500 million pounds. Exhibit 5 is Dr. Jordan P. Yale's clear demonstration of how the continuous development of new uses for the basic material constantly produced new waves of sales. The exhibit shows that in spite of the growth of the women's stocking market, the cumulative result of the military, circular-knit, and miscellaneous grouping would have been a flattened sales curve by 1958. (Nylon's entry into the broad-woven market in 1944 substantially raised sales above what they would have been. Even so, the sales of broadwoven, circular-knit, military, and miscellaneous groupings peaked in 1957.)

Had it not been for the addition of new uses for the same basic material —such as warp knits in 1945, tire cord in 1948, textured yarns in 1955, carpet yarns in 1959, and so forth—nylon would not have had the spectacularly rising consumption curve it has so clearly had. At various stages it would have exhausted its existing markets or been forced into decline

EXHIBIT 5 Innovation of New Products Postpones the Time of Total Maturity—Nylon Industry.

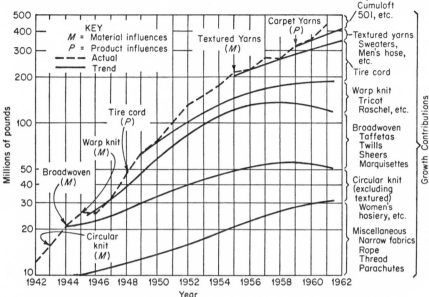

SOURCE: *Modern Textiles Magazine*, February, 1964, p. 33, copyright 1962 by Jordan P. Yale.

by competing materials. The systematic search for new uses for the basic (and improved) material extended and stretched the product's life.

Other Examples

The youthful semiconductor industry provides another recent example of product life extension. As can be seen in Exhibit 6, a combination of new uses and new product forms produced within a very short period a series of new waves of uses and applications that made this a preeminent growth area. Its impact on the life of vacuum tubes, which were replaced by semiconductors, is illustrated in Exhibit 7—a perfect example of the product life cycle in action.[2]

Few companies seem to employ in any systematic or planned way the four product life-stretching steps described above. Yet the successful application of this kind of stretching strategy has characterized the history

[2] See Milton L. Laflen, "Product Life Cycle Analysis of the Semiconductor Industry," *Arizona Business Review*, May, 1967, pp. 122–129.

**EXHIBIT 6   United States Semiconductor Industry Factory Sales.
Data Show United States Production Only. Total Consumption
Would Include Net Imports.**

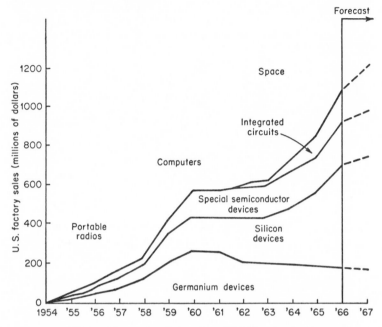

SOURCE: E.I.A., *Electronics Industries, 1966 Yearbook: Economics—
Marketing Facts and Figures,* Motorola, Inc., January, 1967.

**EXHIBIT 7   United States Electronic Receiving Tube Factory
Sales. Data Show United States Production Only. Total Consumption Would Include Net Imports.**

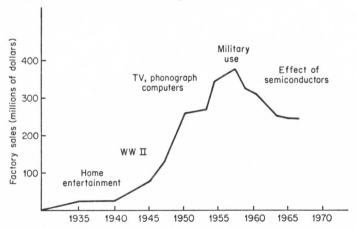

SOURCE: E.I.A., *Electronics Industries, 1966 Yearbook: Economics—
Marketing Facts and Figures,* Motorola, Inc., January, 1967.

of such well-known products as General Foods Corporation's Jell-O and Minnesota Mining & Manufacturing Co.'s Scotch tape.[3]

Jell-O was a pioneer in the easy-to-prepare gelatin dessert field. The soundness of the product concept and the excellence of its early marketing activities gave it beautifully ascending sales and profit curves almost from the start. But after some years these curves predictably began to flatten out. Scotch tape was also a pioneer product in its field. Once perfected, the product gained rapid market acceptance because of a sound product concept and an aggressive sales organization. But, again, in time the sales and profit curves began to flatten out. Before they flattened out very much, however, 3M, like General Foods, had already developed measures to sustain the early pace of sales and profits.

Both of these companies extended their products' lives by, in effect, doing all four of the things Du Pont did with nylon—creating more frequent usage among current users, more varied usage among current users, new users, and new uses for the basic "materials":

1. The General Foods approach to increasing the frequency of serving Jell-O among current users was, essentially, to increase the number of flavors. From Don Wilson's famous "six delicious flavors," Jell-O moved up to over a dozen. On the other hand, 3M helped raise sales among its current users by developing a variety of handy Scotch tape dispensers that made the product easier to use.

2. Creation of more varied usage of Jell-O among current dessert users involved its promotion as a base for salads and the facilitation of this usage by the development of a variety of vegetable-flavored Jell-Os. Similarly, 3M developed a line of colored, patterned, waterproof, invisible, and write-on Scotch tapes, which have enjoyed considerable success as sealing and decorating items for holiday and gift wrapping.

3. Jell-O sought to create new users by pinpointing people who could not accept Jell-O as a popular dessert or salad product. Hence during the Metrecal boom Jell-O employed an advertising theme that successfully affixed to the product a fashion-oriented weight-control appeal. Similarly, 3M introduced Rocket tape, a product much like Scotch tape but lower in price, and also developed a line of commercial cellophane tapes of various widths, lengths, and strengths. The actions broadened product use in commercial and industrial markets.

4. Both Jell-O and 3M have sought out new uses for the basic material. It is known, for example, that women consumers use powdered gelatin

[3] I am indebted to Prof. Derek A. Newton of the University of Virginia for these examples and other helpful suggestions.

dissolved in liquids as a means of strengthening their fingernails. Both men and women use it in the same way as a bone-building dietary agent. Hence Jell-O introduced a "completely flavorless" Jell-O for just these purposes. 3M has also developed new uses for the basic material—from "double-coated" tape (adhesive on both sides), which competes with ordinary liquid adhesives, to the reflecting tape that festoons countless automobile bumpers, to marker strips, which compete with paint.

EXTENSION STRATEGIES

The existence of the kinds of product life cycles illustrated in Exhibits 1 and 2 and the unit profit cycle shown in Exhibit 3 suggests that people involved in new-product work may benefit considerably if they begin planning for the extension of the lives of their products even before these products are formally launched. Planning for new life-extending infusions of effort (as shown in Exhibit 4) at this preintroduction stage can be extremely useful in three profoundly important ways:

1. *It generates an active rather than a reactive product policy.* It systematically structures a company's long-term marketing and product development efforts in advance, rather than each effort or activity being merely a stopgap response to the urgent pressures of repeated competitive thrusts and declining profits. The life-extension view of product policy enforces thinking and planning ahead—thinking in some systematic way about the moves likely to be made by potential competitors, about possible changes in consumer reactions to the product, and about the required selling activities that best take advantage of these conditional events.

2. *It lays out a long-term plan designed to infuse new life into the product at the right time, with the right degree of care, and with the right amount of effort.* Activities designed to raise the sales and profits of existing products or materials are often undertaken without regard to their relationship to one another or to timing—the optimum point of consumer readiness for such activities or the point of optimum competitive effectiveness. Careful advance planning, done long before the need for such activity arises, can help assure that the timing, the care, and the efforts are appropriate to the situation.

For example, it appears extremely doubtful that the boom in women's hair coloring and hair tinting products would have been as spectacular if vigorous efforts to sell these products had preceded the boom in hair sprays and chemical setting agents. The latter helped create a powerful consumer consciousness of hair fashions because they made it relatively easy to create and wear fashionable hairstyles. Once it became easy for women to have fashionable hairstyles, the resulting fashion consciousness helped open the door for hair colors and tints. It could not have happened the other way around, with colors and tints first creating fashion consciousness and thus raising the sales of sprays and fixers. Because understanding the reason for this precise order of events is essential for appreciating the importance of early preintroduction life-extension planning, it is useful to go into a bit of detail.

Setting their hair has been a perennial problem for women for centuries. First, one of the most common ways in which they distinguish themselves from men is through the length and treatment of their hair. Hence to be attractive in that distinction becomes crucial. Second, hair frames and highlights the face, much as an attractive wooden border frames and highlights a beautiful painting. Thus hair styling is an important element in enhancing the appearance of a woman's facial features. Third, since the hair is long and soft, it is hard to hold in an attractive arrangement. It gets mussed in sleep, wind, damp weather, sporting activities, and so forth.

Therefore, the effective *arrangement* of a woman's hair is understandably her first priority in hair care. An unkempt brunette would gain nothing from making herself into an unkempt blonde. Indeed, in a country where blondes are in the minority, to switch from being an unkempt brunette to being an unkempt blonde would simply draw attention to a woman's sloppiness. But once the problem of arrangement became easily "solved" by the use of sprays and fixers, colors and tints could become big business, especially among women whose hair was beginning to turn gray.

The same order of priorities applies in industrial products. For example, it seems quite inconceivable that many manufacturing plants would easily have accepted the replacement of the old single-spindle, constantly mantended screw machine by a computerized, tape-tended, multiple-spindle machine. The mechanical tending of the multiple-spindle machine was a necessary intermediate step, if for no other reason than that it required a lesser work-flow change, and certainly a lesser conceptual leap for the companies and the machine-tending workers involved.

For Jell-O, it is unlikely that vegetable flavors would have been very successful before the idea of gelatin as a salad base had been pretty well accepted. Similarly, the promotion of colored and patterned Scotch tape as a gift and decorative seal might not have been as successful if department stores had not, as the result of their drive to compete more effectively with mass merchandisers by offering more customer services, previously demonstrated to the consumer what could be done to wrap and decorate gifts.

3. *Perhaps the most important benefit of advance, preintroduction*

planning for sales-extending, market-stretching activities later in the product's life is that this practice forces a company to adopt a wider view of the nature of the product it is dealing with. Indeed, it may even force the adoption of a wider view of the company's business. Take the case of Jell-O. What is its product? Over the years Jell-O has become the brand umbrella for a wide range of dessert products, including cornstarch-base puddings, pie fillings, and Whip'n Chill, a light dessert product similar to a Bavarian cream or a French mousse. On the basis of these products, it might be said that the Jell-O division of General Foods is in the "dessert technology" business.

In the case of tape, perhaps 3M has gone even further in this technological approach to its business. It has a particular expertise (technology) on which it has built a constantly expanding business. This expertise can be said to be that of bonding things (adhesives in the case of Scotch tape) to other things, particularly to thin materials. Hence we see 3M developing scores of profitable items, including electronic recording tape (bonding electron-sensitive materials to tape) and Thermo-Fax duplicating equipment and supplies (bonding heat-reactive materials to paper).

CONCLUSION

Companies interested in continued growth and profits should view successful new-product strategy as a planned totality that looks ahead over some years. For its own good, new-product strategy should try to predict in some measure the likelihood, character, and timing of competitive and market events. While predicting is always hazardous and seldom very accurate, done with careful recognition of the historic power of inertia and of our limited capacities to absorb very much newness very rapidly, it is undoubtedly far better than not trying to predict at all. In fact, every product strategy and every business decision inescapably involves making a prediction about the future, about the market, and about competitors. To be more systematically aware of the predictions one is making so that one acts on them in an offensive rather than a defensive or reactive fashion— this is the real virtue of preplanning for market stretching and product life extension. The result will be a product strategy that includes some sort of *plan for a timed sequence of conditional moves.*

Even before entering the market development stage, the originator should make a judgment regarding the probable length of the product's normal life, taking into account the possibilities of expanding its uses and users. This judgment will also help determine many things—for example, whether to price the product on a skimming or on a penetration basis, or what kind of relationship the company should develop with its resellers.

These considerations are important because at each stage in a product's life cycle each management decision must consider the competitive requirements of the next stage. Thus a decision to establish a strong branding policy during the market growth stage might help to insulate the brand against strong price competition later; a decision to establish a policy of "protected" dealers in the market development stage might facilitate point-of-sale promotions during the market growth stage, and so on. In short, having a clear idea of future product development possibilities and market development opportunities should reduce the likelihood of becoming locked into forms of merchandising that might possibly prove undesirable later.

This kind of advance thinking about new-product strategy helps management avoid other pitfalls. For instance, advertising campaigns that look successful from a short-term view may hurt in the next stage of the life cycle. Thus at the outset Metrecal advertising used a strong medical theme. Sales boomed until imitative competitors successfully emphasized fashionable slimness. Metrecal had projected itself as the dietary for the overweight consumer, an image that proved far less appealing than that of being the dietary for people who were fashion-smart. But Metrecal's original appeal had been so strong and so well made that it was a formidable task later on to change people's impressions about the product. Obviously, with more careful long-range planning at the outset, a product's image can be more carefully positioned and advertising can have more clearly defined objectives.

Recognizing the importance of an orderly series of steps in the introduction of sales-building "actions" for new products should be a central ingredient of long-term product planning. A carefully pre-planned program for market expansion, even before a new product is introduced, can have powerful virtues. The establishment of a rational plan for the future can also help to guide the direction and pace of the ongoing technical research in support of the product. Although departures from such a plan will surely have to be made to accommodate unexpected events and revised judgments, the plan puts the company in a better position to *make* things happen rather than constantly having to react to things that *are* happening.

It is important that the originator not delay this long-term planning until after the product's introduction. How the product should be introduced and the many uses for which it might be promoted at the outset should be a function of a careful consideration of the optimum sequence of suggested product appeals and product uses. Consideration must focus not just on optimum things to do, but as importantly on their optimum *sequence*—for instance, what the order of use of various appeals should be and what the order of suggested product uses should be. If Jell-O's first suggested use had been as a diet food, its chances of later making a big and easy impact in the gelatin dessert market undoubtedly would have been greatly diminished. Similarly, if nylon hosiery had been promoted at the outset as functional daytime-wear hosiery, its ability to replace silk as the acceptable high-fashion hosiery would have been greatly diminished.

To illustrate the virtue of preintroduction planning for a product's later life, suppose a company has developed a nonpatentable new product—say, an ordinary kitchen salt shaker. Suppose that nobody now has any kind of shaker. One might say, before launching it, that (1) it has a potential market of x million household, institutional, and commercial consumers, (2) in two years market maturity will set in, and (3) in one year profit margins will fall because of the entry of competition. Hence one might lay out the following plan:

I. *End of first year: expand market among current users*
Ideas—new designs, such as sterling shaker for formal use, "masculine" shaker for barbecue use, antique shaker for "early American" households, miniature shakers for each place setting, moisture-proof design for beach picnics.

II. *End of second year: expand market to new users*
Ideas—designs for children, quaffer design for beer drinkers in bars, novelty design for sadists to rub salt into open wounds.

III. *End of third year: find new uses*
Ideas—make identical product for use as pepper shaker, as decorative garlic-salt shaker, shaker for household scouring powder, shaker to sprinkle silicon dust as a lubricant in machine shops, and so forth.

But all this is only part of the story. As I have suggested earlier, a product is more than its generic self. It consists just as much of all the many things with which it is surrounded—packaging, advertising, service programs, the channels in which it is sold and so forth. This means, therefore, that life-extension strategies must also consider how the product might be modified by various nongeneric augmentation tactics. This, indeed, has been one of the prime reasons for the continued expansion of the computer business. New service programs have augmented the product and expanded the market—extended the product's life. It has been less changes in the generic product than changes in the surrounding service programs that have sustained the computer boom. And some of these augmentation programs were very carefully planned in advance to occur at specific times in order to achieve needed sales expansions later.

Prethinking the possible methods of reactivating a flattening sales curve far in advance of its becoming flat enables product planners to assign priorities to each task and to plan future production expansion and capital and marketing requirements in a systematic fashion. It prevents one's trying to do too many things at once, results in priorities being determined rationally instead of as accidental consequences of the timing of new ideas, and disciplines both the product development effort that is launched in support of a product's growth and the marketing effort that is required for its continued success.

Chapter Nine

Exploiting What Others Have

WE LIVE IN A BUSINESS WORLD that increasingly worships the great tribal god *innovation*. Yet before all our R & D energies and imaginations are too one-sidedly directed at the creation of innovations, it is useful to look at the facts of commercial life. Is innovation all that promising? Is it all that profoundly liberating? More important, how does a policy of innovation compare in promise with more modest aspirations?

In spite of the extraordinary outpouring of totally and partially new products and new ways of doing things that we are witnessing today, by far the greatest flow of newness is not innovation at all. Rather, it is *imitation*. A simple look around us will quickly show that imitation is not only more abundant than innovation, but actually a much more prevalent road to business growth and profits. IBM got into computers as an imitator; Texas Instruments into transistors as an imitator; Holiday Inns into motels as an imitator; RCA into television as an imitator; Lytton into savings and loans as an imitator; and *Playboy* into both its major fields (publishing and entertainment) as an imitator. In addition, though on a lesser scale, we see every day that private brands are strictly imitative, as are most toys and new brands of packaged foods. In fact, imitation is endemic. Innovation is scarce.

This greater abundance of imitation is perfectly understandable. Each solitary innovator sparks a wave of eager imitators. By the time a so-called "new" product reaches widespread visibilty, it has usually been on the market for some time. Its visibility is less a consequence of its actual or temporal newness than of the number of its strident imitators. The newness of which consumers become aware is generally imitative and tardy newness, not innovative and timely newness.

Significant Distinctions

Generally speaking, innovation may be viewed from at least two vantage points: (1) *newness in the sense that something has never been done before* and (2) *newness in the sense that something has not been done before by the industry or by the company now doing it.*

Strictly defined, innovation occurs only when something is entirely new, having never been done before. A modest relaxation of this definition may be allowed by suggesting that innovation also exists when something that may have been done elsewhere is for the first time done in a given industry. On the other hand, when other competitors in the same industry subsequently copy the innovator, even though it is something new for them, this is not innovation; it is imitation. Thus:

- Bubble- or skin-packaging of small fixtures may be "new" for the hardware industry but may have been around for several years in other applications.
- Or it may also be new for a given company in the hardware industry but may have been around among competitors for some time.

These distinctions are not simply academic hairsplitting. They have the greatest significance for how a company develops its R & D budgets, structures its R & D efforts, and directs its product policies. A brief indication of what may be involved will not only clarify the importance of the distinction but also help set the stage for the ideas proposed later.

R & D can be exceedingly costly, time-consuming, and frustrating. When it is oriented to the creation of pure newness, it can involve an enormous commitment of manpower and money—with no assurance of reasonable payout. But when a company's R & D effort is oriented largely toward trying to adapt to its industry or to its organization things that have already been done elsewhere, the character and costs of the commitment are quite different. In the specific case of R & D oriented toward trying to develop for a company something that has already been done by an innovator, the situation is particularly special. There is usually a great premium on speed. One wants not just to catch up quickly with the successful innovator but, more particularly, to do so faster than other would-be imitators who are also working against the clock.

To call the purpose or character of this latter effort "innovation" is to mistake a spade for a steam shovel. The steam shovel is not just a bigger version of the spade; its whole rationale is different. The spade's cost is minuscule; its user requires virtually no training; it has no maintenance costs; and since during a given time period many spades are needed to do the work of a single steam shovel, the spade requires a management setup that is oriented toward the control and direction of many people, rather than toward the full utilization of an expensive and inanimate asset.

Similarly, R & D undertaken to create what might be referred to as "breakthrough newness" is vastly different from R & D that is imitative. The latter is little more than simple "D & D"—design and development. At best, it might be viewed as "reverse R & D"—working backward from what others have done, and trying to do the same thing for oneself.

The importance of these differences in the character of the required effort and commitment (coupled with a sometimes unreasoned faith in R & D and innovation) calls for a more careful self-examination in many companies of their competitive and growth strategies.

Needed: Balanced Policy

Innovation can be a highly productive, if often risky, road to success. In most industries today any company that is not aggressively alert to innovative possibilities is taking a competive risk of which it ought at least to be intelligently aware. Moreover, it is likely to develop an in-company atmosphere and style of behavior on the part of its people that can be dangerously insular. The quest for innovation—particularly in new products, in new-product attributes, and in customer service—is part and parcel of a company's being marketing-oriented.

Hence to have a company style or posture that seeks out opportunities for innovation can make a great deal of sense—whether these innovations are (1) massive ones, such as the new automobile diagnostic repair centers pioneered by Mobil Oil Company, or (2) modest innovations to extend the life cycle or broaden the market of a mature product, such as putting Mead Johnson's Enfamil baby formula into a ready-to-use measured bottle.

And the sense it can make, as pointed out so well in John B. Stewart's perceptive and badly neglected article on the pattern of competitive imitation, is that innovation can be one of the most effective possible means of building a company image of progressiveness and leadership.[1]

---

[1] John B. Stewart, "Functional Features in Product Strategy," *Harvard Business Review*, March–April, 1959, p. 65.

Of course, to come out in favor of innovation these days is about as inspirational as to endorse motherhood. At the same time, seeming to come out *against* innovation probably engenders more preoccupied alarm than being opposed to motherhood. In an age of pills, loops, electric calendar clocks, and early sophistication, unintentional motherhood is a mark of either inexcusable carelessness or unmanageable passion. Similarly, in an age of explosive science, engineering, market research, and rapid consumer acceptance of newness, opposition to innovation is a mark of either irretrievable naïveté or hopeless blindness.

What is needed is a sensibly balanced view of the world. Innovation is here to stay. It is necessary, and it can make a lot of sense. But it does not exhaust the whole of reality. Every company needs to recognize the impossibility of sustaining innovative leadership in its industry and the danger of an unbalanced dedication to trying to be the industry's constant innovator. No single company, regardless of its determination, energy, imagination, or resources, is big or solvent enough to do all the productive first things that will ever occur in its industry and always to beat its competitors to all the innovations emanating from the industry.

More important, no single company can afford even to *try* to be first in everything in its field. The costs are too great. Moreover, imagination, energy, and management know-how are too evenly distributed within industries. Of course, almost everybody implicitly knows this to be true, but my investigations lead me firmly to the conclusion that not everybody clearly acts as if it were true.

Reverse R & D

Once we become self-consciously aware that the possibilities of innovation within any one company are in some important ways limited, we quickly see that each organization is compelled by competition to look to imitation as one of its survival and growth strategies. Imitation is not just something that even the biggest, best-managed, most resourceful company will, by force of competitive circumstances, have to be involved in; it is something it will have to practice as a carefully developed strategy.

This means that the company will, insofar as products and processes are concerned, have to engage actively in reverse R & D—will have to try to create its own imitative equivalents of the innovative products created by others. Moreover, the faster the rate at which entirely new products are launched in any field, the more urgent the need for each company in that field to develop a clear-cut imitative strategy—one that serves to guide not just the business judgments that must be made, but also the way in which the reverse R & D commitments are made.

Since in so many industries the survival and growth of individual companies dictates that they at least quickly imitate the innovator's new products, and since the speed of competitive imitation tends so quickly to cut the margins available to all competitors, the speed with which an imitator enters the market is crucial.

Yet a survey made a few years ago of a range of strongly new-product-oriented companies with strong R & D departments—companies whose products generally required one to three years from the original idea to subsequent market launching—revealed not a single one that had any kind of policy, not even informal or implicit, to guide its responses to the innovations of others. Not a single one of these companies had even given any systematic or sustained thought to the *general notion* of whether it might be useful to have some set of criteria for making commitments to reverse R & D.

This is especially surprising in view of the attendant findings that:

■ Each of these companies had some sort of formal new-product planning process.

■ Each at some time in the recent past had lost considerable profit opportunities because its imitations had been delayed too long.

In other words, while the companies did a very careful job of planning new-product innovations, they had no criteria at all for the much bigger and more crucial job of new-product imitation. Reverse R & D was neither a planned nor a careful process. It merely occurred. It was done entirely at random, and sometimes as an almost blind reaction to what others had done. And, in every recent case in these companies, it was found that the imitator paid a heavy price for imitating either too soon or too late—mostly the latter.

Had any of the tardy imitations been launched about a year sooner, enormous profits would have accrued. The magnitude of these profits would have reflected not simply the acquisition of sales that were otherwise lost, but also the higher prices and profit margins existing in this earlier year.

Risk Minimization

Everybody knows that new products are risky. Predictably, they fail more often than they succeed. This unsettling fact helps explain why there is so much delay in comparative imitation. Would-be imitators sit carefully on the sidelines to watch the innovative product's fate. If it seems finally to take off, they begin a make their own moves.

Watchful waiting is a perfectly legitimate business strategy, particularly because even successful innovations often take a long time actually to become successful.[2] This fact, if none other, confirms the good sense of what I earlier called the "used-apple policy." According to this policy, a company consciously and carefully adopts the practice of never pioneering a new product. It says, in effect, "You don't have to get the first bite of the apple to make out. The second or third juicy bite is good enough. Just be careful not to get the tenth skimpy one." Hence it lets others do the pioneering. If the innovator's product is a rotten apple, the would-be imitator has lost nothing. If it's a healthy, juicy one, the imitator is prepared to move quickly and get an early and profitable piece of it.

But the trick is to be sure to get it early, when competitors are still few and margins still attractive. In some industries it is relatively easy to imitate rapidly because there are few setup problems, the capital requirement is small, and the products are relatively easy and quickly copied. The garment industry is probably the most obvious of such situations. However, when setup problems are great, when capital requirements are big, and when imitation requires lengthy reverse R & D, then getting the second or third juicy bite of the apple may involve several years' time and greatly increased risk.

Imitation of a proved product does not automatically reduce the risk; it merely changes its character. While the innovator faces the risk that his product may not find a ready market, the would-be imitator faces the equally palpable risk of reaching the market when it is already glutted with many competitors—and often rapaciously price-cutting competitors at that. Obviously, the imitator who can substantially shrink his development gestation period below that of other imitators can gain a tremendous advantage. He will encounter fewer competitors and higher and more stable prices during the felicitous duration of his lead over other imitators.

Purposeful Imitation

In most of the larger, better-managed companies, the R & D process, or at least the product development process, gets a great deal of careful attention. In many companies genuine product innovations are the direct consequence of carefully honed corporate strategies. Product innovation is purposeful and planned, not random or accidental. Yet, in these same companies, product imitation tends to be almost entirely random, accidental, and reactive. It is the consequence not of what the *imitator* has planned, but of what his competing *innovator* has planned.

Because others have planned and produced the innovation, it is often, though not always, greeted with a certain amount of understandable

2 See Lee Adler, "Time Lag in New Product Development," *Journal of Marketing,* January, 1966, pp. 17–21.

skepticism by competitors in the same general field. For example, when the electric toothbrush was first brought out several years ago, a number of companies in the portable appliance and "personal care" field reacted quite predictably. Since it was "not invented here," a great many highly plausible-sounding reasons were suggested as to why it would certainly fail. But the electric toothbrush caught on quickly, to become for a time one of the great new booming small-appliance products of the generation.

All companies in the portable appliance field, of course, kept close watch on the new electric toothbrush's progress. Some immediately interviewed users and prospective buyers. But frequently these activities were carried out in the context of extreme skepticism, with management treating the subject with some degree of casualness, if not actual and systematic indifference. At best, it was in some small-appliance companies treated with only idle curiosity. Other "invented here" projects—innovations that were part of a carefully conceived and hard-won corporate plan—seemed both more urgent and more exciting.

Yet had these small-appliance companies had a more formal plan, program, or procedure for handling their approaches to the innovations of competitors, it seems unquestionable that they would have been in the electric toothbrush business sooner and more profitably.

A Suggested System

The remainder of this chapter outlines a positive approach for planning and creating imitations—a formal strategy for *innovative imitation*.

For simplicity, let us assume that the genuinely new product an innovator issues turns out ultimately to be successful, following the more-or-less classic life-cycle curve depicted in Exhibit 1 on the next page. The product is issued at time point 0. Competitor X becomes quickly aware of its existence. Suppose also that competitor X has a requirement that unless the total market for a product in this price range can be expected to be at least 20,000 units per month, he will not attempt to enter the market. If it is 30,000 units, he views it as a highly attractive market.

When the innovation is first seen, the usual pattern in many competitor X firms—whose products require heavy capital expenditures and lots of reverse R & D money and time—is as follows:

At year 0 the decision-making authorities say, "I doubt that it will sell. We'll keep an eye on it." This is all that's done.

At year 1 (or—depending on the industry and situation—at, say, six months), the decision-making competitors may be a bit surprised that the product is still on the shelves. A typical comment at this point is, "Well, it's just hanging on, but not getting anywhere. I told you so."

At year 2 the story is likely to be, "They're getting a bit more business, but I hear company Y is going into it too. There won't be enough for both of them to share. They will go broke on this one."

At year 3 there is nervousness because the curve is definitely headed upward. The reaction is, "George, we'd better take a closer look at this. Get some of your people on it right away."

Somewhere between years 3 and 4, a massive crash program is started.

EXHIBIT 1   The Classic Product Life Cycle

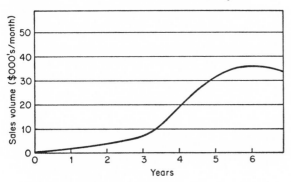

By year 5 company X gets on the market at about the same time as six other companies.

Looking back on what happened, company X, in effect, said at year 0 that the chances of success for this product were 0 percent. The judgment made by company X was zero probability in the sense that nothing was done in any positive way to get ready and launch an imitative product. It suffered from what may be called the "null hypothesis hindrance."

Had the estimated probabilities of success consciously been something above 0 percent, some imitative steps would have been called for, even if only tentative steps. But none were taken at this time, or at years 1 or 2. At each point, in terms of actions taken by company X, a zero probability was attached to the innovator's chances of success. Significantly, however, even though the company X decision makers had gotten exceedingly nervous by year 3, they again at that time said, in effect, that the success chances were still nil.

The reason we must say that company X gave a zero probability to the product's chances of success even in year 3, despite the obviously worried reaction of "George, we'd better take a closer look at this," is that no steps were taken to begin to tackle the most complex and lengthy job associated with imitation—reverse R & D. Nothing was initiated in the one area that would take the most time and most effort if the product were ever to be made. No bets were hedged because the implicit probabilities that were constantly being attached to the innovator's chances of success were still zero. The null hypothesis hindrance had full sway.

Probability Estimates

Actually, few people, deep down inside, are seldom sure of a genuinely new product's commercial fate. Nobody can ever be completely confident at the outset, or at year 1 or year 2, that a competitor's innovation will fail. Deep down there usually lurks some different and more realistic weighting of the probability of failure or success.

This attitude of doubt and tentativeness can and should be translated into sound business practice. There is a way. Suppose that for every genuinely new product issued by a major innovator in its field company X required its marketing vice-president to attach an honest and carefully thought-out coefficient to his estimate of its probable success—success by some measure of, say, unit sales volume. Hence he might in this case have come up with estimates of the chances of success at the successive intervals at which he was required to make a judgment, it would run like this:

```
First at year 0......... 5%
Then at year 1 ........ 10%
Then at year 2........ 15%
Finally at year 3....... 50%
```

Let us call each of these judgments a "success probability estimate" (SPE). Suppose now also that at year 0 the policy of company X was that the marketing vice-president must obtain a rough estimate of the reverse R & D costs involved in developing an effective imitation of the new product. Let us say, for simplicity, that the figure is $100,000, although the accompanying example applies as well for situations where it might be millions of dollars. A proper hedging policy in this case would be that at each interval during which an SPE of the competitor's new product is made, a reverse R & D appropriation is also made in proportion to that estimate (see Exhibit 2).

EXHIBIT 2   Schedule of Reverse R & D Appropriations

Year	Success probability estimate, %	Annual reverse R & D appropriation (based on $100,000 total)	Total appropriated to date
0	5	$ 5,000	$ 5,000
1	10	5,000	10,000
2	15	5,000	15,000
3	50	35,000	50,000

Thus by year 3 half of the required R & D money would have been appropriated, and some share of it would have been spent. While the economics of R & D do vary by industry and project—in some cases $5,000 could not even get a company started, so that perhaps although the year 0 SPE is 5 percent, the appropriation would have to be, say, $10,000—and while other problems would exist in specific cases, the strategy is clear. Namely, it makes a certain kind of good competitive sense to hedge one's bets, to buy at the outset an insurance policy against the success of your competitors' new activities. The face value and premiums of this policy represent an investment in reverse R & D that is designed to get an imitative product to market faster than it would get there otherwise. As time goes on, the face value and premiums would be revised year by year to reflect newly revised estimates of the likelihood of the innovator's success, and also the revised estimates of the imitator's R & D costs.

Imitator's Hedge

Let us call this "insurance program" the "imitator's hedge" (IH). If company X had had such a policy—in short, if its competitive strategies had included an IH—then, instead of getting to market belatedly in year 5, when the rate of market expansion had already slackened and when competition was severe and margins depressed, it would probably have reached market at year 4 and thus more quickly recovered its costs. Indeed, with such a clear-cut and definitive policy, the chances are that the whole process of auditing new products would have become so much more careful and sophisticated that the early signals of probable success or failure would have become much more obvious and meaningful. As a consequence, company X might very well have reached the market sometime in year 3.

There is obviously more to launching a complex (or, at least, a relatively high-technology) imitative product than reverse R & D. Dies must be prepared, plant has to be made available, and numerous other things need time, attention, and money. But the design and development process is often the most heavily time-consuming—particularly in industries where existing production lines can be modified and freed for products that have features similar to the new one's. For example, a plant that makes electric shavers has considerable adaptability to making electric toothbrushes. A plant that makes pneumatic control devices has some adaptability to making laboratory process pumps. But, in either case, there will be great problems and heavy time requirements other than those of reverse R & D. Implementing an IH policy is no simple task. Good intentions will not be good enough. Neither will penury.

It is precisely because the IH often involves so many problems and such vital time considerations that interested companies should seek out all possible ways of minimizing the problems and time inputs associated with a self-conscious program of competitive imitation. We are not talking about something theoretical or arcane. Increasingly in recent years, the military establishments of technically advanced nations have had programs of precisely this kind in their weapons planning and development. For them, a moment saved may be a nation saved. For business, a moment saved may spell many dollars earned. The dollars lost as the result of early support of reverse R & D on products that end up as market failures before the would-be imitator ever produces them will be no less uselessly "lost" than the dollars spent on other forms of insurance that every prudent company very sensibly buys.

The rate of genuine new-product introductions in some industries is obviously too great to justify their companies' installing the IH on each new product that comes along. On the other hand, not every company has ambitions to cover every product opportunity. Still, it is possible to be insurance-poor—to buy too many IHs. This therefore calls for the establishment of insurance criteria. It calls for criteria to select those new competitive products for which reverse R & D should be undertaken and those for which no R & D funds should be allocated. These criteria can take many forms—how close a new competitive product is to the various competences of your company, how near a substitute it is for one of your important products, how big its market potential is, how big development costs might be, how long it might take to achieve reasonable market acceptance, and so forth.

But another and different kind of criterion might usefully be attached to each of these. This might be a policy which says that, except in extreme cases of direct potential threat to one of your central, major products, your company will not, during any single year within the next five years, commit itself to new IHs whose combined first-year costs exceed Y. The company's total IH bill in any year could conceivably far exceed Y, but the aggregate of all new, first-year projects would not exceed Y.

Such a policy might then stipulate that the available Y be distributed among the proposals that score highest at year 0 on an estimated profitability formula that includes among its components each product's SPE. In the case of imitative products that are designed to prevent customers for existing products from switching to a competitor's new substitute, the formula would contain not only a profitability component but also one for "losses prevented." If all this results in the exclusion of projects for which strong IH program demands are being made, then this becomes an indication of the need to review the original criteria, the size of the company's total IH budget, or both, or the possibility that these projects are simply not worth what was claimed.

CONCLUSION

Innovation, new-product development, extending the lives and expanding the markets of existing products by adding new features, styles, packaging, or pricing—all these inexorably belong in the arsenal of devices by which a modern company competes. And innovation is an abundant commodity in our society. But it is probably less abundant than many of us assume. We often mistake innovation for what is really imitation—the large and highly visible outpouring of an imitative product that was genuinely new several years previously when a single innovator first launched it.

Simple arithmetic tells us that there is lots more imitation than innovation. At the beginning a genuinely new product, process, or service generally has only one innovator, but later there are hordes of imitators. No single company can be, or can prudently afford to be, as constant an innovator as it is compelled to be an imitator. And while there are great recognized risks to innovation, there is not today an equivalent recognition of the risks of tardy imitation. When a company comes to market with its imitation at about the same time as the rest of the imitative horde, the risk is great indeed.

Since we live in an age of such unquestioning and often very justified faith in the virtues of innovation, there can develop in the more committed companies a strongly one-sided system of rewards. Plaudits, Brownie points, and promotions go to the clearly innovative individuals—and rightly so. But it is well to be aware of the possible negative consequences. The most unhappily negative effect may be the creation of an environment in which people who frequently suggest imitative practices are viewed as being somehow inferior or less worthy. Taking their cues from the prevailing system of rewards, people may then systematically refrain from championing the imitative strategies upon whose early implementation the continued bread-and-butter success of their companies depends.

Hence an affirmative policy of supporting a strategy of imitation in some organized fashion would have the virtue not only of getting necessary imitative activities into motion early, but also of communicating to the entire organization that while innovators are valued, so are the creative imitators. It would legitimize systematic imitative thinking as much as the more glamorous innovative thinking.

It makes sense, therefore, to have just as clear and carefully developed a method of planning innovative imitation as of planning innovation itself. Such a policy may very well require the institution of the imitator's hedge —the IH factor in product policy.

This suggestion may sound strange and perhaps even vaguely academic to busy men of affairs. Yet it is useful to compare it with what we already do in related areas. Take the field of liability insurance. Its rationale and usefulness are taken for granted as sound practice in personal affairs and also in business. The IH is an insurance policy of similar rationale and usefulness, a policy that is conceptually no more unusual than the rationale of liability insurance. It is no more novel than the concept of budgeting for business success and control.

Perhaps it is an overstatement to say that innovation is the false messiah and a mistake to say that imitation is the new messiah. But to behave lopsidedly as if innovation *were* a messiah, and especially at the awful expense of a realistic appreciation of the fructifying power of more systematic imitation—that would be an even greater mistake.

The Limits of Marketing

Chapter Ten

A Marketing Matrix for a Balanced Business

A GREAT MANY MARKETING EXECUTIVES today are alert, hardhitting, and aggressive. Most of them will quickly admit they wish they got better results. They, like their company presidents above them and their sales managers below them, now fully accept the necessity of being "customer-oriented," not "product-oriented." They agree that the purpose of a business is first to create a customer and then to keep him.

Yet we often deny in deed what we affirm in speech. Robert W. Lear wrote ten years ago that there is "no easy road to market orientation."[1] The translation of that orientation into solidly productive action seems to be an even harder road. Slogans are not enough. They can actually be prophetically dangerous, deceiving their advocates and followers into believing they are doing what they are merely saying. Their companies will get beautifully commendatory headlines—for the resounding speeches of their presidents, for the well-publicized glitter of their marketing programs, for their fetching four-color ads in expensive media, and for their newly revised market-oriented organizational structures. But the narcissistic glare of all this lovely luster can hide an undetected cancer in a company's nerve center. It will confuse form with substance.

[1] Robert W. Lear, "No Easy Road to Market Orientation," *Harvard Business Review*, September–October, 1963, pp. 53–60.

Since so many companies have gotten the marketing message—the simple notion that distinguishes between the narrow nexus of selling and the broadly encompassing meaning of marketing—it may be time for them to take a carefully objective look at exactly where they stand in their efforts to implement the marketing concept. Are these companies merely verbal vigilantes, or are they solidly in the mainstream? The manager may ask himself: "Has our company—have I—done what we've preached? If some ultimate computerized arbiter were scoring us, what grade would we get? With rising profits today, but also with rising pressures and demands for high performance in every phase of the business *right now,* have we drifted away in fact from what we've been resolving in speeches? Have we gotten out of phase with our intentions?"

Grading Yourself

Perhaps fortunately, there is no ultimate computerized arbiter to score or grade us. But there is a way we can do it ourselves. Exhibit 1 is a simple mechanism for doing that job. With it we can grade ourselves not on our marketing orientations but, what is more important, on our actions. Indeed, it can help us grade many things, many people, many functions—a corporation's general posture and practices, a marketing vice president, a sales manager, a product manager, a salesman, a manufacturing vice president, a treasurer, or even a receptionist or telephone operator. And with a little imagination and effort it can even help us relate our grade to its potential profitability.

Exhibit 1 shows what may be called the "marketing matrix."[2] The horizontal scale measures an individual's or a company's concern for customers along a nine-point scale: 1 is the lowest ranking or grading it is possible to get; 9 is the highest. The most famous example of a 1 attitude toward customers is Henry Ford's tarnished declaration that people could have any color car they wanted as long as it was black. A 9 attitude might be illustrated by a salesman's telling a customer without qualification or other consideration, "Any size price cut a competitor can make, we'll make a better one." In short, the salesman wants to give the customer what he wants—regardless.

---

[2] The term "marketing matrix" was suggested to me by Mr. Donald G. Moore, then director of marketing, F. W. Means & Co., of Chicago, who developed it in considerable detail as an outgrowth of his exposure to R. R. Blake and Jane S. Mouton, *The Managerial Grid,* Gulf Publishing Company, Houston, 1964. I am happy to acknowledge Mr. Moore's development of the idea and am indebted to his many suggestions regarding its uses.

EXHIBIT 1   The Marketing Matrix

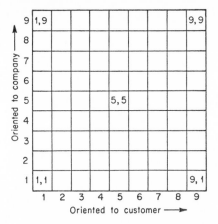

The vertical scale measures concern by the seller for his company or himself. The highest one-sided concern for the company would merit a 9 —for example, the scheduling of flights by an airline company in such a way as to avoid the expense of serving meals, an effective cost-reduction program that cuts customer service at the possible expense of continued customer patronage, a drive to raise return on net worth at the expense of developing programs to hold customers under increasingly more competitive conditions, or a market manager's proposal to reduce his product line drastically because competition in some of the products is making his life personally too difficult.

The lowest concern for the company rates a 1—the attitude that any sum of money should be spent to get the desired results, regardless of the fiscal consequences; that the customer should be given anything he wants; that a reorganization of the market department is necessary so that the new marketing vice-president can show that he's energetic and full of ideas, regardless of whether the company or department is ready for it.

Any company long-term policy, action, program, or attitude and any executive's or department's activities can be located in the matrix. Any given action gets a two-number score, one for the extent of concern for the customer which that action represents, and one for the extent of concern for the company or for the implementing executive. The lower right square is a 9,1—an activity, transaction, or attitude that manifests the highest possible concern for the customer but the lowest possible concern for the interests of the company involved in that transaction. A 1,9 manifests the lowest possible concern for the customer but the highest possible concern for the firm. Some possible examples of various ratings follow.

Location 9,1: High Customer, Low Company

1. Use the computer to optimize the customer's use of your product or service—probably raising his consumption with no possibility of future benefit to the seller.

2. Replace existing company-owned items from service (telephones, leased computers, leased uniforms) as soon as improvements are made, giving the customer the latest improved versions, regardless of the remaining life of the existing items or absence of competitive possibilities and without possible future benefit to the seller.

3. Never charge a lease customer for damages to your equipment, regardless of cost to you.

4. Don't hold the customer to his part of the bargain.

5. Drop everything to answer a customer request, regardless of other commitments.

6. Always keep plenty of extra clerks on the floor in your store in order to give each customer instant service.

7. Put warehouses in every city, town, and hamlet for instant delivery.

8. Produce and have available for quick delivery every possible variation of every product that might conceivably fit into your line, regardless of price and cost considerations.

9. Spend a fortune to study every aspect of a customer's needs and wants, and then promise and give him everything.

10. Show the customer that you are on his side by running down your plant and your management. Be his buddy and a big spender. That will solve everything.

Location 1,9: Low Customer, High Company

1. Set your prices on the basis of all the traffic will bear above your costs, regardless of customer-relations consequences.

2. Never tell a customer where he might get a substitute product that would really serve him better than yours.

3. Never try to develop or distribute substitute products for those you now handle (such as plastics for glass, aluminum for steel, nonwoven fabrics for paper, credit cards for checking accounts) if it costs money and is inconvenient.

4. Don't make direct deliveries, even when the customer is willing to pay the expense, if you have to go to the trouble of setting up a delivery system.

5. Have lots of fine-print protective clauses in all customer contracts so that you are sure to win all arguments, regardless of who is to blame.

6. Don't change your invoice dating terms just because the rest of the industry has changed.

7. In running sales meetings, always tell the gathered salesmen that the manufacturing plant is geared up to run at absolute full capacity and ready to roll. Then show your contempt of the customer by enjoining the salesmen to "go out and get the orders," making sure you enlist lots of aggressive, warlike phrases like "target the customer," "bang away at the market," "roll out the big guns," "march forward," and "now let's get out and fight."

8. As a company president, make sure all annual plans originate from the top down. Get the manufacturing department to decide what the maximum productive capacity is, or the financial department to decide what revenue is needed, and then tell the sales department to sell the output and deliver the cash.

9. As marketing vice-president, never require the sales organization to break down its sales forecasts by market segments or customer categories. Just look at the totals, and let the field organization assume responsibility for delivering it.

10. If you are a service organization, such as a bank, an insurance company, a public utility, a school, or a computer time-sharing firm, always keep the kind of hours that are convenient for your internal needs. Always be sure to overcome all customer objections to your limited hours by pointing to the "obvious" impossibility of accommodation. Never look for ways to adjust your system to the customer's requisites.

11. When a multidivision customer shifts to centralized purchasing, always hold out for your traditional decentralized way of selling. Don't adjust; it's too troublesome. Always look for ways to justify your *status quo*.

12. When launching a complex new product or material, always insist that the prospect take it "as is." Never try to tailor either the product or your traditional selling methods to his problems.

13. Always use lots of extra chrome and questionable doodads on your kitchen appliances so that they will stand out on the sales floor, even though these cause difficult cleaning and adjustment problems for the housewife.

14. As a television station, cram increasing numbers of commercials into the last hour of the "Late Show," after you've got the viewers hooked.

15. As a railroad, stick to standard–time schedules even though the customers have switched to daylight saving time.

16. As a restaurant operator, insist on seating your customers according to prearranged waitress stations, not according to customer preference.

17. Don't respond to a distant customer's request for technical assistance until you have enough requests from that location to make a trip "worthwhile."

18. Don't make the opening and reclosure features of your package more convenient to the customer if this would require changing your package design or your packaging equipment.

19. Don't list prices and discounts on the same catalog page as your product description. The distributors and customers may like it, but it creates a lot of problems when you want to change prices and terms.

20. Always show a picture of your plant or headquarters facade on your letterhead, preferably including a picture of the company founder, and never question how the customer reacts to all this.

21. Put lots of salt in the popcorn at your movie theater so that the viewers get up frequently to buy soft drinks and disturb other viewers.

22. Bind all the textbooks you publish in a single standard color so that you don't have to carry a wide color inventory and, as a consequence, so that you will communicate to students how seriously scholarly (and boring) books really are.

23. If you are in the petroleum refining and retail gasoline business, always fight local building codes so that your standard, historic, low-cost matchbox station design will be accepted for all types of neighborhoods.

24. If you run a multinational corporation, always compel your overseas distributors to report to you in English and in your standard domestic format.

25. In setting your company goals, always set the standard in terms of production volume, revenues, profits, and expanded stockholder equity. Never state them also in terms of market factors, customer need fulfillment, customer-service objectives, or market targets.

Location 1,1: Low Customer, Low Company

An executive functioning in this location might be indifferent, hostile, or just incompetent. A company operating in this corner *is* in a corner—suicidal, self-destructive, hopeless. The company may survive for a time by sheer power of product uniqueness or monopoly position. But it is not capable of long-term survival. Such a posture may work for a company that is organized for a one-shot, in-and-out purpose—a quick killing, after which it closes its doors forever.

Location 5,5: Medium Customer, Medium Company

This is the middle-of-the-road situation. Don't stick your neck out. Always let others do the innovating. At best, be a prudent innovator. Let "meeting competition" be your planning guide. Devote the bulk of your effort to prudential fire fighting. It is a sensible policy, but only if it is followed as a result of a conscious decision, not by accident as a result of drift and thoughtlessness.

Location 9,9: High Customer, High Company

A company that values long-term survival at a high level of expanding profits presumably aspires constantly to the 9,9 location in every aspect of its operation. Advocates of the marketing concept argue with conviction and considerable good sense that a company cannot be effectively marketing-oriented unless the marketing viewpoint infuses its every operation and sector. The manufacturing department may have to become more willing to accept shorter production runs and to customize its output to fit particular customer requests. Finance may have to become more willing to support product development expenditures even if the present line of products is perfectly serviceable. Engineering may have to become more willing to respond to marketing's needs for lower-priced, lower-quality products, even though this may offend the engineer's sense of workmanship and professionalism.

What are some of the operational and policy characteristics that would qualify a company for the ideal 9,9 position?

1. When you have a particular resource base (mineral deposits or a plant with a given productive competence or an established distribution network), you try to capitalize on that resource by:

    a. Studying consumer and customer needs for the purpose of seeing how the resource might be modified or augmented so that it would serve customers better.

    b. Expanding the range of services and benefits to customers so that what cannot easily or quickly be changed in, say, the basic material (e.g., steel, natural gas, automotive service stations) can at least be augmented by truly customer-benefiting peripheral services that make it easier and more beneficial for customers to do business with your firm in your industry.

2. Make tie-in arrangements with producers of other products and ser-

vices in order to provide your prospects with a completed system of benefits, one of which is your specialty. An example is airlines working with computer companies, telephone companies, and freight forwarders to help prospective shippers convert from regional warehousing to direct air cargo.

3. Augment your present generic product line (say, fertilizer raw materials such as phosphate, potash, and superphosphate that you sell to fertilizer mixers and packagers) by helping customers not only with technical services, but also with their forecasting problems, sales-territory planning, sales meetings, sales incentive programs, logistical planning, and even accounting and control problems.

4. Make all your corporate communications integrative, self-reinforcing, and centripetal[3] so that your company is always instantly and easily recognizable, whether it communicates by mail, mass-media advertising, the sign on its buildings, the design and color of its delivery trucks, its annual report, the salesmen's calling cards, its catalog, or its point-of-purchase materials. Hence, give yourself instant identity and, as a result, give the customer the opportunity for instant recognition of your firm.

5. Develop long-term (at least five-year) plans, based both on predictions of external events (competitive practices, customer values and habits, technological developments, government practices) and on assessments of your own internal corporate strengths and weaknesses (manpower, fiscal competence, manufacturing, distribution resources). These audits of the external and internal environments become the basis for determining adaptive changes that are needed to serve properly the existing markets, capitalize on or create new markets, phase out declining products, and provide for the fiscal and organizational resources necessary to do the needed jobs.

The 9,9 Imperative

An appropriate organizational slogan to qualify for a 9,9 ranking is the old but expressive one, "Find a need and fill it." "Find a need" refers to the customer, "and fill it" to the company. The need, of course, has to be a real one, and well understood by the company. Finding it should not consist in identifying things that people could, by hook or by crook, be talked into exchanging for their hard-earned cash. Rather, problem areas, inefficiencies, diluting factors, and opportunities for improving what is valu-

---

[3] See Theodore Levitt, *Innovation in Marketing,* McGraw-Hill Book Company, New York, 1962, chap. 11.

able to the customer should be identified. In the 9,9 location, not only is the need filled with a high degree of competence, but the competence itself derives from a genuine identification of the seller with his prospect's business and problems. The company makes maximum and efficient use of all its available resources, marshaling them expertly and enthusiastically (not grudgingly) for answering the particular customer need in question. And when the company cannot perform the required function efficiently, or cannot reasonably be expected to develop or help others organize the competence to fill it, either it must price its existing product or service at a level that will weaken, if not cancel, the customer need-satisfaction, or it must consciously sacrifice returns to stockholders and employees. Either of these compromises (cutting price or forgoing the business entirely) might disqualify the company from its 9,9 position. But that may not be altogether lamentable or wrong. All that really counts is that the disqualification is conscious and planned—the consequence of thoughtful decision instead of thoughtless drift.

To qualify for 9,9, there can be no captious compromise. Efficient and competent need filling is essential. In such a selling situation, price is only a secondary part of the consideration. What the seller should attempt to do for the customer would be so significant, in terms of the customer's own operation, that the latter could not afford to be without it. He would feel compelled to do business with that seller without feeling that he was trapped. He would feel compelled to deal with him because he offered the best bundle of value satisfactions.

To qualify for 9,9 can easily cause a company to change the entire character of its business. Indeed, the marketing view of the business process requires that a company organize itself to offer a line of products, product options, and service benefits that are dictated by the requisites of the market rather than the present competence or unbending inclinations of the company.

This uncompromising view of business life can make terrible and sometimes perhaps senseless demands on a company. But whether these demands will really be senseless in the long run depends on more than a quick visceral response to undigested and inadequately analyzed facts and trends. The unhappy fate of America's railroads—their loss of passenger business, their losses to trucks and airlines and pipelines—was not really inevitable, in spite of tight government controls and corporate charter limitations. Railroad companies could indeed have defined themselves as being in the transportation business rather than merely in the railroad business. And they could, in the early days, have gotten into pipelining, trucking, and airlines with a genuinely positive and customer-serving orientation. In short, they could have expanded their product line, the options they offered their customers, and the service mix associated with these operations. The constraints imposed on them by regulatory agencies were largely after-the-fact reactions against predatory maneuvers designed to destroy competing carriers.

To become a 9,9 company ineluctably requires a company to ask the ultimate question: What business are we in? Are we in railroading or transportation; in movies or entertainment; in the tool and die business or the parts fabrication and equipment business; in the linen supply business or the customer-support service business; in the computer business, the computer-assisted problem-solving business, or the data-processing business; in the banking business or the fiduciary management business; in the book business, the knowledge business, or the self-development business; in the publishing business or the information business; in the dry-cleaning business or the product renewal business; in the generator business or the energy business; in the sewer-pipe business or the disposal business; in the retailing business or show business?

To be preoccupied, therefore, with being a 9,9 marketing company is preeminently the preserve of the chief executive and the board of directors, and it is preeminently a preoccupation with the encompassing question of the nature and character of your business. That is why marketing is not just a business function, but a consolidating view of the entire business process. Marketing is not concerned with just the facile arts of promotion and selling, but perhaps more importantly with the involuted issues of corporate product policy—with what is to be offered for sale, with the kind of R & D that is to be emphasized so that the right products and the right services may become available for sale—with, in effect, what kind of company is being and should be created.

The marketing matrix is clearly only a device. There is nothing uniquely substantive about it. But it has certain simple virtues:

1. It structures a way of thinking about the corporate marketing effort that takes into account both company requisites and customer requisites.

2. It is a scaling device that provides a company with a benchmark for helping determine how far along the road it has gone toward achieving a proper balance between serving the customer and serving itself and how much remains for it yet to do.

3. Its use will compel a recognition of the fact that different people in a company and different departments have different kinds of responsibilities and different powers of control—some can best serve the corporate purpose by emphasizing cost control and other directly company-oriented

activities, and others by emphasizing sales expansion and directly customer-oriented activities. Seeing more clearly what a particular executive in a particular company can control and what he cannot control, what purpose he can best serve and what he cannot directly serve, makes it easier to judge his performance and easier to direct his efforts for the ultimate best long-term interests of his company.

4. It can be used to stimulate in each job within the organization, and especially at the higher levels, thinking about the appropriate mix in each job of concern for the customer and concern for the company. If the ultimate corporate slogan for a 9,9 operation is "Find a need and fill it," in a small company each key person is likely to be highly involved in both sides of this equation. But in the large company, specialization is inescapable. There will be need finders and need fillers. These will not be the same person. Corporate cupids must exist to make matches between them. Working with the marketing matrix can help individuals within the organization to find where they fit and why, as well as where the "other guy" fits. As a consequence of this structure, people may find that the other guy, who is often viewed as the enemy, may be working toward the same objective and in a not unreasonable, though quite different, manner.

5. Finally, the marketing matrix compels the chief executive to develop a clearer definition of what business his company is in and what directions it must take in product policy, in customer-service activities, in R & D, and in properly orienting the various functional groups and corporate personnel toward making the most meaningful contribution of which they are capable toward the corporation's overall purpose.

But while these are its obvious virtue, the marketing matrix has a powerful hidden virtue. That is its capacity to pinpoint the limits of the marketing concept. This vital and neglected matter is the subject of the next chapter.

Chapter Eleven

The Uses and Abuses of the Marketing Concept

THE MARKETING CONCEPT—the idea that the business of business is to create and keep a customer—is a magnificent idea without which no company can expect to realize its full potentials. It is the constantly expanding recognition of this fact that accounts for the marketing concept's growing popularity. More and more companies are trying it.

Unfortunately, more and more companies are also getting disillusioned, and for good reason. Something is going wrong. The evidence suggests lots of reasons. Two of them are particularly disturbing. The first is that in many cases where the marketing concept is newly inaugurated, there is more enthusiasm and more optimistic talk than there is systematic effort and solid intelligence. The second reason is that the idea has been aggressively oversold. It has promised more than it can deliver.

It is time for a new look at what marketing can and cannot do, what is reasonable for it to achieve and what is not.

The View of the Business Process

The marketing concept views marketing in a special way. Marketing is a business function, but that is not all. Marketing is a very special view of the business process. It views, to repeat, the business enterprise as an organized process designed to create and keep a customer.

Whether the business is on Main Street or on Wall Street, only the creation of a customer can qualify as a suitably actionable statement of the corporate purpose. If you don't create a customer and then continue doing things to re-create (keep) him, the business will fail. The Wall Street enclave of financial institutions most regularly seems to shun the thought of their being in the "marketing game." Yet there is no statement that men of Wall Street make and no action that they take which is not scrupulously directed toward getting customers—customers for an underwriting, customers for advisory services, customers for their trading departments, customers for their contacts and relationships. It is not just the broker in a spacious room full of desks and telephones who is a "customers' man"—it is the entire organization.

The marketing view of the business process means that marketing does more than simply push products and services. That is the primary preserve of selling. Marketing's job is more encompassing. Selling tries to get the customer to want what the company has. Marketing tries to get the company to have what the customer wants. Selling is therefore largely a one-way process—sending outward from the company the things it wants the customer to take. Marketing is a two-way process—sending backward to the company the facts of what the customer wants so that the company may develop and send out appropriate goods and services. In doing that, the company must of course do everything else regarding pricing, packaging, servicing, advising, and delivering that will most effectively balance both the customer's and the company's satisfactions.

This two-way process of mediating between the customer and the corporation clearly gets marketing involved in the most basic of all company questions: What will be its product-line strategy and, derivatively, what kind of company will that make it? If the marketing people learn that the customer would prefer plastic bottles to glass bottles or credit cards to checking accounts, properly responsive actions will greatly change the character of the responding companies.

Who Calls the Corporate Tune?

For marketing to be concerned and involved with these high-level and basic corporate matters seems inevitable and therefore appropriate. But does this automatically mean that the marketing department should also call the corporate tune on these matters—that marketing should have the central say as to whether the bank goes into credit cards or the glass company into plastics?

Marketing undoubtedly must have a say. But to suggest that, simply because it knows the market, it should have the most authoritative say about the company's reactions to the market—this is to go too far. Vigorous but naïve proponents of the marketing concept have gone so far as to suggest that the corporation president's major preoccupation and perhaps even competence should be in the marketing area. To such a formula or job description no knowledgeable man can comfortably subscribe.

Yet that is the job description that seems often implied by energetic devotees of the marketing concept. The resulting demands that the marketing concept has often tried to make on every aspect of some companies' activities have in many cases produced more resistance than results, more agonies than assets. The time has come for defining the limits of the marketing concept.

The frequent failure of enthusiastic corporation presidents and energetic marketing executives to appreciate the marketing concept's limits has led in recent years to a great deal of debilitating abrasiveness, to a lot of interpersonal and interdepartmental conflict, and to terrible troubles in companies where the marketing concept has been newly tried. In some companies there is constant suspicion; in a few cases there is open warfare between departments. In others there is disillusionment and waste—to the extent that the president has been forced to declare a moratorium on the marketing concept. In at least one large corporation the president has been forced to resign.

Promise versus Performance

While in many companies the marketing concept has yet to be recognized as a legitimate way of thinking about business affairs, it is unfortunately true that in many others its actual trial has produced an awful mess. The trouble stems in part from the marketing concept's having been aggressively oversold. In part it stems from an undiscriminating acceptance of a promised panacea—an instant remedy for old and complex maladies. In part it stems from a natural-enough human response—resistance and sabotage by men who see in the marketing concept a threat to what it has taken them years to master. Yet the central cause of trouble is the oversold condition of the marketing concept. It has promised more than it can deliver. In the process it has frightened some managers, alienated others, and disappointed the bosses.

To keep things from getting out of hand, dedicated advocates of the marketing concept must see that while it may be good for a company to be thoroughly marketing-oriented and try for a 9,9 on the marketing matrix, this may not be a good prescription for every department in that company, for every organizational level in that company, or for every individual in that company. As I shall show later, an uncompromising marketing orientation by everyone at all levels and at all times can badly damage a company. What may be good for the corporate goose may not be good for the corporate gander. A lot of a good thing is not always a good thing. Lots of milk may help a youngster grow to healthy maturity. Too much can drown him.

The marketing-oriented disposition that may be appropriate for a company or for its sales organization is seldom fully appropriate for its other departments or for all its employees. The aggressively probing posture of an army's armored division certainly will not be appropriate for the whole army or for its maintenance battalions. It may be good for a company to expand its total fixed assets while its manufacturing department is reducing its. It may similarly be good for a company to be marketing-oriented, but bad for its personnel department or its night watchman to be so oriented.

The complexion, style, and character of an organization are reflections of how its constituent departments and people operate and think. Yet while an organization is composed of its parts, it is more than those parts. Their individual operations and practices do not additively determine or describe the whole organization. A mob is something more than a hundred delinquents; yet the ideas and behavior of a few of its members can shape the mob's entire character.

To what extent should the marketing department's uncompromising dedication to the marketing concept be permitted to shape the corporate character, to call the corporate tune? Where the necessity for imposing limits has not been clearly understood and the marketing viewpoint has been given great corporate power, the marketing concept has sometimes been more of a liability than a liberator. In such cases it has tried with well-intentioned but wrongheaded aggressiveness to make all segments of a company as marketing-minded as the marketing department itself.

The Excesses of Advocacy

Unhappily, this effort has too often been made not by quietly reasoning men but by aggressively emotional men. After years of battle in which they have tried to achieve recognition for their ideas against the bovine density of obdurate colleagues, they are covered with scars. Too often these years have transformed them into excitable apostles who have become insensitive to the human problems of organizations. When they have finally gotten power, they have misused it, tried to move too fast, or at least promised too much. The net result has usually been disastrous. It is time to straighten out the mess, to draw the lines for some sort of productive accommodation between the claims of the marketing concept and the problems of the rest of the company.

Marketing men have to see that marketing has no automatic claim to superior virtue in the business organization. There are two sides to the marketing matrix, not one. It may be right to say that marketing is a consolidating view of the business process. But that is not the same as saying that marketing must therefore and in all cases have the last word. It is a question of balance: What is the proper balance between the demands of the manufacturing department and those of the marketing department? What is the proper balance between the demands of the marketing services department and those of the sales department, between the demands of the marketing vice-president and those of the regional sales manager, between the demands of the treasurer and those of the manager of distributor sales, between the demands of R & D and those of market development?

A Question of Balance

The manufacturing department obviously faces facts and constraints that are quite different from those which confront the marketing department. Every marketing effort to tailor products to customer needs imposes new costs and problems on manufacturing. The efficiency and cost standards against which manufacturing is rightly expected to operate can be seriously affected by the proliferating demands of marketing. To say that marketing should willy-nilly call the entire tune without regard to such costs is obviously nonsense. A company cannot for long be an exclusively 9,1 company (high customer, low company concern), nor can it for long be a 1,9 company. Not even the most one-sided marketing enthusiast would deny that. Unfortunately, such a denial does not always keep him from behaving as if he believed such a ridiculous proposition.

On the other hand, it may be perfectly appropriate for the manufacturing department to call the corporate tune by asserting the intolerability of the costs associated with trying to serve customers better via producing a larger variety of product models and options. Of course, it is true that "high costs" are often not simply fiscal. They can also be personal. The manufacturing department head's insistence on, say, running only one item of one model full blast may reflect not merely the fact that this is the way to achieve minimum unit cost, but also the fact that this results in minimum problems and agonies for him as a manager.

Beyond a point, further product-mix proliferation and further job-shop tailoring are excessively costly. The head of the manufacturing department is expected to do something more than simply produce what the market wants. He is also expected to operate efficiently and to advise the rest of the corporation as to what efficiency's limitations are. His first job is production efficiency, not marketing; getting the most from the least, not giving the most for the least. He knows as well as others that the product needs to find a solvent customer, and that some customers want turquoise cars, not just black ones. But in the end there also needs to be balance and accommodation. The question is: Balance of what, accommodation to what?

The answer is not as simple as it might seem. If it were, there would be less trouble than we see. To get at the root requires a brief departure to a more comprehensive subject—the matter of how one determines the corporate purpose.

The Meaninglessness of Profits

Balance and accommodation in a business organization cannot be achieved by a simplistic appeal to "efficiency" or "profits." The governing consideration is both more encompassing and more prescriptive. "Profit" is neither an encompassing nor a prescriptive statement of business purpose. Profit is merely the result or outcome of business activity. It says nothing about what the activity itself must be. To say that a business exists to produce profit for its owners offers no prescription regarding how to do it. Profits are a consequence of business action. They are not a guide to what that action should be. The only legitimate guide to action, a guide against which to balance and accommodate the inevitably conflicting requisites of the various functional entities within a large organization, is the *corporate purpose*—the goals and ends of the corporation and the strategies that have been devised to achieve them.

Profit cannot be a corporate goal. Indeed, properly viewed profit cannot even be treated as a consequence of business action. Profit is the requisite of corporate life, just as eating is the requisite of human life. Profit is the food without which corporate life cannot be sustained. Hence, to call profit the goal of the corporation is, operationally speaking, silly. It is like saying that the goal of human life is eating. Profit, like eating, is a requisite, not a purpose.

The goals and ends of the corporation cannot appropriately be decided by an operating department of that corporation or by the functional head of a department. The job belongs to the highest councils of the organization —ultimately, the board of directors. In any corporation of size and complexity, the directors will perform this job not by themselves but on the basis of the recommendations of the president and the executive committee. These latter will in turn depend heavily on the advice and recommendations of the corporation's full-time staff departments.

One of the distinctions of staff operations is their freedom from daily operating pressures. They can reflect on the world around them and think quietly about things that others are compelled constantly to do. The fact that others in their companies are compelled to act, not just to think, imposes on the staff the necessity to make the results of its work actionable, not just informative. When helping the president develop a statement of corporate goals and purposes, the staff cannot be permitted to forget that it should be in operational terms—terms that are actionable rather than merely descriptive, terms that show what responsible men must *do* rather than what philosophers believe. The actionable view of a business—any business—describes it as an instrument whose purpose is to create and keep a customer. To create a customer means doing those things which will make people or companies *want* to do business with your company rather than with your competitor. To keep a customer means doing those things which will make him *want* to continue doing business with you. Both situations cover a lot of ground, from pricing, to R & D, to industrial relations.

Unless it can create and keep a customer, a business cannot thrive or survive. While this customer-creating view of the business purpose clearly requires the commanding impact of a marketing viewpoint at the corporate top, it requires lots more besides. It requires the institutionalization of an unexpected paradox. Common sense and experience tell us what logic has only vaguely grasped, namely, that to be a thoroughly effective marketing-oriented company, no company can afford to be a wholly marketing-oriented company. It cannot and must not be uncompromisingly customer-sensitive in its every operational nook and cranny or at every level of its organizational structure. The governing irony is, as we shall see, that marketing orientation produces success only when it is held in check. Only in the countervailing presence of seemingly more parochial considerations can marketing achieve its ultimate aim of customer service.

We have suggested that an inescapable requisite of flourishing corporate survival is the necessity of a constant corporation orientation to the requisites of the marketplace. The very fact that we have defined an ideal corporate posture in marketing terms reflects a view of uniquely unabashed self-assurance regarding marketing's prior appropriateness in any realistic reflections on the corporate purpose. But it is a self-assurance with self-imposed standards of good sense. It intends the business organization to be viewed essentially as an institution pursuing its goals via the process of creating and delivering customer-satisfying goods and services.

To make this view fully effective as a guide to the actions of all sectors of a given company's operations requires a specific supporting statement about two things: (1) its proposed product-line policies and (2) its proposed competitive posture.

Product and Competitive Postures

Regarding product policies, does the company propose to serve all possible sectors of a market—such as the high-priced sectors as well as the low-priced sectors, the high-quality luxury sectors as well as the merely serviceable economy sectors, the small-market specialty sectors as well as the mass-market general sectors, the high-precision product sector or merely the serviceably accurate sector? Does it propose as much as possible to be a full-service company that provides all possible customer-service benefits with its products, or does it propose to be a Spartan, off-the-shelf supplier?

Regarding its competitive posture, does it propose to be a leader and innovator, or a follower and imitator; a company that generally looks to create newness and its own opportunities, or one that generally looks to capitalize on the newness and opportunities created by others?

One measure of the aboriginal state of the marketing arts is the almost automatic assumption in many quarters that when a company adopts the marketing concept it assumes commitment to offer a wide product line, to provide complete customer service, and to dedicate itself to creating resounding innovations. Nothing could be more wrong. Indeed, it is precisely this error which has contributed so much to the antagonism, misunderstanding, and intracorporate troubles to which I have alluded. The marketing view of the business process is consistent with almost any mix of corporate goals, product policies, and strategies. The marketing concept requires only that the best possible customer-oriented job be done consistent with the company's declared goals, policies, and strategies.

The problems that the actual or attempted introduction of the marketing concept has produced have been derived largely from a failure of companies to declare their goals and strategies in an appropriately functional fashion. Well-meaning, sometimes misguided, and often overzealous new marketing executives have been left by default to define implicitly a set of goals and strategies of which nobody else in the company was made explicitly aware, or indeed about which nobody seemed at the time to care. Precisely because no goals or strategies were stated a conflict of goals and strategies resulted. When different people in the same organization hear the sound of different drummers, we should not be surprised that they march in different directions. The result is centrifugal.

Coherence and Function

It need not be supposed that carefully developed and clearly stated corporate goals and strategies automatically produce coherence, harmony, and centripetal thrust. Our chauvinistic faith in the superior virtues of reason and in man's capacity for reasonableness need not be fetishized into blind disregard of our less noble tendencies. Truth has yet to demonstrate its widely declared capacity for making us free. And logic, though regularly celebrated for its cathartic capacity to liberate us from the tyranny of passion and thoughtlessness, has in the affairs of men and their organizations produced not much more than stentorian slogans of reassuring plausibility but operating impotence.

If a company is explicitly stated to be a full-service, full-product-line, innovative producer, the manufacturing department will be much less likely to resist customer-oriented, high-cost product-line proliferation than would otherwise be the case. Indeed, manufacturing's major effort is likely to be transformed from fighting proliferation to fighting for ways to proliferate more efficiently.

A remarkable example of this is the inexplicably uncelebrated feat of the American automobile industry during the 1960s. An extraordinary revolution has occurred in Detroit. It is a revolution that is constantly seen and widely experienced, and yet totally unappreciated and unheralded. It is more revolutionary perhaps than the original assembly line itself. The General Motors Corporation is typical. It produced eighty-one different models of cars in the 1957 model year. Within each of these models it offered a number of simple options—automatic or standard shift, four doors or two doors, convertible or hardtop, and choice of color, trim, and horsepower. By 1967, General Motors offered 177 models, and within each it offered now an almost limitless variety of options, from chartreuse bucket seats to built-in eight-track tape playback machines. While head of the Chevrolet Division, Edward Cole declared that with little extra effort and virtually no additional cost, each of the 2.1 million cars his division produced could have been in some aspect different from every other car.

Detroit is now capable of producing with remarkable ease a different car for virtually every wrinkle in the American personality. Moreover, a buyer can get his personally designed, specially equipped chariot delivered in only a few weeks and at a price that, for what he gets, is cheaper than ever.

The mighty colossus of the Detroit assembly line, the old symbolic whipping boy of technology's implacable pursuit of production efficiency at the expense of consumer choice and distinction, has organized the assembly line to produce both unlimited choice and extraordinary economy. The production engineers, the computer programmers, and the corporate controllers have by a mighty determination and with dazzling results combined their resources to show that product proliferation does not automatically equal cost proliferation. Instead of fighting proliferation with the simple logic that the more items of a kind you can produce, the more efficiently you can produce them, they have responded to the corporation's determination to serve the proliferating preferences of the public by developing ways to do the job efficiently and well.

The key to this achievement was not so much the skill of Detroit's engineers as it was the congruence of departmental goals within Detroit's gigantic corporations. Everybody worked diligently and enthusiastically to achieve the corporate objectives of serving every involved portion of a highly segmented market.

Goal Congruence

Where goal congruence is not automatic within an organization—as it seldom is, and has not always been in Detroit—conflict and inefficiency will prevail. In most large organizations characterized by a clear division of departmental functions and some operating autonomy, there will be conflict if there are not explicitly stated goals and strategies and where goal congruence is not automatic. Moreover, the conflict will intensify as the claims of conflicting departments are more vigorously advocated.

It is the special character of our times that the claims of the marketing department are the most vigorously and often the most uncompromisingly advocated. As a result, marketing today has often gotten itself into the position of creating more corporate troubles than solid sales. It has often caused trouble because it has insisted that the rest of the corporation do things that it has neither been in the habit of doing nor had any taste for doing. Thus it has wanted manufacturing to be marketing-oriented, not product-oriented; finance to be marketing-oriented, not money-oriented; R & D to be marketing-oriented, not engineering-oriented. In short, it has insisted that other departments make a major switch by behaving according to the code that governs its own special affairs. Too commonly, the result has been bitterness and conflict between departments.

To refer to interdepartmental conflict is to make a strong statement. "Conflict" is a word that is neither edifying in its implications nor descriptive of everyday life as we see it in the business organization. To use it in this setting is to invite suspicion regarding one's familiarity with what actually happens inside business and regarding his competence to prescribe for its well-being. It is more common to speak euphemistically of "differing viewpoints" and "unresolved issues." Society is more successful in civilizing its language than its deeds. To mute conflict in word is not to eliminate it in fact.

To appreciate the fact of the pervasiveness of conflict in the corporate organization one need only look at the enormous edifice of administrative machinery and surrounding euphemisms marshaled to get the corporate job done. What is the purpose of committees, policy memorandums, and the office copying machine if not to obtain interdepartmental and interoperational congruence—in a word, to meliorate conflict, or at least to prevent the further proliferation of incongruence and disparity?

The language we use often says more about what we actually do, feel, and fear than about what we openly admit. The approved language of organizational life turns naturally to such words as "agreement," "approval," "coordination," "accommodation," "resolution," "consistency," "harmony," "unity," and "consent," and to the conversion of the neutral noun "team" into a prescriptive organizational prefix or adjective—"teamwork" and "team effort." It is well to understand that each of these words implies the existence or the imminence of its opposite—disagreement, disapproval, inconsistency, unconformity, misunderstanding, incongruence, discord, dissension, opposition—in short, conflict. Since we are fated to live together, we have devised machinery and words to make the process as congenial as possible and to sound as smooth as pudding. Underlying it all is the natural prevalence of complicated competition in the organization.

The clear fact is that the word "conflict" is both more descriptive of what goes on and more divisive in its implications than the terms "unresolved issues" and "differences of viewpoints." Unrequited organizational conflict is infinitely more destructive of an organization's good health than any of us likes to admit. That is why we work so hard at inventing words to pretend it does not exist. But its existence persists and corrodes. The massed power of cunning competitors is not the only thing that kills.

Conflict is the pervasive condition of the animal world.[1] Man distinguishes himself from other animals by his capacity to mitigate if not always to eliminate this condition. He has even found a name for this capacity—"civilization," as if he had invented civilization and as if its invention were a sign of superior merit. That is why we refer to all other animals as being

---

[1] See Konrad Lorenz, *On Aggression*, Harcourt, Brace & World, Inc., New York, 1966.

of a "lower order." But civilization is not an invention. It is itself a condition of human life. Indeed, it is a necessary condition. Man requires society to create a man—to conceive a child. But to sustain man, civilization is needed. The infant must be nurtured into self-sufficiency via the inescapable unity of itself and its mother. Without some such relationship the helpless infant perishes.

Society and civilization are antecedent requisites of human life, not its purposeful inventions or accidental creations. Society and civilization are possible only with the prior existence of a high degree of goal congruence among men. At minimum, they are possible only with the help of some machinery or rules for achieving order and accommodation. That is what mores, culture, values, government, and the Ten Commandments are all about.

The marketing concept is closely related in origin and purpose to mores and the Ten Commandments, which represent an attempt to enforce civilization—i.e., goal congruence. The marketing concept is the civilizing consequence of the large business organization. It asserts a goal and advocates supporting strategies designed to consolidate a large organization behind a single purpose that is more meaningful and specific than the old idea of profits. The marketing concept could not have originated in the small, compact organization where there tends to be almost implicit and automatic coordination between the requisites of the market (the external environment) and the requisites of the company itself (the internal environment). The emergence of the marketing concept in the large corporation expresses that organization's need for a new way of finding order and achieving accommodation among the conflicting claimants to which it has given operating autonomy.

The Purposes of Functions

The large organization is distinguished from the small organization by facts more significant than size. The large business organization spawned the separation of business functions, such as manufacturing, finance, R & D, and law. It separated them because that is the only way it could manage its complex task. In the small organization a few intimates passing one another in the hall or plant several times a day can, almost on the run, make all the decisions or know all the facts needed to run the company. In the large organization this is impossible. Functions are the province of specialists, often geographically or organizationally quite remote from one another. Communication therefore becomes formalized, and consequently in important respects distorted. Putting things on paper clarifies but also obfuscates. Written communication makes things explicit but also makes them different. The mere fact that it is specialists who do the work creates a problem of translation—the language barrier of specialist jargons.

In the strict sense not even the upper-level bosses are generalists who speak a language common to everybody. The top general managers are themselves specialists in that they manage special or limited operations— say, manufacturing or the consumer-products division or the administrative department or the controller's office. Even the ultimate general manager, the chief executive officer, has the job description of a specialist, emphasizing perhaps long-term planning and capital decisions. He is not in charge of operations.

As a consequence of the almost inescapable necessity of specialization, and especially as enormous amounts of money become committed to specific specialized departments, each department is operated more in terms of the inner logic of its needs than in terms of the related needs of other departments. The treasurer's department will become more concerned with developing capital hurdle rates and holding, say, the manufacturing department to its particular rate than with helping it find ways to improve that rate. Manufacturing's preoccupation with its own operating efficiency will create a preference for long production runs that can greatly raise the distribution department's warehousing and inventory-carrying costs. Distribution, on the other hand, may resist small-order handling for the same reason that the manufacturing department wants a simple, long-production-run assembly line.

The fiscal leverage of long runs and large-volume warehouse takedowns will be highly persuasive in an organization characterized by heavy capital commitments. The result of all this is the creation within such companies of what we may characterize as product-oriented distortions. There develops a strong preference for doing things mainly in response to the internal demands or logic of the operation—cutting manufacturing costs, improving warehousing efficiency, reducing development expenses, and cutting package-size options. It is the unhappy competitive consequences of those distortions that produced the marketing concept—a return to the primeval idea that in the end you cannot sell what people will not buy, that the business firm exists to create and keep a customer.

But in order that the marketing concept might make its point against the entrenched positions of powerful functional forces in the organization, forces endowed with responsibility for great aggregates of capital and accustomed to an old and up-to-now apparently successful routine, it has often been sold in a way that has led to oversell. The result is that it has produced distortions of one kind while trying to correct those of another.

Goals Are Not Enough

It should not be supposed that a mere statement of corporate goals and strategies, no matter how carefully developed or systematically stated, will by itself produce harmony, coherence, or fully effective commitment. Goal congruence is an essential requisite to harmony and commitment, but it does not exhaust what needs to be done.

At least three facilitating conditions must be fulfilled:

1. There must be within the organization a full-time marketing vice-president. He must have an effective staff, and he must be a prudent, patient, skilled executive capable of obtaining the confidence of line sales management and of his corporate peers.

2. All levels of the organization must constantly be taught what in fact is the meaning and rationale of the marketing concept in respect to their particular functions.

3. The chief operating officer must constantly be helped to produce the right signals to the entire corporation regarding its continuing commitment to the marketing concept.

The head of the marketing organization must assume the responsibility for seeing that items 2 and 3 are carried out. He is the relevant center of energy on which everything else depends. His most critical task will be item 2—constantly helping others to understand the "what" and "why" of specific marketing-oriented activities and strategies: in short, helping people understand in meaningful detail how marketing-mindedness translates into specific activities in their particular shops.

Problems of Translation

The dimensions of this task are greater than is usually supposed. It has not been uncommon even for sympathetic sales managers, sympathetic manufacturing vice-presidents, and sympathetic treasurers to resist well-conceived and highly appropriate and promising marketing proposals and programs. The reason is that the rationale for these proposals and programs was not always communicated. Thus, one treasurer, as a member of his company's operating budget committee and charged with helping find ways to fight a profit squeeze, argued strongly against the establishment of a full-time retailing task force whose function was to provide free merchandising help to retailers. The marketing vice-president's theory was sound. It was that self-service retailing had led to an emphasis by many chains on opening new stores at the expense of better merchandising and controls in existing stores. The results were bad and worsening: frequent stockouts in the department carrying this company's products; shabby displays and seemingly shoddy products; and, due to a lack of better advice from experienced salespersons, frequent failure of interested customers to buy the products even though their interest was piqued.

The proposed task force was to create better displays and police them on a scheduled basis, develop attractive automatic merchandisers and informative point-of-sale self-help communicators for the customer, and constantly detail the stores for inventory checks and display correction. The marketing vice-president failed to get support for this costly but promising program. The basic reason was that he failed to educate the treasurer and the company president properly about the urgent need for his proposal, which he felt was so promising in its payout. He explained in detail what he was proposing, but he did not support that explanation with evidence of the retailers' willingness to accept help or with a pro forma payout of his scheme. The following year that company's chief competitor did exactly what had failed to pass the treasurer's strict surveillance. The competitor's market share rose nearly 30 percent in just over a year.

In another case, the marketing vice-president's proposed market-segment reorganization plan was rejected by the sales department. The plan called for rearranging sales territories primarily along customer rather than along geographic lines. The idea was to specialize the sales force in order that salesmen could provide their customers with more knowledgeable systems and applications help. The proposal would have created many transitionary problems for the sales organization. The sales manager's resistance to the proposal was not a matter of his being particularly stubborn, lazy, or insensitive. The trouble was that the marketing vice-president made neither a sufficiently careful nor a properly documented presentation about the increasingly specialized application needs of the market, nor did he suggest a method for dealing with the difficult transition period.

In both of these cases, the marketing vice-president and his staff committed the same inexplicable error: They tried to *sell* a program to their colleagues rather than trying to get them to want to *buy* a program. They violated their own first principle: Do those things which will make the customers *want* to do what you would like them to do. They did not properly educate their own organization about how the marketing concept translates into specific customer-getting activities. They then amplified the dissonance of this failure by failing themselves to do the kind of completed and responsible staff work that would have satisfied their peers that the programs were something more than costly and disruptive pie-in-the-sky gimmicks.

Good ideas are not enough. Neither is brute energy or enthusiasm. The chief marketing executive and his staff must be eternally sensitive to the central organizational fact of their existence, namely, that their presence is a constant threat to the autonomy of practically every other operating segment of the company. Nowhere is this more true than in companies in which the concept of a truly customer-minded marketing effort is newly launched. The threat will seem especially imminent in multiproduct, multidivision companies and in companies historically noted for their aggressive selling methods.

The Uneasy Road of Marketing

When the marketing concept is properly launched, there will be established a chief marketing executive at the headquarters level. The nature of the threat he will represent to others becomes enormously clear when we look at the prescription for the role of the marketing head as developed by Robert W. Lear while he was marketing vice-president of the Carborundum Company, a multiproduct, multidivision, technical products company:

> The key role in developing market-oriented plans, and in seeing that the plans are effectively carried out, must be played by the chief marketing executive. He and members of his staff must devise plans which have adequate promise of securing greater long-term sales and profits; they must do the bulk of convincing both top management and product division management that these plans are sound; they must be able to penetrate into the lower echelons of marketing management, both in divisional headquarters and in the field, and see that roadblocks to a successful conclusion are removed. If such results are to be forthcoming, the chief marketing executive must have at least equal rank with the operating division manager; because of his staff capacity, he may need even more rank to overcome line division insularity. And it almost goes without saying that he needs the complete support and backing of the company president.[2]

Lear's emphasis on "plans" and their origin means, for most companies, nothing if not a shift of power to a new and differently oriented center of organizational energy. But, as he also says:

> Perhaps one of the most dangerous pitfalls of the market-orientation approach is involved in the unwarranted assumption that an organizational reshuffling alone can and will produce results. If it involves the same old people and the same old procedures, not much of a change will occur. To a great extent, market orientation is a state of mind, a posture, an attitude. It requires aggressive policing and pursuit in fact as well as in theory.[3]

[2] Robert W. Lear, "No Easy Road to Market Orientation," *Harvard Business Review,* September–October, 1963, pp. 59–60.

[3] *Ibid.,* p. 59.

The "pursuit in fact" requires the planning and policing to which Lear refers. And plans, if they are to be useful and implementable blueprints for action and therefore provide something policeable, must be specific, detailed, and responsible. This requires a great deal of concentrated labor —no job for the dilettante or the verbal acrobat who equates the word with the deed. It is this descent from the lofty generalities of the new marketing rhetoric to the detailed operating specifics of responsible plans and programs that some advocates of the marketing concept apparently find difficult or distasteful. The result is that they either have very little to sell to the colleagues they seek to persuade, or are disinclined or unfit to make the effort to educate them properly about the merits of what they should buy.

Manufacturing versus Marketing

What the automotive industry's mass-production-minded manufacturing executives were able to accomplish in order to accommodate marketing requisites should be a profound lesson about what is possible—possible not only for manufacturing, but also for sales and all other corporate functions. But to say this is not to absolve marketing of the necessity of facing facts. Manufacturing and sales and administration cannot do just anything. It will not help to intone the cliché that "Where there's a will, there's a way." To have a will takes more than understanding the marketing concept. The man in charge of manufacturing also has a budget. The quarterly review to which he is subjected is more palpable to him than the company's customers. While a great deal more tailoring of products to the vast variety of customer wishes is possible within the implacably volume-oriented requisites of his plant than often seems possible at first glance, the manufacturing vice-president cannot be expected to embrace this possibility eagerly or without a fight. His job is to run an efficient plant. Unless there is a clear corporate statement regarding the market requisites against which this efficiency is to be attained, there is every reason for him to fight costly product-line proliferation.

Manufacturing represents a mission and a commitment. Its job is manufacturing, and doing it efficiently. The manufacturing vice-president knows things about manufacturing—its limitations, its powers, and its resources —that the marketing vice-president does not and need not know. The manufacturing chief's job is the management of machines, materials, and men. To be fully expert in that mission is to be less than fully expert in, say, marketing. To be expert in both is to be an expert in neither. His job is to be an advocate for the manufacturing process and viewpoint. He should appreciate and understand marketing, but should not be automatically or fully submissive to its every desire.

To proffer an opposite prescription would be to suggest a course that could lead to the most awful inefficiencies—inefficiencies that could ultimately hobble the marketing function itself. This is precisely what happened in one famous consumer packaged-goods firm. The president was so relentlessly intent on his marketing mission that he failed even to include his manufacturing vice-president on his top-level product planning committee. He felt, on the basis of his previous experience in another company, that manufacturing would always be disruptive, saying what could not be done rather than how to do what should be done. For awhile the manufacturing vice-president's loyalty and extraordinary ingenuity kept output coming and costs in reasonable line. But finally deliveries slowed down, quality became impaired, and costs ran wild. With operating margins deeply depressed, the huge advertising and promotion funds needed to continue the company's aggressively successful marketing activities dried up. Only when that happened—when the president faced the visible absence of the gross margins he needed most to pursue his single-minded marketing momentum—did he face the facts of manufacturing's claims.

Problems Inside Marketing

Just as the manufacturing head cannot possibly be a fully marketing-minded executive, neither can certain individuals within the marketing organization itself. A field sales manager has no control over product-line development, such as the marketing head does. He has a fixed line of products to sell, and he must sell them. Hence, he cannot fully tailor the product to the customer, except insofar as the product itself can be modified as a normal part of the company's activities. He can tailor the product to the customer by selecting from a given line, and under certain circumstances the right marketing orientation can indeed cause him to recommend the more suitable product of a competitor. Airlines do this regularly with commendable good cheer by recommending a competitive carrier to fit a customer's time constraints. Insofar as this is done, that is as marketing-minded as one might be able to get.

The business functional areas or operations over which an individual has been given control can limit both his power and his inclination to be fully marketing-minded. Within this marketing department only the marketing chief can achieve this eventuation. Only he is in a position effectively to influence the wide range of activities that marketing encompasses. His subordinates may argue for and help influence certain practices or product-line strategies; but once things are decided, they have no choice but to do what is decided, even if that means offering customers less than what they want or in a way that they do not prefer.

On the other hand, the marketing chief is in a position to decide what is to be done and what is to be offered. But clearly even his power is limited. The ultimate decisions are the chief executive's. Hence, only he can achieve the ultimate in marketing orientation. But it is precisely because only he has enough authority to be totally effective in his marketing orientation that he must limit the exercise of that authority. The reason is that his function transcends marketing. He must strike a proper balance between the wishes of the marketplace and the resources and objectives of the total corporation. Like many obvious truths, this one is often overlooked precisely because it is so obvious.

The Role of a Balance Wheel

Balance between the requisites of the various functional departments must be provided by the corporate balance wheel—the chief executive or his first lieutenant. He must decide on what is finally right in order to work toward the desired marketing posture. But he cannot be effective in that decision and he cannot get proper support and understanding for it unless all functional departments have indeed developed some capacity to appreciate that the corporation's ultimate mission is marketing—that its function is to create and keep a customer in a profitable fashion. Unless everyone fully appreciates this, and understands what this means in an operating sense, there will be a great deal of recrimination, hostility, and ineffectiveness.

The various parts of a large corporation are capable of a great deal more accommodation to the often difficult and troublesome things that effective market orientation generally requires. Unfortunately, this accommodation has not been facilitated by advocates of effective market orientation, who have too often insisted on too much from the rest of the corporation, while providing too little in the way of persuasive argument for doing it. Marketing does not exhaust business, even if the marketing view of the business process must in some way predominate.

The chief executive has the responsibility and the authority to strike the best balance between serving the market and serving the company's own need for operating efficiency. His insistence on efficiency at all points means that there will have to be compromises within the organization between the demands of marketing and those of everyone else. Otherwise, a company's vigorous quest to achieve a better marketing orientation can result in making customer-oriented demands on departments and individuals that they cannot and often should not meet. The result will be chaos and recrimination.

To avoid this, one of the essentials imposed upon a company that is determined to be more energetically marketing-oriented is a clearer definition than is customary of each department's, each individual's, and each operating level's functions and responsibilities within the company's declared intentions. Such definitions would describe what is reasonable to insist from everybody in order to achieve an optimum balance between customer-oriented effort and the constraints, needs, and policies of the company.

In recent years in Detroit this has meant that the design, product planning, and manufacturing departments have viewed their tasks as consisting chiefly of finding efficient mass-production ways of maximizing the number of options and features that marketing could offer the consumer. With that as a clear-cut objective and challenge, the usual strains between marketing and manufacturing have been greatly reduced. As everyone knows, the mere fact that manufacturing and marketing are both part of the same company is no automatic assurance that they work smoothly together. They may both be interested in maximizing the company's profits; but while marketing may be convinced that the best way is via greater product-line tailoring to customer wishes, manufacturing may view such activities as costly product-line proliferation that undermines profits. Only after a firm decision is made at the organization's summit that a certain range of product-line tailoring is to be sought will manufacturing and marketing stop bickering and start cooperating.

The Veil of Problems

The extent to which this kind of costly bickering exists is frequently hidden behind a veil of other problems. In one company the product development department habitually ran at least a year behind its scheduled completion of designs for new variations on existing products. Marketing constantly complained and constantly tried to get the product development department at the outset to make more realistic estimates about the length of the development period. But however much its original estimates were extended, it would still be late.

Careful study traced the delays in part to manufacturing. The latter was closely consulted about the production requisites of the proposed changes. No matter what the product development department did, manufacturing constantly suggested the necessity of modifying various components lest costs be too high, rejects too great, and maintenance too difficult. Fair enough. Unfortunately, manufacturing never suggested how the problems might be solved—only that they must be. Yet manufacturing knew more about how to solve them than product development did. While it offered no real assistance, it was adamant that things needed improvement. Delays followed delays, and the product development department was blamed. Manufacturing certainly should get some of the blame. But blame for what? Sabotage? No. Deliberate withholding of help? No. Things were both more innocent and more insidious. No help was given product development because that sort of cross-departmental cooperation was not contemplated in the company's decentralized way of doing things. Development was "their business," and "we've got our own problems." Besides, everybody knows that the longer it takes for development to finish its work, the fewer problems manufacturing will have later. It is a very sensible rationalization. Everybody works for the same company with presumably a single set of objectives, but nobody seems to be helping anybody else. The opposite is more descriptive. Best of all, nobody feels any guilt.

Statement of Product-line Strategy

The intercession of coordinating committees might help, but it would not be adequate. As long as each department hears the sound of a different drummer, each will march in a different direction. What is needed is a more explicit statement of the company's product-line strategy, with detailed supporting statements of what this means for each of the involved departments, functions, and at times even job titles. These statements would then give the appropriate superiors in each case a reasonbly explicit standard against which to judge the performance of subordinates. In the case just cited, the cause of the trouble was that each department head had set his own standards and goals. Each wanted to do what was "right," but his "right," unfortunately, was not the same as somebody else's, even though they were all paid by the same company. If manufacturing has the implicit standard of doing almost anything to keep its operating costs and its management problems at a minimum, then it may indeed engage in unconscious sabotage of marketing's implicit standard of offering the market the widest possible selection of products. And if marketing has this as its major standard, it may insist on practices that unconsciously sabotage the company's budgets by insisting too uncritically that there is no choice but "to do what the marketplace demands."

No department in any company can be permitted to have its way at all times against the claims of other departments. One of the ironies of the marketing concept is that while it argues in favor of the uncompromising need of companies to be marketing-oriented, the excessive assertion of that orientation is capable of doing as much damage as the insular product orientation it is generally trying to replace. On major matters such as product-line policy and marketing budgets, the chief executive will have to make decisions and take actions that keep the marketing concept from running wild. A reasonably clear and regularly reviewed statement of the company's product strategies and market goals is an essential first step. It will help prevent the president from being confronted with the necessity of making decisions that might otherwise be made at lower levels, and it will prevent his decisions on these matters from appearing arbitrary and capricious.

Strategies for Marketing Restraint

On less global matters within the marketing department itself, the chief marketing executive will likewise have to set standards and make decisions to keep the marketing concept from running wild there. Such action will have the further virtue of preventing the marketing concept from making demands on various members of the marketing organization that they cannot possibly meet.

For example, the salesman of a company that produces only polyethylene resin cannot properly serve a customer where analysis shows that polyvinyl chloride is best for him. The company's limited line limits the salesman's capacity to fulfill the marketing concept's injunction that you provide the customer with what he really needs—what is best for him. A properly trained salesman will point out to his company that such situations are occurring with an increasing frequency, which suggests that it ought to consider broadening its line. Still, it is his job to sell as much as he can, not cling to every possible fragile excuse for not being able to sell what he has. It is therefore the responsibility of the marketing chief to train the salesman to handle this situation such that the salesman may tell the customer: "What I have really doesn't suit your needs. You might try the XYZ Company for it. I can give you the name of a man there to call, and I am sure he will help you out. On the other hand, have you considered altering your product to use our polyethylene? There are some real advantages. Let me show you and explain what is involved, how you will benefit in the marketplace, and what both the equipment cost and material cost differences will be. . . . Those, in summary, are the alternatives. Of course, you should do what's best for your business. We will be more than glad to work with you on your product design and equipment planning. We believe there is an honest argument in favor of our material, or else we would, I am sure, · be offering other materials as well. . . ."

With this approach, the salesman will have done everything he is empowered to do. He can go no further, to help either the customer or his company. He will have achieved an optimum balance of sound marketing orientation and proper concern for the health of the company he represents.

The marketing concept deserves all the attention and plaudits it has gotten. Unhappily, it also deserves many of the troubles it has generated. Some of these are the normal troubles and agonies of change. Some are the fruits of oversell, mismanagement, irresponsibility, and sloppiness. Good intentions are not enough to improve the situation. Neither is energy, commitment, or even being right. It takes care, patience, restraint, education, completed staff work, and now, more important than all, an honest effort to appreciate the limits of the marketing concept.

Looking Ahead

Chapter Twelve

Trends Without a Future

NOTHING CONCERNS THE business manager so much as the future. That's what all his decisions are about, and never about anything else. In a world that seems in such constantly monumental turmoil, it is not surprising that so many business magazines and convention speeches attend so constantly on the future—what lies ahead.

Unfortunately, almost everything being said and written is wrong—or, at least, badly misleading.

Activity is mistaken for change. Incidents are misinterpreted as trends. Change in a few visible things is rhetorically magnified into the appearance of massive transformations in all things. The future in all things is falsely projected as the linear extrapolation of the present in some things.

Business decisions are inescapably about the future—the past is gone and done with; the present is here and irrevocable. Understandably, decision makers are eager consumers of every futuristic pronouncement that fills the air. They cannot afford not to listen, lest they miss what might hurt them or an opportunity that might help them.

Before the business manager's eager consumership of the futurist's plausible predictions gets him into trouble, he might profitably apply some skeptical consumerism to these blandishing pronouncements.

Every prediction's plausibility resides in its listener's concurrence about

something that already exists. The predicted exhaustion of natural resources resides in the fact of our currently rising consumption and the
plausible assumption of their limited supply. The predicted decline of
assembly-line discipline and productivity resides in the publicized discontent of youthful workers on the most advanced of all assembly lines, the
Vega plant at Lordstown. The decline of the so-called "work ethic" resides
in the loud and visible presence of so many youthful dropouts. The futuristic dominance of the managerial sciences in business resides in the expanding presence of so many of its advocates in the nation's business
schools and business professional journals. Predicted new markets in educational technology, pollution control, in-home shopping via interactive
CATV hookups, skyrocketing leisure markets, huge new service industries,
drastically shorter discretionary work weeks, enormous quantities of female
employees working on par everywhere with men, huge new opportunities
in mass urban transportation—all these and many more that fill the air
with urgent warnings and titillating promises for executives told to make
decisions now before it is too late reside in some currently existing conditions or events.

But before any decisions are made, let alone the wrong ones, it is well
to consider some other facts. First, in the social universe, the future does
not necessarily reside in the present, as in the organic universe. In the
organic universe, change is generally concomitant with the passage of
time. As time passes, a small cabbage will, more or less predictably, become a large cabbage. In the social universe, a small event seldom pres-
ages a predictably larger occurrence. Riots seldom become civil wars. A
period of escalating criminality seldom turns in time into all-out anarchy.
The granting of women's suffrage fifty years ago has produced few con-
gresswomen, and there is today not a single female U.S. senator, and no
woman has yet been a seriously considered candidate for a major party's
presidential nomination. Televised baseball has not curtailed live attendance—in fact, the opposite has happened, with both the leagues and the
ball parks expanded. So also with football, basketball, and hockey. Nor
has television killed the movies, though it killed some of the old movie
companies which refused to make the relatively minor adaptations which the
situation called for. Neither the rise of industrial unionism nor the increasing governmentalization of business affairs in the 1930s has visibly impaired the private enterprise system's capacity to manage its affairs, to
grow, or to prosper. And our children, about whose lethargy, passivity,
and lack of interest in the world around them we agonized so much as
they lay stupefied and transfixed in front of the television tube in the 1950s
(one of the most avidly bought books of the time, Rudolph Flesch's *Why*

Johnny Can't Read, was a sign of our desperate worries about their future)—these are the same children who ten years later made riots at the political conventions in Chicago and Miami and revolutions on our campuses. Meanwhile, President Nixon was elected in 1968 on a platform of vigorous anticommunism, fiscal integrity, decentralization of government, and getting government out of business. In less than four years he was ceremoniously drinking tea in Peking and vodka in Moscow, was running the largest federal deficit in the nation's history, had centralized the federal machinery into the White House as no other President ever had, and had become the first U.S. President ever to impose peacetime wage and price controls.

Nor is it simply in social and cultural matters that prediction is so fragile and experts are so quickly defrocked by events. In 1953, to commemorate the fiftieth anniversary of man's first heavier-than-air flight by the Wright brothers, the prestigious *Aeronautical Engineering Review* did the obligatory thing: it published a Fiftieth Anniversary issue. Half was dedicated to a nostalgic review of the past fifty years; the other half consisted of articles looking toward the next fifty years. Contributors were the crème de la crème of the aeronautical profession, men like Willie Ley and Wernher von Braun. The future of air travel was seen by these celebrated experts working on the very frontier of aeronautics as remarkably limited: nothing about intercontinental ballistic missiles, nothing about space travel. Rocketry was nimbly projected as consisting of winged atmospheric missiles, as they had been when von Braun's U-2s tried to annihilate London in 1941. Four years after the 1953 predictions, suddenly there was Sputnik—and a new era. The ultimate irony is that the *Aeronautical Engineering Review* no longer exists. It has been transmogrified into *Aeronautics and Astronautics.* One wonders what name and emphasis will follow its next unreliable predictions.

And who would have predicted that affluent, liberal 1973 would witness an explosive national nostalgia for the fashions, cars, movies, music, and radio programs of depression-ridden, racist, dark, hopeless, and catastrophic 1933?

And what of the somber, catastrophic warnings in *The Limits of Growth,* the Club of Rome's project published under the leadership of Dennis Meadows? The elegant hysteria of this computerized projection of a people-crowded world of depleted natural resources seems at first irrefutable. What it does not consider, as linear projectionists rarely do, is the possibility of alternatives. For example, geothermal energy is available, for all practical purposes, in unlimited quantities, and it is more than a theoretical availability. With that it is possible through hydrocarbonization to create any mineral in any quantity man might wish. But when presented with that suggestion, one Nobel Prize scientist responded: "True, but geothermal energy will be too expensive." Thus the physical scientist set himself up as a prescriptive social scientist telling the world it could never afford what is necessary for its survival.

The engineer seems no more reliable than the economist or sociologist or, for that matter, the business executive, in advising the world where the world is headed. The slightest bit of sensible review of history tells us that the world does not move on perfectly parallel railroad tracks laid down by rational social engineers.

Before we fall into fiscal error on the admonitory advice of fluent prophets, it is well to ask each time, "What conditions have to be fulfilled for the predicted events to happen?" What else must happen first? What immemorial social codes must change; what historically abiding business practices have to be abandoned; what ancient human prejudices, habits, tastes, folklores, and dogmas have to be dropped, or modified, and by how much? What intervening compromises and adjustments are possible and likely? What, indeed, is not changing? Is what we see change or merely activity? Boiling water in a sealed kettle is full of activity but little change, and such change as exists precipitates in time back from steam to water.

Have fluent futurologists who depend so much for their high-priced popularity on a lively imagination and a facile command of the active verb mistaken activity for change, incidents for trends; confused the passage of time with the march of events? Indeed, how much certifiable change is there, or has there ever been? Do the ancient mythical Greek tragedies tell us anything different about man than the real tragedies of today? Did imperial Caesar, without the benefit of computers and management scientists, govern differently or less well than do the industrial Caesars of today? Were ancient, pastoral Sodom and Gomorrah essentially any different in their fundamental mores and maneuvers than modern, industrial Siberia and Gotham? Did people then respond to different incentives, march to different drummers, harbor different ambitions, pursue different sexual prey?

Or do learning, education, and science make all that much difference? The Western world has alive today more scientists than have died altogether in man's previous history. Yet we witness today an enormous recrudescence of mysticism, astrology, tarot cards, Jesus freaks, Hari Krishnas, and witchcraft. We live in the so-called "technocratic age," yet multiplying in open abundance are back-to-nature communes living stoically (and, I will predict, temporarily) off the barren land inadequately replenished from season to season with nature's own recycled, biodegradable materials.

We see everywhere around us the simultaneous abundance of opposite and opposing conditions, coexisting without competing. Even a brief list is long:

1. Frozen prepared foods, and elaborate from-scratch cooking, complete with exotic herbs, condiments, and the televised and published advice of Julia Child.

2. Two- and three-car families, plus ecologically benign bicycles for husband and wife.

3. Booming spectator sports, and booming participation sports.

4. Romantic and lyrical folk music, plus raucous and cynical rock.

5. Popular revival of classical baroque music (Vivaldi and Telemann), plus the growing popularity of the twelve-tone atonality of Stravinsky and Schönberg.

6. The familiar poetic lyricism of John Betjeman versus the jarring strangeness of Allen Ginsberg.

7. Miniskirts versus jeans, and sleek Pucci gowns versus full peasant patch dresses.

8. Full-shouldered, heavily textured, tailored Edwardian suits versus colorfully casual body shirts and slacks.

9. Computerized scientific management versus entrepreneurial venture teams.

10. Mass-merchandizing discount stores side by side with full-markup specialty boutiques.

11. Simultaneous booms in contemporary and antique furniture.

12. Mass production by thousands of workers in factories, and personalized production by individual artisans in craft shops.

13. Passive, indulgent vacations in luxurious seaside hotels, and actively dangerous trips down the rapids of the Colorado River.

We see over the course of many years not only an enormous persistence of fundamental styles of social behavior and practical practice, not only the quick denial of predictions recently made and early frustration of hopes lately entertained, but also the simultaneous existence against all popular logic of profoundly opposite conditions at precisely the same time.

But it is not surprising that so many opposites thrive so abundantly—that events do not, as professional predictors would have us believe so often, move undeviatingly in any clear direction. Since the beginning of man, man has known, feared, and celebrated the simultaneous presence of opposing forces in his environment and the erratic conditions of his existence.

In the beginning there was darkness and light, good and evil. Both concepts are firmly enshrined in the sacred literature of all religions and folk history. The prevalence of competing opposites is a persisting theme in man's history: God has Lucifer, Odysseus had the Cyclops, Jesus had Judas, Othello had Iago, Jefferson had Hamilton, Lenin had Stalin, the id has its ego, and man's rational component has its contending aesthetic component.

It is not necessary to understand exactly why so many opposites have always thrived simultaneously, or why so many seemingly vigorous incidents have failed to mature into trends, why so much of what concerns us the most is so temporary, and why, indeed, we appreciate so little what is abiding. It is only necessary to know that these are the historic facts— necessary that the manager brings some perspective to the events he witnesses and the advice he receives.

Yet to have some modest understanding about these conditions makes perspective more meaningful and its utilization more reassuring. It helps answer the question we have asked before: What conditions have to be fulfilled for certain forecasts to come true?

Let us seek some understanding by looking at several areas in modern life that have been particularly popular subjects of business prediction: the future markets for leisure, housing, education, and pollution control.

The Illusory Leisure Market

Few things in recent years have been more confidently hailed than the magnificent opportunities offered by the so-called "leisure market." To repeat the ecstatic hyperboles would be to commit a major redundancy.

It is true that sales of skis, boats, and Coleman heaters are in unprecedented ascendance. But whether it is because of leisure or of affluence is another question. It is a highly relevant question. Its attribution to leisure is generally accompanied by expansive forecasts of expanding leisure for our population. More leisure (defined as time uncommitted to obligatory work) is generally assumed to mean more free time, and more free time means bigger markets. Yet the facts are contradictory.

In 1973 the U.S. working population actually had substantially *less* leisure than in 1939, and even less free time. In 1939 the average U.S. factory worker spent 37.7 hours at his job each week. In 1973 he spent 40.6 hours. Yet, in 1939 we were still in a deep depression, with nearly 12 million willing and able men walking the streets searching for non-existent jobs. Those with jobs clung to their meager savings against the possibility they would have no job next week. In 1973 they had jobs; and instead of working a partial week, they worked overtime. They had less leisure, but they spent more money and more time on leisure activities. To be sure, in 1973 they had more paid vacation time. But if it were paid-vacation leisure time on which the so-called leisure industry had to depend for its prosperity, it would limp along no better than the pencil business.

More leisure does not automatically mean more free time. The 40-hour week of 1973 actually leaves less time than the 40-hour week of 1940. Where in the bad old days it took a steelworker five minutes to walk to work, or fifteen minutes on a streetcar, it now takes him a half-hour on a clear day driving a late model car on a superhighway. Even with freeways to speed the worker along his urban path, for the next ten years any reduction in the work week is likely to be more than consumed by the lengthening of the commuting time, even if more plants and offices move to the suburbs.

Even when there is more leisure and a briefer commute, whether there will in the foreseeable future be more time is sufficiently questionable to require serious attention. What counts is not absolute time, but discretionary time. The relevant question is: How much time will be left over to consume all the splendidly expanding artifacts of business's fertile imagination?

The answer requires a look at how man becomes acculturated. When in his less affluent years he bought a bottle of whiskey on rare ceremonial occasions such as New Year's Eve or weddings, a Saturday night blast was a special indulgence. When he finally reached the stage of buying a bottle cyclically every Saturday night, the weekday drink became the indulgence. When the weekday before-supper drink finally became a regularity, it became viewed as a civilized necessity. Drinking ceased to be discretionary. It was obligatory—a routine style of life, like three meals a day. New styles of life tend quickly to become habitual. Consumption patterns that at first seem indulgent and discretionary tend in time to become routine and necessary. Once patterns develop and commitments get made, the so-called leisure (nonworking) hours into which they are fitted are no longer so easily part of the available time.

More so-called leisure-time products and services will indeed be demanded in the years ahead; but it is affluence, not leisure, that will produce most of the demand. Yet the extent of affluence is itself a weak predictor of the style of leisure life.

Income Levels Deceptive

Consider today's Detroit auto worker who earns $9,500 a year and whose working wife brings home another $5,000. This family income of $14,500 is well above that of the new M.I.T. graduate with an M.S. degree in electrical engineering. The traditional taxonomy places both families in the upper middle class. But in operative, consuming terms, the taxonomy fails to fit.

The Detroit family actually belongs in a new and perhaps anomalous category: the overachieving working class. Its income qualifies it for inclusion in *Time* magazine's high-income subscriber list. Yet its consumption style hardly makes it an attractive audience for *Time's* Literary Guild book advertisements. In its buying habits it will be more like other $9,500 Detroit auto worker families than like young $14,500 Bloomfield Hills auto executive families. It will spend less on gin and more on bread, more on bowling and less on entertaining, less on clothing and more on credit. Yet, according to the Conference Board, half the U.S. families with $10,000 to $15,000 income owe this status to working wives.

Just as income is not a functional guide to the pattern of consumption, so any reduction in the length of enforced on-the-premises work time is not a functional guide to the availability of discretionary time. As man gets more liberated from on-the-job obligations, he creates for himself new off-the-job obligations. For instance, one reason for the reduction in the formal work-week is improved productivity, based on increased knowledge, but to keep up with the advancing knowledge a man must spend increasing time in off-the-job study.

Thus it is probable that the demands on a person's off-the-job time will accelerate more rapidly than the expansion of the time itself. Time that is not consumed by the necessities of study and of keeping up with the new uses of knowledge will rapidly be consumed by commitments modern man makes to other patterns of time usage, such as new recreation patterns and social service programs. What remains for discretionary distribution among other goods and services is not likely to produce some of the magnitudinous leisure-time consumption booms that are so confidently predicted. It is not time, but life-style preferences and income that the so-called leisure boom is all about.

But not even money alone is a sufficient explanation for the obvious boom in certain leisure products. Why, for example, do people spend money on skis, golf, sailboats, camping equipment, sports cars, do-it-yourself workshops, oil paintings, Hawaiian vacations, and trips to Europe? Why not more on better home furnishings, tithes to the church, or dinner parties at home?

A clue comes from the character of the booming leisure-time activities themselves. They have one thing in common: they are activities possessed of a highly individualistic, personal, nongroup character. The skier, the golfer, and the painter are each engaged in a solitary activity whose credit for mastery will be uncontestably his own, unshared by others, and not lost deep in the bowels of some cooperating task force or team. The husband who produces a lamp in his basement workshop will have engaged in an act of creation that is unquestionably his own personal achievement, just as the wife with her cookbooks, herbs, and condiments produces a gourmet meal that is her own personal output, not that of some factory kitchen in Minneapolis. Indeed, often now these stereotyped roles are reversed.

Today's discretionary market is selectively engaged in activities that may be characterized as representing a silent revolt against, or at least an escape from, the organized, structured, mass-production quality of modern life. It is an act of self-assertion in a world of group assertiveness, of trying to find personal distinction in a homogenized environment, of testing and demonstrating one's own private powers of mastery in a visible way in order to offset the dissatisfactions of a life where one's personal contributions are never fully measured and are generally hidden deep inside some committee, task force, assembly line, laboratory, or other essentially group effort. Seldom in his daily job does anyone ever do a complete job of anything all by himself. Seldom does anybody do all the things himself that need to be done to start and finish a job. Gone is the age of the master craftsman, the solitary inventor, the executive who carries all his facts and tools in his hat. In today's advanced societies, the individual increasingly sacrifices his personal identity to the machinery of a system. And it works uncommonly well. Yet it is a system whose confinements and rules are oppressively demanding. Work starts at 8:30, not 8:35, because 8:30 is when the assembly line starts running, when the task force meets, when the boss starts dictating, when the time-shared computer becomes available. Lunch is equally tightly programmed, down to a specific reservation at the Pinnacle Club. Airplane schedules are fixed, and vacations are programmed and coordinated months in advance.

Nor does life at home escape this benign regimentation. Man's home has ceased to be his castle. It is an extension of his attachment to the economic machine. Breakfast is programmed to fit the school and commuting schedule; dinner is squeezed between the hurried daytime schedule and the punctual appearance of Walter Cronkite at dusk; weekends become an elaborate linear program to optimize the benefits of the competing claimants for the family car or cars; an accommodating mealtime is scheduled for a family whose members are each programmed into a separate series of obligations, duties, and escapes. Even God's work must be planned to fit a highly institutionalized Sunday routine lest congestion in the parking lot deprive Him of communicants and contributors.

Everywhere that modern man turns, he is the captive of rules, clocks, schedules, traffic lights, confining customs, and rigid routines of other people's demonic making. Not even the president of a large corporation or nation can escape; perhaps he especially cannot.

All this helps explain why modern adults are so agitated about hippies and the life styles of their rebellious children. By all external evidence, adults are worried because their children seem to reject the customs, norms, morality, values, and routines of an orderly adult world. Yet in actuality it is not order, routine, custom, or morality that the adults want to preserve. Their real problem is that they envy their children's easy escape from these confinements. They are reacting against the rebellion of their children, and of all others whom their children admire, because others are achieving a degree of envied freedom without seeming to have earned it, while hardworking adults who believe themselves to have earned it see themselves unfairly deprived by comparison. Hence the "young" are seen as having "no right" to rebel against, or legitimately comment on, a world others work so hard to keep intact. The children don't really understand the adult world, and hence the adult trauma, because they have neither fully experienced nor tried seriously to work with the demanding adult world.

No matter how solemnly he explains or rationalizes his opposition to what he sees in the younger generation, the adult is actually engaged in a love-hate dialectic. He loves the idea of freedom, irresponsibility, and the looseness he sees in the young, but he actually hates the young for their unearned and enthusiastic access to these amenities. The world has been set on its head. The "kids" unjustly get the just desserts of which he is deprived.

This also explains why today's parents are so particularly upset with some of the ideas and opinions their children bring home from college. The children often question the absolute legitimacy or total utility of what the adult world does and values, a world no individual adult sees himself as having made or seems himself capable of escaping. Youth not only questions the legitimacy of this world, and questions it with self-assured Christian self-righteousness, but then disappears happily at night to play with magnificent abandon at the Psychedelic Circus. On weekends they're off to the beach, the slopes, and other master symbols of sybaritic freedom. The abandoned parents, having worked so diligently to make it all possible, reap nothing but scorn and the compelling necessity to keep the machine going.

Youth is "free" because it is not yet totally enmeshed in the modern machine. Its every deed and word of unrestrained freedom rudely remind the parent, as nothing else can, of his own comparative captivity. In part to prevent this constant reminder, the parent, who has sent the child to college to be educated, wants from the college the opposite of education. He wants acculturation. He wants his child to learn to be as solidly respectable and as firmly committed to the "realities" of the world as he himself has been forced to be. When the parent gets revolt for what he has so dearly paid, it is understandable that he takes his animus out on the schools.

Yet the modern adult is not all that imprisoned. As his life gets more regimented and homogenized, and as his own personal contribution to getting things done in this world is increasingly less identifiable in a world where things are increasingly done by groups, he has found ways to assert his own personal worth. Leisure-time activities of a highly personal character are his "out." They are his ersatz freedom.

To appreciate the point, one needs only to look at how few of the leisure activities in which he so actively engages are team activities or are passive in character. They are personal and active, not group and passive. He is not playing basketball on a local church team, not organizing a neighborhood adult hockey league. He is engaged in solitary activities where his own personal contribution is highly visible and unambiguous. When he does join a team, it is something like bowling, where his personal contribution is absolutely clear and not dependent on the help or contribution of his teammates.

This insistence on personal distinction and self-expression surfaces in many ways—the great variety of color, accessory, and power options demanded in cars; the rising variety of sartorial styles, colors, and designs; the search for new and varied vacation experiences; the expanding cosmopolitanism in culinary and drinking tastes; and, yes, the growing taste for more varied sexual experiences. Thus, when we talk of the leisure life or the leisure market it provides less guidance than if we look more carefully behind the surface indicators, because unless we do we may lose the value of the advice we thought we gained by listening to superficial indicators.

The Housing Market

Thinking ahead must not be a simple exercise in linear extrapolation. It requires a creative synthesis. When that synthesis is absent, the result can be catastrophic. In recent years one of the most illuminating examples of such a bitter harvest has been the experience of the industries associated with residential construction.

The extravagantly optimistic extrapolations of the mid-1950s regarding the imminent boom in family formation and babies proved almost totally false, even though the young people who were to produce this boom already existed. A huge national industry spent billions developing products and productive capacity that stood wastefully idle as the eagerly anticipated housing boom refused to materialize.

What went wrong? Retrospective wisdom reveals the pitfalls of extrapolation and illustrates what we mean by creative synthesis. A complex series of changes knocked historic trends off their optimistic course. For one thing, people married later than expected. Marriages were postponed partially because of the new tendency for people to go on to college and partially because they stayed there longer. Birth control became easier and more legitimate, greatly lengthening the period between marriage and parenthood. The college boom itself was facilitated by three interrelated things:

1. The sheer abundance of so many young people competing for jobs gave those with superior educational credentials access to better jobs.

2. Hence the accepted formula for personal career success shifted from personal energy to formal knowledge.

3. Society became willing to tax itself far beyond any previous levels to provide itself with more higher education at lower prices.

More education and more birth control resulted not only in postponing childbearing, but also in giving young people greater access to a wider labor market. Suddenly jobs beckoned not just in the old hometown but out there in the entire nation. A childless couple could more easily travel and avail itself of more distant opportunities. With better transportation—the speed of the airplane and the privacy of the automobile—uprooting and moving ceased to be the logistical trauma of the past. Gone too was the psychological trauma of departing from the folks at home. They themselves had reasonably secure jobs; assured pensions; telephones for long-distance, conversational visits; and fast airplanes for weekend access to the grandchildren. Besides, leaving home was not a solitary adventure. Everybody was doing it.

With booming times and all this access to a national labor market, young couples were doubly encouraged to preserve their career mobility as long as possible early in their working lives. The result was a life style totally different from that of the young couples of the period immediately after World War II. The war veterans, reared in depression and dispersed into the peripatetic uncertainty of a terrible war, eagerly returned to the solid stability of a home of their own in their familiar hometowns. Their children of the 1960s sought the opposite—the freedom to pull up stakes, to explore their own world, and to live their own independent experimental lives. And they preferred the mobility of apartments to the restrictions of home ownership. The result was the creation of sick and enormously chastened residential construction and construction-materials industry.

The Slippery
Public Market, Education

Nothing today excites the business community more than the prospect of a huge new market in what has typically been called the "public sector"—education, pollution control, mass urban transportation, medical care. And nothing is more likely to produce the frightful disappointments that have already begun.

General Electric and Time, Inc. organized the General Learning Corporation in 1965 with elaborate fanfare. Dr. Francis Keppel, the newly resigned U.S. Commissioner of Education and former dean of Harvard's Graduate School of Education, was put at the helm of an enterprise funded with $10 million in cash, lots of electronic equipment from GE, a huge library of educational materials from Time, and an enormously talented and energetic staff. Two lears later General Learning was a shambles. It had to be fully reorganized, its strategy entirely repositioned, its targets severely lowered, its staff ruthlessly cut. General Learning's only comfort was that many of its similarly optimistic competitors suffered a similar ignominy.

The reason for these massive failures is not that the forecasters were wrong. There *is* indeed a huge education market. There *was* a need for what General Learning proposed to sell. But there can be needs without markets—that is without willing or solvent customers.

The reason companies such as General Learning, Raytheon, Westinghouse, RCA, and IBM covet the education market with such acquisitive anticipation is that they correctly recognize the enormous pedagogical power of technology in education—equipment for language labs; interactive computerized equipment for instruction in reading skills, in mathematics, and in a huge range of subjects that have been taught since their origin in the undeviatingly inadequate face-to-face fashion of the ancient little red schoolhouse. This, coupled with the obvious need to find more efficient educational methods in the face of manpower shortages, makes the new technology a hard prospect to resist. But in spite of the palpable presence of an expanding education market, it remains a market that is devoid of customers for so much of the new technology that would solve the manpower problem.

There is no customer because the product that is most sensible to produce is also too costly to produce and hence too costly to buy. With no customer large enough to buy it, the product does not get produced. It took dozens of educators and scientists in Harvard University's Project Physics over five years to produce a brand new, one-year basic high school physics course. The course employed sophisticated modern technology, not just for classroom laboratories but also for transmitting the material to the student and for feeding his work back to the source for correction, modification, and reinforcement. It required extensive teacher training.

The development bill was over $12 million. This compares with the $50,000 or so that it costs a publisher now to produce a conventional physics book. In the latter case, however, most of the development cost is hidden. It is borne by the author, who takes it "out of his hide" working weekends and evenings. But there are not enough weekends in a hundred thousand lifetimes to produce and test an electronically sophisticated basic physics course such as the one Harvard produced. It takes a large group of dedicated specialists who must be financed directly with real money, not just with moonlighting personal commitment.

The New York school system is the nation's largest, with approximately 470,000 high school students, yet it is too small either to underwrite the creation of a basic physics course or to encourage private companies to do it. Its ironclad promise to use and annually pay for the use of such a new course for the next twenty years, even without modifications in the course to include new knowledge during all that time, would not be sufficiently enticing to produce even a second sales call from the company eager to be its developer. Within any reasonable range of annual costs, no single school system is big enough to amortize the development cost.

Perhaps only all the combined public school systems of the entire state of California are really large enough for a promise to use a truly sophisticated, high-technology, new course to encourage a private company to develop and produce it. But no state's public schools operate in this manner. And no private company is large enough, or has yet reached a sufficiently charitable state of public-service mindedness to produce such a course on speculation the way textbooks are produced. Moreover, if a combined California system could afford the program, it would still have to build special classrooms, build special labs, buy enormously expensive equipment, and train hundreds of teachers.

This explains why the constant refrain of companies such as Raytheon at education conferences is, "We can do it; just give us the money." They will not develop the basic courses or the needed equipment on speculation. And it is not really that the cost is too high—they have spent more than that on other fragile speculations. It is that there is no customer. The school systems simply cannot afford the product. Even if they could, it would take years for inertia and resistance finally to yield to its use. The world will beat no path to this mousetrap. As a consequence, Dean Theodore R. Sizer, then of Harvard's Graduate School of Education, wrote in his 1968 *Annual Report* that major industrial organizations which had hoped to make educational technology a new area of activity and profits had already begun to scale down their expectations and budgets.

Until there is massive public support for developing such courses—on the order of the federal government's $1.8-billion contribution to the $2-billion supersonic transport—the brave new world of electronic education is unlikely to materialize. Only one customer can cause the product to be produced, and that is the most unpopular and suspected of all U.S. customers, Uncle Sam.

The school systems cannot do it, not just for lack of money, but also because they will not join together to create the size needed to encourage the developers. The school systems will not get together because their entire reason for existence is that they be separate. There are over 19,000 school districts in the United States. There are more than twenty-five in the Chicago metropolitan area alone. Each, in effect, was created in order to be autonomous from every other one. Each represents the efforts of some town or suburb to have a self-controlled system of its very own, uncontaminated by the standards and tax bases of surrounding towns and cities. The long struggles for school system consolidation by educators and money-wise politicians have produced an unblemished record of total failure. And new Supreme Court rulings designed to equalize educational expenditures among different school systems will not help because they cannot compel agreement on educational technologies or teaching methods.

The Pollution-control "Market"

The same absence of a customer existed for years in air and water pollution. While individual companies can now be compelled to scrub clean their air and water effluences, only the pressure and money finally of the federal government got things going. Even so, there is resistance. If costly pollution abatements mean the risk of factories closing, of their competitiveness being reduced, of a loss of local jobs, many local authorities will find ways of letting pollution continue. It takes a different authority than the local one to convert the need into a market.

Who, for example, finally underwrote cleaning up the shamefully contaminated Charles River in Massachusetts that looked so beautiful and smelled so awful to the Harvard-Radcliffe lovers on its banks? It is abutted by Cambridge, Watertown, a half-dozen Newtons, Allston, Brighton, Waltham, West Roxbury, Dedham, Dover, and several other independent towns. It deposited its unseemly float into hapless Boston—a city with a real estate tax already stratospheric beyond redemption. All the abutting communities suffered the river's beautiful but terrible presence.

Yet none of them could by themselves afford to clean it. Not one town, even if it could have afforded to do the job, could in fact have gotten it done. It was an area problem, not a town problem.

As long as each community existed to escape the problems and taxes of every other community, the job simply could not get done without a separate intervention. There was no customer for the obviously compelling need to clean the Charles River. None of the abutting communities would, on this matter, join forces to create a single financially viable and workable customer. Indeed, many years ago the abutting communities thought they had actually created the administrative machinery to solve the problem. They created the Metropolitan District Commission, a super, area-wide governmental unit with, among other things, responsibility for the care and management of the Charles River over its entire course. But the MDC wasted away. The communities refused to pay the taxes the MDC needed to do its job. Each community was convinced the others were most culpable for the river's contamination. None wanted to pay any more than it already did.

Significantly, however, these same communities have effectively joined forces on one major matter of mutual concern—urban transportation. Just as New York created the Port Authority, so eastern Massachusetts has created the Massachusetts Bay Transit Authority. It operates a gigantic, reasonably efficient, and highly convenient network of buses, streetcars, and subways. With enormous efficiency and dispatch, the MBTA brings Wellesley's stockbrokers to their splendid State Street offices in Boston each morning and swiftly returns them each afternoon to comfortable, settled, domestic surroundings characterized by handsome and progressive public schools and excellent snow removal.

Wellesley, Newton, Lexington, Beverly, Marblehead, and all the other polished suburbs agreed eagerly to the good sense of cooperation and sharing with Boston in the creation and support of this single customer, the MBTA. The stockbrokers, professors, and razor-blade executives needed each day to get into the city in a hurry, and out of it even faster. What could have made better sense than to do the civic thing, to cooperate in providing appropriate facilities?

Unfortunately, most big-market-potential problems are not viewed as being equally compelling. Only pollution control has finally gotten the attention it requires. But significantly it came from Washington, which passed the laws and, for the most part, has provided the money and the tax incentives. Before that, needs went unfulfilled. There were no viably solvent customers for visibly huge markets. The suburban self-interests which had so thoroughly fragmented metropolitan-area government in every U.S. city prevented the solution of problems which this fragmentation was largely designed to escape. Even now, attitudes are not getting better, even at the official level. When William F. Haddad was on the New York City Board of Education, he argued for a further fragmentation of the city's metropolitan public school system into even more separate and autonomous enclaves: "If we had local control of the schools on the West side of Manhattan [where he lived], I'd feel a lot better about putting my kids in the schools here because . . . I'd go down there and I'd damn well make that school function for my child."[1]

Federal Help Needed

Private enterprise will not properly benefit from the huge public market represented by education, areawide pollution control, and other major public problems until there is a viable customer. Because of the strong and probably irremediably parochial interests of the numerous small governments that prevail so powerfully in the urban areas of the nation, it is unlikely that they will willingly reconstitute themselves into viable customers.

The magnitude of the problem of creating a viable customer for any number of public projects that require massive areawide effort is illustrated by the fact that in the greater Chicago metropolitan area there are 1,060 different and not necessarily cooperating local governmental units.

But federal involvement is precisely what the business community has generally rejected almost as an article of faith. Washington is almost automatically viewed as bad and to be resisted. The only reason its monopsonistic powers have not been resisted in national defense is because national defense is aimed at external threats. Internal threats are not generally viewed by the business community as warranting any similar suspension of customary opposition to the expansion of Washington's activities.

Yet perhaps, with a more realistic appreciation of what is possible, the needed changes may be achieved more readily than now appears possible. The fact is that Washington's activities in these areas can be greatly expanded without an equal expansion in its powers. This is not generally recognized, even where it has already happened.

Thus we have a national system of unemployment insurance that is purely states-rights in character and administration. It is the result of a highly instructive federal innovation. To get all states to institute the system, and to obtain some sort of national uniformity and minimum standards, the Unemployment Compensation Act provided for a federal

The New York Times, Sept. 1, 1968.

tax on payrolls. But 90 percent was rebatable to the states on condition that they establish and operate an unemployment compensation program of a clearly stipulated character. The administration was to be, and still is today, by the states. The incentives for establishing a proper system were obvious. Every state quickly did its duty.

The same principle also operates in a variety of other areas, and it has merit for education and area pollution control. Whatever merit there may be to the old arguments about states rights and local autonomy, the necessities imposed by modern times require new views about how to accommodate these necessities. Until the very men who live in Wellesleys, the Upper Montclairs, the Wilmettes, and the Santa Monicas recognize the compelling need for federal customer-creating machinery for the achievement in the twentieth century of what modern technology and knowledge both demand and make achievable, these men will not achieve for their businesses the thriving benefits from the public market that they now so optimistically covet. That, at least, is one condition that must be fulfilled.

The Lesson for the Learner

Man's greatest continuing preoccupation is with the unknown. As his condition becomes ever more pervasively characterized by change rather than convention, he increasingly draws that much closer to those who claim some sort of comforting prescience. Predicting the future has therefore become an industry all its own, indeed one of our more thriving growth industries. Its most avid customers are corporate executives who have no choice but to deal with the future. The higher their rank the greater their required concern with the future.

Yet, as we have seen, predictions served up to them in such splendidly expensive packages are often either banal or fatuous. All are, of course, carefully staged to be properly provocative. Some are solemnly inspirational. But few are actionable. They stimulate, if not always thought, at least adrenaline. This has some virtue, but generally lasts about as long as it takes to get back to the pressing problems at the office.

To be told that in the year 2000 at least 30 percent of our food supply will be harvested in the ocean does of course alert us to the possibilities of marine biology and the competition to surface food sources. It may even suggest a possible course of action for the International Harvester Company, for Ralston Purina, for the Bath Iron Works, for Bolt, Beranek & Newman, and for anybody else who seeks growth opportunities. The prediction has its uses, especially if it is grounded in some imminent truths about science and life.

Yet it is precisely this grounding which is so often weak. The sea may harbor a huge food supply, but the consuming public is not likely to embrace any great fondness for strange new foods. Food habits are among the most difficult of all to change, even in the face of extraordinary privation. No better and no more discouraging examples are the singular disappointments suffered in recent years by companies that have created new, low-priced, high-protein foods for consumption by undernourished masses in South America and India.[2]

Clearly, a prediction about the future of the ocean's contribution to our lives may be misleading if it is based solely on scientific or technological possibilities but without regard to how people live, what they value, and how they change their accustomed habits. Thousands of wretched people starve daily in India amidst the world's largest roving supply of edible cattle. The capabilities of technology form perhaps the least realistic basis for predicting what we will consume or how we will live.

There can be a need, but no market, or a market, but not enough customers to make things happen.

The lesson is clear enough: Beware of the fluent prophet—especially the expert who makes his living offering provocatively plausible prophesies to men who cannot afford not to listen.

Man generalizes in order to make life tolerable, even possible. Otherwise, each problem he faces, each task that demands action, would require him to start all over again from scratch. Every generation would have to learn from the beginning and by itself all that it needs to know for its effective survival and progress. Such a style would be disastrous. It would have prevented man from ever descending from the trees. The Kwakiutl Indians suffer from precisely this restriction. Their language has no transitive verbs. This deficiency keeps them from making useful generalizations. One generation cannot pass concepts on to the next. The most important things it knows go with it to the grave. Each generation must start all over on its own.

The capacity to generalize is an essential requisite for progress. It is this capacity that distinguishes man from animals. Literate man has generational memory—the capacity to transmit ideas and concepts to succeeding generations, such that they start where their predecessors left off. Literate man inherits from preceding generations formulas or principles or recently useful tactics that are available for application to his own generation's world. He does not, like the animals, have to start from scratch each time.

[2] See Ray A. Goldberg, "Agribusiness for Developing Countries," *Harvard Business Review*, September–October, 1966, p. 81.

The attraction of principles and formulas is therefore immense. That is why management textbooks sell so well, as do management-development seminars that promise to provide instant answers, liberating checklists, and other spurious shortcuts.

The danger is obvious. We need to learn from the past lest we become restricted to our generational capacities. Yet as long as we learn from and progress beyond the past, we run the risk of employing obsolete dogmas for new times. The issue is not whether knowledge and know-how are transferable. It is whether they are applicable.

In business, as in war, the applicability of specific concepts, strategies, and tactics to specific situations is not automatically self-evident. The transferability of an experience or generalization from one generation or situation to another is a function not just of the details of the situation or generation, but also of the environment in which it occurs and of the objectives of the people involved. The situations may be similar, but not the objectives.

The essential managerial skill is not to be a good memorizer of principles, as is so often the case in medicine and law, but to be able to determine what the problem really is. It is the ability to do this job which distinguishes the chief executive from the janitor. Details are more important than dogma.

Of course the experienced manager knows that "you've got to take one situation at a time." But what he knows is not always reflected in what he does. The prevailing fact is that it is precisely because he knows he has to take one situation at a time that he is so magnetically drawn to medicine men who promise liberation from that kind of particularism. He has so many things to deal with, so many situations constantly calling for decision, so many problems constantly demanding resolution, that he looks for easy, or at least fast, ways out. His numerous daily pressures make the attraction of generalizations and principles very tantalizing indeed. They help him get his work under control—applying general principles where he can—thus making available more time for the less tractable situations that remain. In the case of marketing, this reliance on general principles or derived formulas is particularly virulent. It thrives because in marketing so many ungovernable and unpredicted things seem constantly to be happening with such simultaneous regularity.

What we have seen in this book is that Murphy's law remains virile and unrepealed: "If anything can go wrong, it will." Aubrey Menen once pointed out that a soldier does not have to know right from wrong as long as he knows right from left. His commander, however, must know what the soldier need not know. And just as right and wrong have no absolute moral content, neither do business rules or principles. In the end there are no rules or principles. The commander must struggle alone to decide what is right for the situation that he must analyze for himself. The burden is on his capacity to open up his pores for all the subtle inputs that characterize the "situation" and what is appropriate to the objectives on which he has decided.

The management of a large organization is far more difficult than most men who manage are themselves aware. Few in fact are managers. They are custodians. Somehow things get done decently well, but only because their competitors are of approximately equal caliber. Most managers unfortunately do very little thinking in the course of their work. They are entirely unaware of how much they manage by formula, dogma, principles, textbook maxims, and resounding clichés; of how much in the process they are forfeiting the one distinction by which we tell man from animal. Their resort to easy generalization is explained by the heavy burdens of their job. But to explain it is not to condone it. When you reach some stage of maturity, you want to look into the mirror and be sure *you* are there. You want to know that it is you and not some ancient soothsayer who is really running things. There comes a time in the life of every business when you have to abandon principle and do what's right.

Chapter Thirteen

The Morality(?) of Marketing

AMERICANS CONSUME ABOUT $20 billion of advertising a year, and very little of it because they want it. Wherever we turn, advertising is forcibly thrust on us in an intrusive orgy of abrasive sound and sight, all to induce us to do something we might not ordinarily do, or to induce us to do it differently. This massive and persistent effort crams increasingly more commercial noise into the same, few, strained twenty-four hours of the day. It has provoked a reaction as predictable as it was inevitable. A lot of people want the noise stopped, or at least alleviated.

Advertising is marketing's most visible feature. A lot of people equate advertising with marketing. When they say they want advertising cleaned up and corrected, it is also marketing they are talking about.

As more and more products enter the battle for the consumer's fleeting dollar, advertising increases its boldness and volume. Industry offers the nation's supermarkets about a hundred new products a week, equal, on an annualized basis, to the total number already on their shelves. Where so much must be sold so hard, it is not surprising that advertisers have pressed the limits of our credulity and generated complaints about their exaggerations and deceptions.

Only classified ads, the work of rank amateurs, are presumed to contain solid, unembellished fact. All the rest is suspect of systematic and egregious distortion, if not often of outright mendacity.

The attack on advertising comes from all sectors. Indeed, recent studies show that the people most agitated by advertising are precisely those in the higher income brackets whose affluence is generated by the industries that create the ads.[1] While these studies show that only a modest group of people are preoccupied with advertising's constant presence in our lives, they also show that distortion and deception are what bother people most.

This discontent has encouraged the enactment and proposal of a lot of consumer-protection and truth-in-advertising legislation. People, they say, want less fluff and more facts. They want description, not distortion, and they want some relief from the constant, grating, vulgar noise.

Legislation seems appropriate because the natural action of competition does not seem to work, or, at least, not very well. Competition may ultimately flush out and destroy falsehood and shoddiness, but "ultimately" is too long for the deceived—not just the deceived who are poor, ignorant, and dispossessed, but also all the rest of us who work hard for our money and can seldom judge expertly the truth of conflicting claims about products and services.

The consumer is an amateur; the producer is an expert. In the commercial arena, the individual consumer is an impotent midget. He is certainly not king. The producer is a powerful giant. It is an uneven mat
In this setting, the purifying power of competition helps the consumer very little—especially in the short run, when his money is spent and gone, gone from weak hands into strong hands. Nor does competition among the sellers solve the "noise" problem. The more they compete, the worse the advertising din.

A Broad Viewpoint Required

Most people spend their money carefully. Understandably, they look out for larcenous attempts to separate them from it. Few men in business will deny the right, perhaps even the wisdom, of people today asking for some restraint on advertising and various sharpshooting marketing practices, or at least for more accurate information on the things they buy and for more consumer protection.

Yet, to speak in the same breath about consumer protection and about marketing's distortions, exaggerations, and deceptions is often to confuse two quite separate things—what is legitimate and what is abuse. Rather than deny that distortion and exaggeration exist, it is fair to argue that

[1] See Raymond A. Bauer and Stephen A. Greyser, *Advertising in America: The Consumer View,* Harvard Business School, Division of Research, Boston, 1968; see also Gary A. Steiner, *The People Look at Television,* Alfred A. Knopf, Inc., New York, 1963.

embellishment and distortion are among marketing's legitimate and socially desirable purposes; and that illegitimacy consists only of falsification with larcenous intent. And while it is difficult, as a practical matter, to draw the line between legitimate distortion and essential falsehood, it is useful to take a long look at the distinction that exists between the two. This I shall say in advance—the distinction is not as simple, obvious, or great as one might think.

The issue of truth versus falsehood, in business or in anything else, is often complex and fugitive. Anyone seriously concerned with the moral problems of a commercial society cannot avoid the necessity of pursuing the complexity to its philosophic end.

What Is Reality?

What, indeed? Consider poetry. Like advertising, poetry's purpose is to influence an audience, to affect its perceptions and sensibilities, perhaps even to change its mind. Like rhetoric, poetry's intent is to convince and seduce. In the service of that intent, it employs without guilt or fear of criticism all the arcane tools of distortion that the literary mind can devise. Keats does not offer a truthful engineering description of his Grecian urn. He offers, instead, with exquisite attention to the effects of meter, rhyme, allusion, illusion, metaphor, and sound, a lyrical, exaggerated, distorted, and palpably false description. And he is thoroughly applauded for it, as are all other artists, in whatever medium, who do precisely this same thing successfully.

Commerce, it can be said without apology, takes essentially the same liberties with reality and literality as the artist, except that commerce calls its creations advertising, or industrial design, or packaging. As with art, the purpose is to influence the audience by creating illusions, symbols, and implications that promise more than pure functionality. It is not cosmetic chemicals women want from Helena Rubenstein, but the seductive charms promised by the alluring symbols with which these chemicals have been surrounded—hence the rich and exotic packages in which they are sold, and the suggestive advertising with which they are promoted.

Commerce usually embellishes its products thrice: first, it designs the product to please the eye, to suggest reliability, and so forth; second, it packages the product as attractively as it feasibly can; and then it advertises this attractive package with inviting pictures, slogans, descriptions, songs, and so on. The package and design are as important as the advertising.

The Grecian vessel, for example, was used to carry liquids, but why did the potter decorate it with graceful lines and elegant drawings in black and red. A woman's compact carries refined talc, but why does the manufacturer make these boxes into works of decorative art?

Neither the poet nor the ad man celebrates the literal functionality of what he produces. Instead, each celebrates a deep and complex emotion which he symbolizes by creative embellishment—a content which cannot be captured by literal description alone. Communication, through advertising or through poetry or any other medium, is a creative conceptualization that implies or produces a vicarious experience through a language of symbolic substitutes. Communication cannot be the reality it talks about. All communication is in some inevitable fashion a departure from reality.

Poets, novelists, playwrights, composers, graphic artists, fashion designers —they all have one thing in common. They deal in symbolic communication. None is satisfied with nature in the raw, as it was on the day of creation. None is satisfied to tell it exactly "like it is" to the naked eye, as do the classified ads. It is the purpose of all art to alter nature's surface reality, to reshape, to embellish, and to augment what nature has so crudely fashioned, and then to present it to the same applauding humanity that so eagerly buys the manufacturer's exotically advertised cosmetics.

Does anyone accept the natural state in which God created him? We scrupulously select our clothes to suit a multiplicity of simultaneous purposes, not only for warmth, but manifestly for such other purposes as propriety, status, and seduction. Women modify, embellish, and amplify themselves with colored paste for the lips and powders and lotions for the face; men as well as women use devices to take hair off the face and others to put it on the head. Like the inhabitants of isolated African regions, where not a single whiff of advertising has ever intruded, we all encrust ourselves with rings, pendants, bracelets, neckties, clips, chains, and snaps. God's original creation is not good enough for anybody.

Man lives neither in sackcloth nor in sod huts—although these are not notably inferior to tight clothes and overheated dwellings in congested and polluted cities. Everywhere man rejects nature's uneven blessings. He molds and repackages to his own civilizing specifications an otherwise crude, drab, and generally oppressive reality. He does it so that life may be made for the moment more tolerable than God evidently designed it to be. As T. S. Eliot said: "Humankind cannot bear very much reality."

No line of life is exempt. All the popes of history have countenanced the costly architecture of St. Peter's Basilica and its extravagant interior decoration. All around the globe, nothing typifies man's materialism so much as the temples in which he preaches asceticism. Men of the cloth have not been persuaded that the poetic self-denial of Christ or Buddha— both men of sackcloth and sandals—is enough to inspire, elevate, and hold their flocks together. To amplify the temple in men's eyes, they have systematically sanctioned the embellishment of the houses of the gods with the same luxurious design and costly decoration that Detroit puts into a Cadillac automobile.

One does not need a doctorate in social anthropology to see that the purposeful transmutation of nature's primeval state occupies all people in all cultures and all societies at all stages of development. Everybody everywhere wants to modify, transform, embellish, enrich, and reconstruct the world around him—to introduce into an otherwise harsh or bland existence some sort of purposeful and distorting alleviation. Civilization is man's attempt to transcend his ancient animality; and this includes both art and advertising.

But civilized man will undoubtedly deny that either the innovative artist or the grande dame with chic "distorts reality." Instead, he will say that artist and woman merely embellish, enhance, and illuminate. And he will mean something quite different by these words when they are applied. to the fine arts and when they are applied to the more secular world.

But the distinction is sophistry. It is a mark of civilized man's superior sensibilities that he has invented a great many subtle distinctions to distinguish between things that are objectively indistinct. Let us take a closer look at the difference between man's "sacred" and "secular" distortions.

The man of sensibility will want to canonize the artist's deeds as superior creations by ascribing to them some special virtue and almost cosmic significance. He will almost certainly refuse to concede any constructive, let alone cosmic, virtues to the production of the advertiser. And though the artist and the advertiser employ identical crafts and similar methods, he will likely charge that advertising uniformly deceives us while the artist at least seeks to elevate us.

If we assume for the moment that there is no objective, operational difference between the embellishments and distortions of the artist and those of the ad man—that both men are more concerned with creating images and feelings than with rendering objective, representational, and informational descriptions—then the greater virtue of the artist's work must derive from this intention.

It will be said that art has a higher value because it has a higher purpose. In other words, it is the ends which determine the morality of the means. True, the artist is interested in philosophic truth or wisdom, and the ad man in selling his goods and services. Michelangelo, when he designed the Sistine chapel ceiling, was interested in the inspirational elevation of man's spirit. Edward Levy, who designs cosmetics packages, is interested primarily in creating images to help separate the unwary consumer from his loose change. So the argument goes.

But is the presence of a "higher" purpose all that redeeming? Consider the reverse proposition: the marketing man seeks only to convert people to his commercial custom. Michelangelo sought to convert their souls. Which is the greater blasphemy? Who commits the greater affront to life —he who dabbles with man's animal appetites, or he who meddles with man's soul? Which act is the easier to judge and justify?

How much sense does it really make to distinguish between similar means on the grounds that the ends to which they are directed are different—"good" for art and "not so good" for advertising? The distinction produces zero progress in the argument at hand. How willing are we to employ the involuted ethics whereby the ends justify the means?

Apparently, on this subject, lots of people are very willing indeed. The business executive seems to share with the minister, the painter, and the poet the doctrine that the ends justify the means. The difference is that the businessman is justifying the very commerical ends that his critics oppose. While his critics justify the embellishments of art and literature for what these do for man's spirit, the businessman justifies the embellishment of industrial design and advertising for what they do for man's purse.

Taxing the imagination to the limit, the businessman spins casuistic webs of elaborate transparency to the self-righteous effect that promotion and advertising are socially benign because they expand the economy, create jobs, and raise living standards. Technically, he will always be free to argue, and he will argue, that his ends become the means to the ends of the musician, poet, painter, and minister. The argument which justifies means in terms of ends is obviously not without its subtleties and intricacies.

The executive and the artist are equally tempted to identify and articulate a higher rationale for their work than their work itself. But only in the improved human consequences of their efforts do they find vindication. The aesthete's ringing declaration of "art for art's sake," with all its self-conscious affirmation of selflessness, sounds hollow in the end, even to himself; for, finally, every communication addresses itself to an audience. Thus art is very understandably in constant need of justification by the evidence of its beneficial and divinely approved effect on its audience.

The Audience's Demands

The compulsion to rationalize even art is a highly instructive fact. It tells one a great deal about art's purposes and the purposes of all other communication. As I have said, the poet and the artist each seek in some special way to produce an emotion or assert a truth not otherwise apparent. But it is only in communion with their audiences that the effectiveness of their efforts can be tested and truth revealed. It may be academic whether a tree falling in the forest makes a noise. It is *not* academic whether a sonnet or a painting has merit. Only an audience can decide that.

The creative person can justify his work only in terms of another person's response to it. Ezra Pound, to be sure, thought that ". . . in the [greatest] works the live part is the part which the artist has put there to please himself, and the dead part is the part he put there . . . because he thinks he ought to"—i.e., either to get or to keep an audience. This is certainly consistent with our notions of Pound as perhaps the purest of twentieth-century advocates of art for art's sake.

But a review of his life shows Pound spending the greater part of his energies seeking suitable places for deserving poets to publish. Why? Because art has little merit standing alone in unseen and unheard isolation. Merit is not inherent in art. It is conferred by an audience. The fact that it should be an informed and learned audience does not diminish the point. The point also holds in advertising: if it fails to persuade the audience that the product will fulfill the function the audience expects, the advertising has no merit.

Where have we arrived? Only at some common characteristics of art and advertising. Both are rhetorical, and both literally false; both expound an emotional reality deeper than the "real"; both pretend to "higher" purposes, although different ones; and the excellence of each is judged by its effect on its audience—its persuasiveness, in short. I do not mean to imply that the two are fundamentally the same, but rather that they both represent a pervasive, and I believe universal, characteristic of human nature— the human audience demands symbolic interpretation in everything it sees and knows. If it doesn't get it, it will return a verdict of "no interest."

To get a clearer idea of the relation between the symbols of advertising and the products they glorify, something more must be said about the fiat the consumer gives to industry to "distort" its message.

Symbol and Substance

As we have seen, everywhere man seeks to transcend nature in the raw. Everywhere, and at all times, he has been attracted by the poetic imagery of some sort of art, literature, music, and mysticism. He obviously wants and needs the promises, the imagery, and the symbols of the poet or the priest. He refuses to live a life of primitive (or even noble) barbarism or sterile functionalism.

Consider a sardine can filled with scented powder. Even if the Ralph Nader Bureau of Standards were to certify its contents as identical to those sold in a beautiful paisley-printed container, who would buy it? Not even the proper Boston matron celebrated for exaggerated penury. While she may deny it in self-assured and neatly cadenced accents, she obviously desires and needs the promises, imagery, and symbols produced by hyperbolic advertisements, elaborate packages, and fetching fashions.

The need for embellishment is not confined to personal appearance. A few years ago, an electronics laboratory offered a $700 testing device for sale. The company ordered two different front panels to be designed, one by the engineers who developed the equipment and one by professional industrial designers. When the two models were shown to a sample of laboratory directors with Ph.D.'s, the professional design attracted twice the purchase intentions as the engineers' design. Obviously, the laboratory director who has been baptized into science at M.I.T. is quite as responsive to the blandishments of packaging as the Boston matron.

And, obviously, both these customers define the products they buy in much more sophisticated terms than the engineer in the factory. For a woman, dusting powder in a sardine can is not the same product as the identical dusting powder in an exotic paisley package. For the laboratory director, the test equipment behind an engineer-designed panel just isn't as "good" as the identical equipment in a box designed with finesse.

Form Follows the Ideal Function

The consumer refuses to settle for pure operating functionality. "Form follows function" is a resoundingly vacuous cliché which, like all clichés, depends for its memorability more on its alliteration and brevity than on its wisdom. If it has any truth, it is only in the elastic sense that function extends beyond strict mechanical use into the domain of imagination. We do not choose to buy a particular product; we choose to buy the functional expectations that we attach to it, and we buy these expectations as "tools" to help us solve problems of life. Our actions are directed to our expectations.

But under normal circumstances, we are compelled to judge a product's utilities before we actually buy it. It is rare that we choose an object after we have experienced it; nearly always we must make the choice before the fact. We choose on the basis of promises, not experiences.

Whatever symbols convey and sustain these promises in our minds are therefore truly functional. The promises and images which imaginative ads and sculptured packages induce in us are as much the product as the physical materials themselves. To put this another way, these ads and packaging describe the product's fullness for us: in our minds, the product becomes a complex abstraction which is, as Immanuel Kant might have said, the conception of a perfection which has not yet been experienced. But all promises and images, almost by their very nature, exceed their capacity to live up to themselves. As every eager lover has ever known, the consummation seldom equals the promises which produced the chase. To forestall and suppress the visceral expectation of disappointment that life has taught us must inevitably come, we use art, architecture, literature, and the rest, and advertising as well, to shield ourselves, in advance of experience, from the stark and plain reality in which we are fated to live. I agree that we wish for unobtainable unrealities, "dream castles." But why promise ourselves reality, which we already have? What we want is what we do *not* have!

Everyone tries in his special personal fashion to solve a primal problem of life—the problem of rising above his own negligibility; of escaping from nature's confining, hostile, and unpredictable reality; of finding significance, security, and comfort in the things he must do in order to survive. Many of the so-called distortions of advertising, product design, and packaging may be viewed as a paradigm of the many responses that man makes to the conditions of survival in the environment. Without distortion, embellishment, and elaboration, life would be drab, dull, anguished, and at its existential worst.

Symbolism, Useful and Necessary

Without symbolism, furthermore, life would be even more confusing and anxiety-ridden than it is with it. The foot soldier recognizes the general by the insignia he wears, not by the name he bears. The general without his stars and aides-de-camp to set him apart from the privates would suffer in authority and credibility as much as perfume packaged by Dracula or a computer designed by Rube Goldberg. Any ordinary soldier or civilian who has ever been in the same shower with a general can testify from the visible unease of the latter how much "clothes make the man."

Similarly, verbal symbols help to make the product; they help us deal with the uncertainties of daily life. "You can be sure . . . if it's Westinghouse" is a decision rule as useful to the man buying a turbine generator as to the man buying an electric shaver. To label all the devices and embellishments companies employ to reassure the prospective customer about a product's quality with the pejorative term "gimmick," as critics tend to do, is simply silly. Worse, it denies, against massive evidence, man's honest needs and values. If religion must be architectured, packaged, lyricized, and musicized to attract and hold its audience, and if sex must be perfumed, powdered, sprayed, and shaped in order to command attention, it is ridiculous to deny the legitimacy of more modest and similiar embellishments to the world of commerce.

But still, it will be said that commercial communications tend to be aggressively deceptive, often with intent that moderate mortals might legitimately view as bordering on larceny. Perhaps, and perhaps not. The issue is more complex than the ordinary critic believes. Man wants and needs the comforting satisfactions of attractive surroundings and handsome packages, the reassurances of hopeful promises. He needs the assurances projected by well-known brand names, and the reliability suggested by salesmen who have been taught to dress by Oleg Cassini and to speak by Dale Carnegie. Who would rather deal with certifiably honest but autistic skid-row bums? Of course there are blatant, tasteless, and willfully deceiving salesmen and advertisers, just as there are blatant, tasteless, and willfully deceiving artists, preachers, and even professors. But before talking blithely about deception, it is helpful to make a distinction between *things* and the *description* of things.

The Question of Deceit

Poetic descriptions of things make no pretense of being the things themselves. Nor do advertisements, even by the most elastic standards. Advertisements are symbols, not the real things, nor are they intended to be, nor are they accepted as such by the public. A study some years ago by the Center for Research in Marketing, Inc., concluded that deep down inside the consumer understands this perfectly well and has the attitude that an advertisement is an ad, not a factual news story.

Even Professor Galbraith grants the point when he says that ". . . because modern man is exposed to a large volume of information of varying degrees of unreliability . . . he establishes a system of discounts which he applies to various sources almost without thought. . . . The discount becomes nearly total for all forms of advertising. The merest child watching television dismisses the health and status-giving claims of a breakfast cereal as 'a commercial.' "[2]

This is not to say, of course, that Galbraith also discounts advertising's effectiveness. Quite the opposite: "Failure to win belief does not impair the effectiveness of the management of demand for consumer products. Management involves the creation of a compelling image of the product in the mind of the consumer. To this he responds more or less automatically under circumstances where the purchase does not merit a great deal of thought.

[2] John Kenneth Galbraith, *The New Industrial State*, Houghton Mifflin Company, Boston, 1967, pp. 325–326

For building this image, palpable fantasy may be more valuable than circumstantial evidence."[3]

Linguists and other communications specialists will agree with the conclusion of the Center for Research in Marketing that "advertising is a symbol system existing in a world of symbols. Its reality depends upon the fact that it is a symbol . . . the content of an ad can never be real, it can only say something about reality, or create a relationship between itself and an individual which has an effect on the reality life of an individual."

Consumer, Know Thyself!

Consumption is man's most constant activity. It is well that he understands himself as a consumer.

The object of consumption is to solve a problem. Even consumption that is viewed as the creation of an opportunity—like going to medical school or taking a singles-only Caribbean tour—has as its purpose the solution of a problem. At a minimum, the medical student seeks to solve the problem of how to lead a relevant and comfortable life, and the person on the tour seeks to solve the problem of loneliness.

The "purpose" of a product is not what the engineer explicitly says it is, but what the consumer implicitly demands that it shall be. Thus the consumer consumes not things, but expected benefits—not cosmetics, but the satisfactions of the allurements they promise; not quarter-inch drills, but quarter-inch holes; not stock in companies, but capital gains; not numerically controlled milling machines, but trouble-free and accurately smooth metal parts; not low-cal whipped cream, but self-rewarding indulgence combined with sophisticated convenience.

The significance of these distinctions is anything but trivial. Nobody knows this better, for example, than the creators of automobile ads. It is not the generic virtues that they tout, but more likely the car's capacity to enhance its user's status, pride and ambitions.

Whether we are aware of it or not, we in effect expect and demand that advertising create these symbols for us, to show us what life might be, to bring the possibilities that we cannot see before our eyes and screen out the stark reality in which we must live. We insist, as W. S. Gilbert put it, that there be added a "touch of artistic verisimilitude to an otherwise bald and unconvincing narrative."

Understanding the Difference

In a world where so many things are either commonplace or standardized, it makes no sense to refer to how we handle them as false, fraudulent,

---

[3] *Ibid*, p. 326.

frivolous, or immaterial. The world works according to the aspirations and needs of its actors, not according to the arcane or moralizing logic of detached critics who pine for another age—an age which, in any case, seems different from today's largely because its observers are no longer children shielded by protective parents from life's implacable harshness.

To understand this is not to condone much of the vulgarity, purposeful duplicity, and scheming half-truths we see in advertising, promotions, packaging, and product design. But before we condemn, it is well to understand the difference between embellishment and duplicity and how rare the latter is in our times. The noisy visibility of promotion in our intensely communicating times should no more assume to reflect an equivalent proportion of malevolence or mendacity than the number of books published each year should reflect an equivalent level of American intellectuality.

Thus the issue is not the prevention of distortion. It is, in the end, to know what kinds of distortions we actually want so that each of our lives is, without apology, duplicity, or rancor, made bearable. This does not mean we must accept out of hand all the commercial propaganda to which we are each day so constantly exposed, or that we must accept out of hand the equation that effluence is the price of affluence, or the simple notion that business cannot and government should not try to alter and improve the position of the consumer vis-à-vis the producer. It takes a special kind of perversity to continue any longer our shameful failure to mount vigorous, meaningful programs to protect the consumer; to standardize product grades, labels, and packages; to improve the consumer's information-getting process; and to mitigate the vulgarity and oppressiveness that surface so much in our commercial affairs.

But the consumer suffers from an old dilemma. He wants "truth," but he also wants and needs the alleviating imagery and tantalizing promises of the advertiser and designer.

Business is caught in the middle. There is hardly a company that would not go down in ruin if it refused to provide fluff, because nobody wants or will buy pure functionality. Yet if it uses too much fluff and little else, business invites possibly ruinous legislation. The problem therefore is to find a middle way. And in this search, business can do a great deal more than it has been either accustomed or willing to do:

- It can exert pressure to make sure that no single industry finds "reasons" why it should be exempt from legislative restrictions that are reasonable and popular.
- It can work constructively with government to develop reasonable standards and effective sanctions that will assure a more amenable commercial environment.
- It can support legislation to provide the consumer with the informa-

tion he needs to make easier comparisons between products, packages, and prices.

- It can support and help draft improved legislation on quality stabilization.

- It can support legislation that gives consumers easier access to strong legal remedies where justified.

- It can support programs to make local legal aid easily available, especially to the poor and undereducated who know so little about their rights and how to assert them.

- Finally, it can support efforts to moderate and clean up the advertising noise that dulls our senses and assaults our sensibilities.

It will not be the end of the world or of capitalism for business to sacrifice a few commercial freedoms so that we may more easily enjoy our own humanity. Business can and should, for its own good, work energetically to achieve this end. But it is also well to remember the limits of what is possible. Paradise was not a free-goods society. Even the forbidden fruit was gotten at a price.

Index